Du's
Handbook
of
Classical Chinese
Grammar

An Introduction to
Classical Chinese Grammar

On the Contributors

The core of this work is the previously unpublished *Introduction to Classical Chinese Grammar*, written in 1978 by Archie Barnes, who taught Classical Chinese at Durham University for over 20 years. It has been significantly reworked and expanded for publication by Don Starr (currently Spalding Lecturer in Chinese Language and Civilisation at Durham University) and Graham Ormerod (a former Modern/Classical Chinese student).

Archie Barnes: Head of the Chinese Department of Durham University from 1961-1984; author of *Chinese Through Poetry*, the first book to approach learning Classical Chinese through verse instead of prose. The work was completed just before his death in 2002.

Don Starr: Former Head of the Department of East Asian Studies at Durham University, Don Starr has over 30 years' experience of teaching Modern Chinese, Classical Chinese and Japanese language. He was President of the British Association for Chinese Studies and is a Committee member of the British Chinese Language Teaching Society.

Graham Ormerod: Graduated in 1984 in Modern and Classical Chinese at Durham University. Graham Ormerod's past 25 years have been spent in the Far East based in Hong Kong, Taiwan and Singapore.

Du's
Handbook
of
Classical Chinese
Grammar

An introduction to
Classical Chinese grammar

Contributors

Archie Barnes
Head of Chinese Department
Durham University
(1961-1984)

Don Starr
Spalding Lecturer
in Chinese Language & Civilisation
Durham University

Graham Ormerod
Modern & Classical Chinese graduate
Durham University

First published in Great Britain 2009 by Alcuin Academics, an imprint of WritersPrintShop

ISBN 1904623743

Cover Design: Gisele Malenfant
(www.timelessdigital.org)

Cover characters: 子曰：學而時習之［不亦說乎？］ *(zǐ yuē: xué ér shí xí zhī [bú yì yuè hū?])* 'The Master said: "[Is it not pleasant to] learn with a constant perseverance and application?" This is the first line of the 論語 *(lún yǔ)* or *Analects* of Confucius.

Contents

Preface

This handbook has it origins in material produced by Archie Barnes in the late 1970s for undergraduate students of Classical Chinese at Durham University. Following Archie's death in 2002, Graham Ormerod, a member of one of the last classes of students Archie taught before his retirement, agreed with Archie's wife, Marie, who also happened to be a member of the same class, to prepare for publication some of the works Archie had produced in manuscript. The first was: Archie Barnes, *Chinese through Poetry: An Introduction to the Language and Imagery of Traditional Verse*, published in 2007, and very enthusiastically received. This is the second work.

Archie was attracted to many aspects of Chinese studies, but of all of them Classical Chinese was his favourite. He was fascinated by language itself and taught himself new languages as a hobby, for fun, in order to expand his linguistic horizons. For example, when he devised for struggling students a systematic vocabulary learning method (VOLATS – Vocabulary Learning And Testing System) he learnt Gaelic in order to test it out. Although Archie's fascination with grammar was not necessarily shared by all his students, they were all touched by his inspiring teaching and infectious enthusiasm. Only he had the temerity to go on teaching long into the lunch break. At that time, grammar was already in serious decline as part of language teaching methodology. I remember Archie's incredulity as he described how he had tried to help one of his children, studying "new Latin" at school, revise for his exams. He discovered that in spite of having studied Latin for several years, his child did not know about the existence of declensions for nouns, and was under the impression that the different case endings were different words. Archie was horrified.

In the 1970s at Durham, we were using Mrs Y.C. Liu's *Fifty Chinese Stories* (London: Lund Humphries, 1960) as the basic textbook for teaching elementary Classical Chinese. This was a compilation of some of the best known excerpts from Classical Chinese texts, provided with GR romanisation, a Modern Chinese version in characters and romanisation, and a classical Japanese version in romanisation. *Fifty Chinese Stories* was originally compiled for traditional teaching methods with the teacher giving an exposition of each text in a classroom setting. It provided an excellent selection of texts, but, in the context of changes in language teaching methods taking place at the time, lacked the structured approach being applied to Modern Chinese language courses. Archie set about remedying this, writing instalments over weekends for the following week's classes and distributing them in his elegant handwritten script versions.

He adopted a three-pronged approach. He added pīnyīn romanisation and both word-for-word trot translations and regular English translations of the texts of the *Fifty Chinese Stories*, which remained the core of the teaching material. To supplement the texts, he produced a structure-based analysis of how

Classical Chinese Grammar

Classical Chinese expresses some key linguistic concepts (the copula, numerals, demonstratives, tenses, adverbs, relative clauses, etc.). This was based on the grammar and vocabulary of the *Fifty Chinese Stories*, but, instead of working from Chinese, it started from the English linguistic concepts and explained how Classical Chinese expressed these. In the original version, each section was followed by exercises. The first part of the present volume is a revised version of Archie's original grammar course with the exercises reworked as reference material (since it is now conceived primarily as a reference / self-study work). The third part of Archie's original work was a composition course, i.e. writing in Classical Chinese. Although active language production is indicative of the highest skill level in a language, even English public schools have abandoned efforts to get pupils to turn *Times* leaders into Latin. The exercise was undoubtedly very beneficial, but asking students to translate into Classical Chinese seemed idiosyncratic even in the 1980s, and would probably be viewed as sadism now.

During the course of editing Graham Ormerod became convinced, and I agreed, that it would be very useful to supplement the grammar with a section on 虛詞 (*xūcí*) 'empty words', i.e. words whose function is primarily grammatical. There are many reference works in Chinese that offer analyses of 虛詞 (*xūcí*) and example sentences, but this is an area poorly catered for in English. We hope readers will find our efforts in this respect helpful. We have tried to steer a middle course between, on the one hand, making the definitions and examples so simple that they fail to cover many examples of usage and, on the other, making them so complex, in an attempt at comprehensiveness, that the main functions become lost in a mass of examples of very minor or exceptional usage. Among the Chinese works used for this part should be mentioned:

呂叔湘 (Lǚ Shūxiāng), 文言虛字 (Wényán Xūzì). 香港 (Xiānggǎng/Hong Kong): 大光出版社 (Dàguāng Chūbǎnshè), 1971;

徐豫生 (Xú Yùshēng), 郁誠煒 (Yù Chéngwěi) eds. 實用古漢語大辭典 (Shíyòng Gǔhànyǔ Dà Cídiǎn). 河南人民出版社 (Hénán Rénmín Chūbǎnshè), 1995;

白玉林 (Bái Yùlín), 遲鐸 (Chí Duó) eds. 古漢語虛詞詞典 (Gǔhànyǔ Xūcí Cídiǎn). 中華書局 (Zhōnghuá Shūjú), 2004.

This work will be followed by a new version of the *Fifty Chinese Stories* based on Mrs Liu's original selection of texts with Archie Barnes' translations and pīnyīn, plus grammar notes added by the editors. We should like to thank warmly Mrs Liu, who sadly died earlier this year, and her daughter Dr Tao Tao Liu for agreeing to this. Finally we should like to pay tribute to Archie Barnes, a wonderful colleague and teacher.

Don Starr (in Durham)   October 2008

Acknowledgements

A few years ago, I suggested at a lunch with some Durham graduates, one of whom was the widow of Archie Barnes, Marie, that Archie's handwritten Classical Chinese 'trots' and grammar notes should be saved for future Classical Chinese students.

I volunteered, having absolutely no idea what I was letting myself in for. All I knew was that I had once thoroughly enjoyed Durham University's Classical Chinese courses, that after 25 years in Hong Kong, China and Taiwan, my Chinese was probably still up to the challenge, and that I probably had the necessary computing skills to ensure that the project could be brought to completion. At the time, little idea did I have of the heinous complexity of desktop publishing for a book let alone one with simplified and traditional characters, pīnyīn and the trot format. At every turn there was a problem. It was certainly a great deal more work than I had ever expected. In the end, I decided that it was probably better to split up the work into two stand-alone books, of which this, *Du's Handbook of Classical Chinese Grammar*, is the first.

Fortunately for me, I was not on my own in this endeavour. Twenty-five years of speaking and reading Modern Chinese meant that picking up Classical Chinese again was not too difficult, but still I could not possibly complete a task of such magnitude without help. To my rescue came the combined forces of the Chinese Department of Durham University. In a mad travesty, the University may well have abandoned one of the most successful Chinese courses in the United Kingdom for the sake of saving a few pennies, but at least our lecturers realised that a lifetime's teaching material was worth saving.

I would like to thank Spalding Lecturer in Chinese Language and Civilisation at Durham University, Don Starr, for agreeing to mastermind the project. I also breathed a sigh of relief when Caroline Mason volunteered to help with the editing process. Both had taught the Classical Chinese course at Durham University and both were very familiar with the original material. I also need to thank David Barnes, who was a major help in the proofing process - not an easy task by any means.

I would also like to thank the following people who helped in ways small and large to bring this book to fruition either through their technical knowledge, their ideas or their general support: Marie Barnes, Hugh Baker, Keith Pratt, Peter Kahrel, Ilyas Khan, Chas Jones, and Pinyin Joe. Donald Sturgeon's website, the 'Chinese Text Project' (www.chinese.dsturgeon.net), was also a huge aid.

And finally, a big thanks to my family for seeing me through what is still an on-going marathon. To Helen, whom I love dearly and who has been extremely supportive throughout, and to Cherine and Myles, to whom I dedicate this handbook.

Graham Ormerod (in Hong Kong)   October 2008

Introduction to the Handbook

The Du Experience

The main material for this book was used continuously for close to thirty years by Durham University's Classical Chinese students. Archie Barnes's grammar work has been edited and in places re-worked for the lone student. It has also been complemented by new sections on *Exposure*, *Interrogatives* and *Function Characters*. A dictionary and index are also provided.

We also include the first five annotated stories of Mrs Y.C. Liu's *Fifty Chinese Stories*, which was first published in 1960. This re-worked version uses original Chinese character texts, 'trots' (a translation of each character in context together with its pīnyīn transcription), comprehensive footnotes, and a full translation into English. Going forward, it is intended that all fifty stories will be treated in a similar way in order to provide a comprehensive Classical Chinese primer. This is currently a work-in-progress and is based closely on the hand-written trots of Archie Barnes, which were used as first-stage Classical Chinese teaching materials at Durham University.

Traditional versus Simplified

With the rise of modern China as an economic and increasingly a political powerhouse, it is undoubtedly important to learn the simplified forms of Chinese characters. However, for any student or budding sinologist, one cannot and should not dismiss the traditional forms of characters or *fántǐzì* (繁體字/繁体字). Even in China, examples of traditional forms can be found everywhere. Moreover, almost all of the original written reference material for works over 50 years old is in traditional characters. At some stage, the student will find that knowledge of the simplified form needs to be complemented by familiarity with the traditional and vice-versa.

The reality is that of the 50,000-55,000 characters in China's most comprehensive dictionaries, only around 2,200 were simplified and of those, only around 350 were simplified beyond recognition, such as the character for 'listen' (*tīng*), which was re-written as 听 from the original 聽. The 800 or so examples in this handbook use the traditional form exclusively, but the simplified characters can be found in the dictionary at the end should the reader need them. It will not take too much effort on the part of the student to get to grips with the recognition of traditional characters, if simplified is the starting point, and vice versa.

On Pronunciation and Tones

China's main spoken language is Mandarin. In China, it is known as Pǔtōnghuà (普通話/普通话); in Taiwan, as Guóyǔ (國語/国语). They are essentially the same, but after 50 years of following their own paths, slight changes in pronunciation and sometimes tone can now be detected for a small number of characters. For example, the character for 'and' is 和. In China, it is pronounced *hé*. In Taiwan, it is pronounced *hàn*; it is only pronounced *hé*, when it is in the compound character for e.g. 'peace', *hépíng*, (和平). Another example is the common character for 'know', 'recognise', 識 / 识. In China, the tone is second and is pronounced *shí*; in Taiwan, it is pronounced in fourth tone, *shì*. Such complications are noted where appropriate.

In addition to Modern Chinese variations in pronunciation and tone, Classical Chinese also has its own traditional alternative pronunciations for certain characters. For example, the usual pronunciation for 車 / 车 meaning vehicle or chariot is *chē*, but traditionalists will likely insist on it being pronounced *jū*. In some cases, a character may take on a different tone depending on whether it is functioning in a sentence as a noun or as a verb, e.g 雨 the character for 'rain' is traditionally pronounced in third tone, *yǔ*, if it is a noun and fourth tone, *yù*, if it is acting as a verb. Since in Modern Chinese the character 雨 is always a noun, the only time a student would hear it in fourth tone is when a Classical Chinese text is being read aloud and even then it might just be a third tone pronounced 'incorrectly'.

In modern Chinese-English dictionaries in China, even the more comprehensive ones, such tonal and pronunciation variances may no longer be shown. This is the case with 焉 , which when used as an interrogative is traditionally pronounced as a first tone *yān*, but as a contraction of 於 + 之 (*yú + zhī*), it takes a second tone *yán* (it should be noted that for ease of differentiation, we have decided to maintain this tonal distinction for 焉 *yān*/*yán* throughout this handbook). In standard Chinese-Chinese dictionaries from China, such as the *Cíhǎi* (辭海 / 辞海) or *Cíyuán* (辭源 / 辞源), such tonal variations may still be shown. Modern Chinese-English

dictionaries from Taiwan have also tended to keep traditional alternative pronunciations and their meanings distinct.

In addition, the Chinese character 'one', 'a', 一 , is usually written in pīnyīn with its basic first tone, *yī*. However, the reality is that the tone for this character changes depending on the tone of the character following it. The same applies for the character for 'no', 'not' 不 (*bù*). We follow the standard tonal changes for these two characters in this handbook.

The rule for 一 (*yī*) is as follows: on its own or at the end of a phrase, 一 is pronounced as a first tone, *yī*. Before a character in fourth tone, 一 is pronounced as a second tone, *yí*. Before a character with any other tone (i.e. a first, second or third), 一 is pronounced in fourth tone, i.e. *yì*. The tonal change for 不 (*bù*) is straightforward in comparision; it changes to a second tone, *bú*, before a character with a fourth tone.

In spoken Chinese, there are other rules for tonal changes, but only 一 (*yī*) and 不 (*bù*) are character specific. Consequently, the pīnyīn for all other Chinese characters in this primer are given with their full basic tones. Further, it is only where Modern Chinese compound words are transcribed that the pīnyīn for the different characters runs together to form words, as in the earlier use of the word for the national language of China, Pǔtōnghuà (普通話 / 普通话). It is also common in names not to use pīnyīn tone marks. This is unfortunate, since the more tonal reinforcement that a student of Chinese language has, the better. In this book, all pīnyīn transcriptions show their tones.

On Alternative Characters

The more Classical Chinese one reads, the more one will become aware of the pervasiveness of alternative characters. There are two kinds. The first is where two or more characters have the same meanings and are effectively interchangeable, e.g. the character for 'bed', 床 (*chuáng*) is also found written as 牀; the character for 'old man' 叟 (*sǒu*) may also appear as 叜 or 傁. Footnotes or a good Classical Chinese dictionary are usually the only sources for such variants.

The other type of alternative character is, for want of a better term, a 'borrowed' character. The 'borrowed' character has its own basic set of meanings and so will look 'out of place' until it is read in the sense of the replaced character. For example, 女 (*nǚ*) is the character used for 'woman', 'female'. However, in early Chinese writings, 女 is the common alternative character for 汝 (*rǔ*) which in Classical Chinese means 'you', 'thou'. When 女 means 'you', 'thou', it is correct to pronounce it *rǔ* rather than *nǚ*. Another alternative met in this handbook is 有 (*yǒu*) 'have', 'there is', which when read *yòu* is the alternative character for 又 (*yòu*) 'and', 'also', 'in addition'.

As a general rule, when a character looks totally 'out of place', it will turn out to be either a person's name, a place name or an alternative character. Often such characters are annotated in commentaries, if there are any, to the the original texts. In this handbook, all occurrences of alternative characters are highlighted either in the text or in the dictionary.

On Translations

Taken out of context, a short phrase or sentence in Classical Chinese may well produce a myriad of differing, but still technically 'correct' interpretations and translations. Classical Chinese tends to be much less specific than English in its use of pronouns, tense, case, number, gender, etc. We are forced into choices in the English version that limit the meaning compared to the original.

This poses a problem when we translate some of our simpler examples. For those where there is no subject, but which are obviously sentences, we have tended to use 'he' as default rather than 'she', 'they', 'you' etc. In addition, for ungendered Chinese terms, such as 人 (*rén*), we have tried to use an English equivalent, i.e. 'person', 'people' where appropriate, but otherwise, 'he' is the default. Please bear in mind, it could equally be 'she'. For case, number, tense, etc., we have simply taken what we consider to be the most obvious translation.

Abbreviations

A_1	adverbial placed before subject (if explicit)	interr.	interrogative
		irreg.	irregular
A_2	adverbial placed between subject (if explicit) and verb	lit.	literally
		MC	Modern Chinese
A_3	adverbial placed after object (if explicit)	MW	measure-word
		myth.	mythical
adj.	adjective	neg.	negative
adv.	adverb	nom.	nominalisation
aka	also known as	NB	*nota bene* (take notice)
alt.	alternative	n.	noun
attrib.	attributive	O / obj.	object
BCE	before common era	occ.	occasionally
b.f.	bound form	opp.	opposite
Budd.	Buddhism	orig.	original
ca.	circa	p	page
CC	Classical Chinese	part.	particle
Cent.	century	pass.	passive
cf.	compare	pers.	personal
cop.	copula	pl.	plural
c.o.s.	change of state	postpos.	postposition
dem.	demonstrative	poss.	possessive
eds.	editors	pp	pages
emph.	emphatic; emphasis	pr.	pronunciation
exclam.	exclamation	prep.	preposition
exp.	exposure	prob.	probability
express.	expression	pron.	pronoun
dial.	dialect	ps-pron.	pseudo-pronoun
dir.	direction	rel.	relative
fin.	final	sim.	similar
func.	function	sthg	something
fus.	fusion	S / subj.	Subject
fut.	future	sx	suffix
GR	Gwoyeu Romatzyh (an archaic pīnyīn system)	temp.	temporal
		trad.	traditional
imp.	imperative	var.	variant
init.	intitial	V / vb	verb
interj.	interjection	/ ... /	grammar formula

Introduction
to
Classical Chinese Grammar

Introduction

Classical Chinese refers to a language with its origins in the second millenium BCE. This developed by the latter part of the first millenium BCE to a relatively mature state. This form of language, which dates from the Warring States and early Hàn periods (5th — 1st Century BCE), endured basically unchanged for the next two millenia until the early 20th century. Throughout this period most formal writing was in Classical Chinese, a language that increasingly diverged from the spoken language. In the early 20th century, with pressure for universal education and 'modernity', it was replaced by a vernacular written language based on the spoken language of Běijīng.

The definitions and examples here are mostly taken from texts from the Warring Sates and Hàn periods, the age of the great philosophers and early historians. Some of the basic characteristics of Classical Chinese are outlined below.

Lexical Ambiguity

The wide geographical distribution and long period of development of Classical Chinese has resulted in a large number of vocabulary items. In terms of investment, this means that one has to spend time and effort learning a large number of tautological words that give only a small return. In addition, the characters one learns, especially the more common ones, turn out to have a wide range of meanings, often unrelated to one another. This is best illustrated with a concrete example. The following characters all mean 'you' or 'your',

but each one has a number of distinct, separate meanings as well:

而	*ér*	you; and; but; if
爾	*ěr*	you; this; that; thus; only
乃	*nǎi*	you; then; only then; but; be
戎	*róng*	you; weapons; war; chariot; Róng (surname)
汝	*rǔ*	you, thou; the River Rǔ; Rǔ (surname)
女	*nǔ*	you; daughter; woman; she
若	*ruò*	you; like; seem; as; if

Incidentally, none of the pronouns for 'you' above is a polite form. In the case of an inferior talking to a superior, the above characters for 'you' would be avoided in favour of a term denoting the real or honorifically conferred status of the addressee. For example 君 (*jūn*) 'ruler' was conventionally used by inferiors for 'you' when addressing superiors.

In literary Chinese, the situation of common characters taking on a variety of different meanings was exacerbated by a very special development, that of prose parallelism. In the West, we tend to think of parallelism in terms of Old Testament poetry, but in China it was more akin to euphuistic prose in that it involved repeating the same thing (or something very similar) in different words, as a literary fashion. But what happened when one could not find an appropriate synonym? One roped in a near-synonym, a character with a similar but not identical meaning. A trivial example from 賦 (*fù*), a genre halfway between verse and prose, is having two words for 'and' between clauses. The traditional prose character was 而 (*ér*); to avoid repeating it in the parallel line the character 以 (*yǐ*) was used, even though it did not originally mean 'and' at all, but 'in order to ...'. From then on, it took on both meanings.

This process led to an increase in vagueness and ambiguity, an opposite development to that of semantic precision in the West (the Jesuit '*distinguo*', for instance). Although this development was most noticeable in prose, it inevitably affected verse as well, the end result being a semantic dilution of individual vocabulary items in the literary language as a whole for both prose and verse. The result of this process is a literary language with infinite variety; the loss is the reduction in precision - a headache for the student who wants to know exactly and with certainty what a line of prose or poetry means.

At this point, to prevent the learner being overwhelmed by tangles of this kind, the principle of 'one word, one meaning' is followed both here and in the *Five Classical Chinese Stories* (pp 90-99). It should be noted that the ability to distinguish meanings comes from context, familiarity and practice, as has been the case for over two millennia of Chinese learners.

Optional Precision

It is important to introduce early a very important feature of Classical Chinese as compared to many other languages: the principle of optional precision. In English, we almost always have to specify whether a noun or pronoun is singular or plural, even when this is perfectly clear from the context. For instance, we have to say three dogS, where the '-s' means 'more than one';

but we already know from the 'three' that there is more than one, so from a logical point of view the plural '-s' here is redundant. The existence of cases like 'three sheep', where no '-s' is required, demonstrates this. But, in general, the obligatory distinction between singular and plural in English is something we feel more comfortable with, especially as it saves us deciding in each case whether the context has already made it clear whether we are dealing with 'one' or 'more than one' and whether that distinction is important in this case.

Another category of possible redundancy is the indication of tense. When describing a past event (unless we are using the 'historic present' as in '... so he says to me ...'), we put all the finite verbs into the past tense, typically by adding '-ed'. But, once we have established that the story we are telling happened in the past, we do not really need to keep reminding our listeners of the fact by using the past tense in every sentence. Whereas English tends to err in the direction of over-redundancy here and elsewhere, Classical Chinese errs in the opposite direction and under-indicates distinctions that most languages find essential.

An area which may well cause the student the most difficulty in Classical Chinese is the tendency not to specify who is doing something to whom, partly due to the limited use of pronouns. European languages tend to use pronouns far more. We shall meet first- and second-person pronouns later, but at this stage we shall restrict ourselves to statements in the third person. The first thing to notice is that whereas Classical Chinese has common equivalents for third-person object pronouns ('him, her, it, them') and possessive pronouns ('his, her, its, their'), it has, perhaps surprisingly, no common third-person subject pronouns ('he, she, it, they').

When European works of the last two centuries were translated into Classical Chinese (e.g. the Delegates' Version of the *New Testament* made in 1853), there was often a tendency to use a rather un-Chinese "translatese" that was littered with pronouns like their English originals; the English 'he' became 其 (*qí*), originally 'his', or 彼 (*bǐ*) literally 'that (person)'.

Where English would use a third-person subject pronoun, Classical Chinese either used a noun or nothing at all, depending on the clarity requirements. For instance, 'when Mr X entered the room, he saw ...' would be expressed as 'when Mr X entered the room, saw ...'; this is quite clear, since the subject has not changed. If the subject does change, a noun or pronoun may be necessary; for example, 'when Mr X asked his wife about it, she said ...' would become 'when Mr X asked his wife about it, the wife said ...'. But the context or situation may make it clear that the subject has changed, in which case no noun or pronoun will be needed; e.g. 'he struck a blow at him, but he dodged out of the way' could be expressed as 'struck a blow at him, dodged out of the way'. Similarly 'he gave her the jade; she was delighted' could become 'gave her the jade, was delighted'. Whether or not a pronoun or noun is used is the writer's free choice, whereas in English a subject pronoun is obligatory.

Another area where Classical Chinese requirements are simpler than English ones is

that of possessive pronouns. In 'he stretched out his hand' the 'his' is not essential, since one does not normally stretch out someone else's hand, so Classical Chinese says 'extend hand'. But, 'he took hold of her hand' would normally include the Chinese for 'her'. In other words, 'his' more often means 'someone else's' rather than 'one's own'.

In English, we are obliged to use articles e.g. 'a', 'the', 'some', 'any' even when they are non-distinctive. Classical Chinese occasionally uses equivalents of these, but not regularly. As well as meaning 'his' etc., 其 (*qí*) can also mean 'the ... concerned'. 一 (*yī*) means 'one' and sometimes 'a'. We shall see under Section V on *Numerals* that there are also plural equivalents of these. Usually, though, Classical Chinese indicates neither definiteness nor plurality, so that 馬 (*mǎ*) can mean 'a horse', 'some horses', 'the horse', 'the horses' or 'horses (in general)'.

In English, a predicative adjective requires the copula (am, is, are, was, etc.) before it. This is not so for Classical Chinese, where most equivalents of English adjectives are qualitative verbs which also contain a copula, e.g. 馬 白 (*mǎ bái*) means 'the horse is white', because 白 (*bái*) means not 'white' but 'be white'. However, when characters such as 白 (*bái*) are placed before the noun, they function like an English adjective, hence 白 馬 (*bái mǎ*) means 'white horse'.

The problem here is not that Classical Chinese cannot clearly express tense, number and person, but that it is not obliged to, hence the use of the term 'optional precision'. Since economy of words (minimalism) is an ideal in Chinese prose and particularly verse, it is perhaps hardly surprising that writers take full advantage of this optionality, even if it reduces clarity for the Western reader (and often for the Modern Chinese reader or translator as well). In fact, when the works were written, they probably caused few problems to contemporary readers.

Exposure

In prose, we meet the phenomenon of exposure. In this, some element of a clause, which may normally occur in a medial or final position, such as expressions of time or place, or the object of the main verb, occurs instead in the initial position. Exposure is common in Classical Chinese and is used for either of two reasons:

i) *Rhetorical*: to isolate the key point of a message through preliminary orientation. The exposed element becomes the 'topic' of the sentence; the rest of the sentence will be the point of the message, the 'comment'. An English parallel would be, instead of saying 'I went to see my brother Jim last week', to say 'You know my brother Jim? Well, I went to see him last week.' Jim, the object of the visit, has been exposed as the topic of the news of a visit and the hearer's attention is now focused on him as the point of departure; then follows the actual news of the visit to him. This may be compared to setting the scene on a stage as a background to the action.

ii) *Stylistic*: to create an aesthetically more pleasant rhythm and flow. An important principle in Chinese literary style, both in verse and in prose, is that one should endeavour to avoid long, clumsy sentences, and in particular complicated objects; these should be got out of the way by exposure purely for aesthetic reasons. Long qualifiers are also avoided and replaced with predication. The distance between intimately connected components should also be kept to a minimum. The preferred Chinese style has always been to break discourse down into short, self-contained chunks.

To be clear, we note here that when a topic is exposed, it is not the topic that is being emphasised. The emphasis, in fact, falls squarely on the rest of the sentence or the 'comment'.

Basic Word Order

The languages of East Asia basically have two kinds of word order: *Subject → Verb → Object*, i.e. /S V O/ and *Subject → Object → Verb*, i.e. /S O V/. Chinese, like its southern neighbours, Vietnamese, Thai and Cambodian, is /S V O/, while its other neighbours, Japanese, Korean, Mongolian, Eastern Turkish, Tibetan and Burmese, are /S O V/. Most modern European languages, including English, are also predominantly /S V O/ in word order so the word order of Classical Chinese should present few difficulties.

There is one exception to this: /S V O/ languages tend to place relative clauses after their head-noun, e.g. 'the man, who ...', but Chinese places them in front, similar to the /S O V/ languages. Unlike Modern Chinese, Classical Chinese is sparing in its use of such attributive clauses and they are not usually long.

Main Features
of
Classical Chinese Grammar

Main Grammar Features

(I) Methodology and Structure

Apart from the three possible main components of a clause or sentence: subject (S), verb (V) and object (O), i.e. /S V O/, there are a plethora of secondary components, which we refer to here as 'adverbials' (A) and which may but need not include actual adverbs. The difference between /S V O/ and these secondary components is that whereas /S V O/ answers the question 'Who is doing what to whom?', adverbials answer all the other questions about the action being performed, e.g. when, where, why, how, with whom, for whom, how often, and with what result.

To be clear, 'main' and 'secondary' are used here in a purely structural sense as a matter of convenience in exposition: they should not be understood as meaning more or less important for the point of the statement. Any component can function as the essential part of the answer to the question, whether real or imaginary, that prompted the statement to be made. To some extent there is a tendency in Classical Chinese prose for the topic of a statement to precede the comment, for the known to precede the unknown, for the background to precede the foreground, but this tendency is in competition with other structural requirements and by no means always prevails. In verse, by comparison, the greater freedom in word order weakens this tendency even more, so that we have to be prepared for the emphatic components occuring in any position.

Adverbials consisting of adverbs usually occur immediately before the verb they are qualifying or before another adverbial in this position, so that we can have several such verb-qualifiers in a row, just as a noun can be qualified by a demonstrative, a quantifier and a verb. Non-adverb adverbials, on the other hand, may occur in any of three positions, thus:

i) A_1-*type adverbials*: These are placed before the subject (S) or if the subject is not explicit, before the verb;

ii) A_2-*type adverbials*: These are placed between subject (S), if explicit, and verb (V) - this is the usual adverb position;

iii) A_3-*type adverbials*: These are placed after the object (O) or after the verb if the object is not explicit.

This gives the total possible range of main and secondary clause-components as:

$$/A_1 \ S \ A_2 \ V \ O \ A_3/$$

An English clause illustrating this is '(A_1) Nowadays (S) we (A_2) never (V) see (O) him (A_3) alone', where each position is occupied by a single word. A longer example: '(A_1) Three days after that (S) John and I (A_2) both (V) telephoned (O) the suppliers (A_3) independently of each other', where some of the positions are occupied by phrases. This formula will be found useful for describing most of the clause structures of Classical Chinese prose and also for comparing Chinese and English structures.

(II) How Groups of Nouns Relate

In Classical Chinese, there are three kinds of relationships between nouns and pronouns:

i) *Addition*: 'A and B', e.g. 牛與馬 (*niú yǔ mǎ*) or 牛及馬 (*niú jí mǎ*) 'cattle and horses';

ii) *Attribution* (*qualification, limitation*): 'A's B' or 'B of A' or 'A-B', e.g. 馬之頭 (*mǎ zhī tóu*) 'the horse's head';

iii) *Apposition*: 'A, B' or 'A, viz. B', e.g. 我友李氏 (*wǒ yǒu lǐ shì*) 'my friend, Mr Lǐ'.

If that were all there would be no difficulty, but in practice the 與 (*yǔ*) or 及 (*jí*) - both meaning 'and' here - along with 之 (*zhī*), equivalent here to /...'s/, are very often omitted, particularly in customary compounds, and this can create ambiguity, which can only be resolved by:

i) *Technical knowledge of Chinese culture*: e.g. 山林 (*shān lín*) 'mountain forest' could theoretically mean either 'mountains and forests' or 'mountain forests'; but since Chinese forests are associated with mountains (the lowlands being tilled), the latter meaning 'mountain forests' is to be expected.

ii) *Common sense*: e.g. 手足 (*shǒu zú*) 'hand foot' obviously cannot mean 'the feet of the hands', so must be 'hands and feet' (extended to mean 'brothers'), whereas 雁足 (*yàn zú*) 'wildgoose foot' does not make sense as 'wild geese and feet', so must be 'the foot of a wild goose' (extended to mean 'a letter').

iii) *Experience*: In the case of 山水 (*shān shuǐ*), only experience can tell one that it means 'mountains and rivers' (extended to mean 'landscape'), not 'mountain rivers'.

However, if we wanted to say 'mountains and forests' we could reinstate the character for 'and', i.e. 山與林 (*shān yǔ lín*), and the phrase would be quite unambiguous. Similarly, if we wanted to say 'mountain rivers' we could use a postposition to clarify it, e.g. 山上 [之] 水 (*shān shàng [zhī] shuǐ*) 'the rivers on the mountains' or 山中 [之] 水 (*shān [zhōng] zhī shuǐ*) 'the rivers in (or among) the mountains'.

The combination of /Pronoun + Pronoun/ implies 'and', e.g. 我汝 (*wǒ rǔ*) 'you and I (lit. I and you)', whereas /Pronoun + Noun/ implies attribution (possession), e.g. 我弟 (*wǒ dì*) 'my younger brother'.

In many cases the inclusion or omission of words for 'and' or 'of' will be determined by idiom. Often, it is a matter of taste; the writer will be guided by considerations of genre, rhythm, emphasis, clarity and so on. For example, these words will often be omitted in compressed styles (verse, book titles), but kept in less compressed styles (expository prose, narrative). Figure 1 provides more examples.

(III) Personal Pronouns

Personal pronouns are used far less than in Western languages. Where we might expect them to be used, we often find nouns (including names) or zero, i.e. nothing at all.

Figure 1: Examples of Relationships between Nouns [1]

Original	Ellipsis	Meaning
子女 (zǐ nǔ)	子 [與] 女 (zǐ [yǔ] nǔ)	sons and daughters
狗肉 (gǒu ròu)	狗 [之] 肉 (gǒu [zhī] ròu)	meat of a dog, i.e. dog meat
草木 (cǎo mù)	草 [與] 木 (cǎo [yǔ] mù)	grass and trees
海水 (hǎi shuǐ)	海 [之] 水 (hǎi [zhī] shuǐ)	sea's water, i.e. seawater
夫妹 (fū mèi)	夫 [之] 妹 (fū [zhī] mèi)	husband's younger sister; sister-in-law
弟妹 (dì mèi)	弟 [與] 妹 (dì [yǔ] mèi)	younger brothers and sisters
夫妻 (fū qī)	夫 [與] 妻 (fū [yǔ] qī)	husband and wife
矛盾 (máo dùn)	矛 [與] 盾 (máo [yǔ] dùn)	spears and shields; weapons
妻子 (qī zǐ)	妻 [與] 子 (qī [yǔ] zǐ)	wife and son; wives and sons
馬賈 (mǎ gǔ)	馬 [之] 賈 (mǎ [zhī] gǔ)	dealing in horses; a horse trader
天命 (tiān mìng)	天 [之] 命 (tiān [zhī] mìng)	heaven's mandate; destiny; fate
父子 (fù zǐ)	父 [與] 子 (fù [yǔ] zǐ)	father and son
天地 (tiān dì)	天 [與] 地 (tiān [yǔ] dì)	heaven and earth
宋人 (sòng rén)	宋 [之] 人 (sòng [zhī] rén)	a man from Sòng (lit. Sòng's man)

Note: (1) With no indication of number or article, there may be many possible translation permutations.

First- and second-person pronouns

In Classical Chinese, first- and second-person pronouns do not normally distinguish either number or case. In pre-Hàn Chinese (writing up to circa 206 BCE), 吾 (*wú*) and 我 (*wǒ*) were largely distinguished: 吾 (*wú*) was used as subject ('I' or 'we'), pre-verbal object ('me' or 'us'), or possessive ('my' or 'our'), while 我 (*wǒ*) was used as post-verbal object ('me' or 'us') or topic ('as for me' or 'as for us'). Similarly with the words for 'you', 爾 (*ěr*) and 汝 (*rǔ*) respectively. In later writing, this distinction was largely lost.

Other words for 'I' are 余 (*yú*) and 予 (*yú*). For 'you' there are 若 (*ruò*), 而 (*ér*), 乃 (*nǎi*), 戎 (*róng*), 汝 (*rǔ*) and its variant 女 (in this meaning read *rǔ* not *nǔ*). The royal 'we' is 朕 (*zhèn*). Plural forms include 我儕 (*wǒ chái*) 'we', 吾等 (*wú děng*) 'we', 我輩 (*wǒ bèi*) 'we' and 爾曹 (*ěr cáo*) 'you'. But these are little used and usually the singular form is used for the plural (if at all). Possessive forms have an optional 之 (*zhī*), e.g. 我之手 (*wǒ zhī shǒu*) is the same as 我手 (*wǒ shǒu*) 'my hand(s)' or 'our hands'.

Nouns used as pseudo-pronouns are also employed for the first and second person. They may refer to actual status or function, or may be extended metaphorically. They are best seen as ostensible references to a third person, like the French 'monsieur' used pronominally. We list some of the more common ones below:

王	*wáng*	king; prince; Your Majesty
陛下	*bì xià*	lit. [those] below the throne; Your Majesty

子	*zǐ*	viscount; you
臣	*chén*	[your] subject; [your] minister, I
君	*jūn*	[my] ruler; [my] lord; you, sir
妾	*qiè*	[your] concubine; I (used also by wives and unrelated women)
卿	*qīng*	[my] minister; you (husband to wife)
夫子	*fū zǐ*	[my] master (disciple to teacher); you, sir (to elder stranger)
叟	*sǒu*	the old man; you, sir
兄	*xiōng*	[my] elder brother; you (to brother, cousin or friend)
弟	*dì*	[your] younger brother; I

Third-person pronouns

Third-person pronouns distinguish case, but not number or gender:

i) **Subject pronoun**: 彼 (*bǐ*) 'he', 'she', 'it', 'they' (emphatic), but usually zero (i.e. nothing at all); 其 (*qí*), 伊 (*yī*), 渠 (*qú*) and 厥 (*jué*) are also used in later Classical Chinese. The plural form, 彼等 (*bǐ děng*), is unusual.

ii) **Object pronoun**: 之 (*zhī*) 'him', 'her', 'it', 'them'.

iii) **Possessive pronoun**: 其 (*qí*) or 厥 (*jué*) 'his', 'her', 'its', 'their'.

The object and possessive forms are sometimes also used for the first or second person ('me', 'you', 'my', 'your'). In the list of third-person pronouns above, note the absence of individual characters for 'he', 'she', 'it' or 'they' as the subject of a sentence. There are three possible equivalents:

i) The person's name;

ii) A common noun, e.g. 婦 (*fù*) 'the woman', 'she'; 其人 (*qí rén*) 'the person concerned', 'he', 'she', 生 (*shēng*) 'the gentleman', 'he';

iii) Most commonly zero, i.e nothing at all, e.g. 視之 (*shì zhī*) 'looked at it' can mean 'he (etc.) looked at it' or even 'I looked at it'.

Self

i) 自 (*zì*) is an A₂-type adverb positioned before the verb and means 'myself', 'yourself', 'himself' etc. as subject or object, e.g. 我自 視之 (*wǒ zì shì zhī*) 'I'll look at it myself'; 自殺 (*zì shā*) 'he killed himself'. With 其 (*qí*) 'his (etc.)' preceding the object, it means 'own' referring to the object, e.g. 自 視其手 (*zì shì qí shǒu*) 'he looked at his own hands'.

ii) 己 (*jǐ*) (pronoun) means 'myself (etc.)' as subject or object, in the normal subject and object positions, especially in contrast with 人 (*rén*) 'other people' (see below). It also means 'my (etc.) own', e.g. 汝出己 錢 (*rǔ chū jǐ qián*) 'pay it out of your own pocket'. In sentences involving causative verbs, noun clauses etc., 己 (*jǐ*) may have a different reference from English, e.g. in A 請 B視己 (*A qǐng B shì jǐ*) 'A asked B to look at him', the 'him' refers back to A not to B.

3) 身 (*shēn*) means 'body'; 'one's body'; 'oneself' (etc.). It is used contrastively, e.g. 身至，而妻不至 (*shēn zhì, ér qī bú zhì*) 'he himself came, but his wife did not'.

One another

相 (*xiāng*), 互 (*hù*) or 交 (*jiāo*) meaning 'one another' are all A₂-type adverbs positioned before the verb, e.g. 夫妻相視 (*fū qī xiāng shì*) 'husband and wife looked at one another'. 相 (*xiāng*) is also sometimes used as a plain third-person object pronoun instead of 之 (*zhī*); in such a case, it is still placed before the verb. 相 視 (*xiāng shì*), then, may also mean the same as 視之 (*shì zhī*), i.e. '[they] looked at him'.

One, people, others

人 (*rén*) means 'one', 'people', 'others', e.g. 損人以利己 (*sǔn rén yǐ lì jǐ*) 'he harmed others in order to benefit himself'.

Word order for pronouns

In a negative clause, an object pronoun often precedes the main verb (including modal verbs), though the usual position after the verb became more common in later language, e.g. 我識之 (*wǒ shì zhī*) 'I know him', but 我不之識 (*wǒ bù zhī shì*) 'I don't know him', or later 我不識 之 (*wǒ bú shì zhī*). This 不之 (*bù zhī*) could also appear as 弗 (*fú*) 'not him', i.e. 我弗識 (*wǒ fú shì*). Similarly with negatives other than 不 (*bù*), e.g. 未 (*wèi*) 'never yet': 我未之 見也 (*wǒ wèi zhī jiàn yě*) 'I've never seen him'.

Creating noun-phrases *(nominalising)*

A character never changes in form. Sometimes, though, the tone and very occasionally the pronunciation of a character change, depending on whether the character is acting as noun or verb, e.g. 王 (*wáng* = king; *wàng* = to rule over) or 乘 (*shèng* = a carriage; *chéng* = to ride [a carriage]). However, when the change is grammatical (i.e.

not lexical), this is indicated by the character being preceded by a function particle such as 之 (*zhī*) or 其 (*qí*), thus:

either: /Noun + 之 (*zhī*) + Verb/

or: / 其 (*qí*) + Verb/

e.g. 人死 (*rén sǐ*) 'the man died' but 人之死 (*rén zhī sǐ*) 'the man's death', 'the man's [act of] dying', 'the fact that the man died' and 其死 (*qí sǐ*) 'his death', 'his dying', 'the fact that he died'. Creating noun-phrases has two main uses:

i) *As topic*: At the start of a sentence, the noun-phrase is often followed by 也 (*yě*), a pause marker, and means 'as for', 'in the event of', 'if', 'when' etc., e.g. 李氏之死也，人皆患之 (*lǐ shì zhī sǐ yě, rén jiē huàn zhī*) 'when Mr Lǐ died, everyone was upset about it', or 其死也 (*qí sǐ yě*), 'when he died' etc.

ii) *As the object of certain verbs*: With verbs such as 知 (*zhī*) 'know', 患 (*huàn*) 'be upset about', 見 (*jiàn*) 'see', 聽 (*tīng*) 'allow' etc., this nominalisation usually corresponds, in English, to a noun-clause ('that he did...'), e.g. 我知其死 (*wǒ zhī qí sǐ*) 'I know (that) he died', 我患其死 (*wǒ huàn qí sǐ*) 'I'm upset about his death', 'I'm upset that he died', 勿聽狗之入屋內 (*wù tīng gǒu zhī rù wū nèi*) 'don't let the dog inside the house', literally 'don't allow the dog's entering the house'.

The reader should note that both uses may occur together, in which case the first 之 (*zhī*) is usually omitted, e.g. 我 [之] 見狗之弗食也，怒甚 (*wǒ [zhī] jiàn gǒu zhī fú shí yě, nù shèn*) 'when I saw that the dog would not eat it, I was very angry'.

Figure 2: Examples involving Pronouns (1)

此人有槍 (*cǐ rén yǒu qiāng*)	This man has a spear.
取人之物 (*qǔ rén zhī wù*)	take someone else's things
我儕之友 (*wǒ chái zhī yǒu*)	our friends
我自為之 (*wǒ zì wéi zhī*)	I did it myself.
子食己李 (*zǐ shí jǐ lǐ*)	Eat your own plums!
爾曹之言 (*ěr cáo zhī yán*)	your words i.e. what you (plural) said
其人以己槍自殺 (*qí rén yǐ jǐ qiāng zì shā*)	He killed himself with his own spear.
彼自知其非 (*bǐ zì zhī qí fēi*)	He himself knew that he was wrong.
我弟與汝弟相見 (*wǒ dì yǔ rǔ dì xiāng jiàn*)	My younger brother met your younger brother.
子不之識 (*zǐ bù zhī shí*)	You don't know him.

子之盾與我之矛 (zǐ zhī dùn yǔ wǒ zhī máo)	your shield and my spear
未之視也 (wèi zhī shì yě)	He has not (yet) looked at it.
我與其友 (wǒ yǔ qí yǒu)	his friend and I (lit. I and his friend)
子弗能為乎? (zǐ fú néng wéi hū?)	Can you not do it?
君知之乎? (jūn zhī zhī hū?)	Do you know it?
其自殺也, 家人弗知 (qí zì shā yě, jiā rén fú zhī)	His family did not know that he had killed himself.
臣友請見 (chén yǒu qíng jiàn)	My friend requested an interview.
予見其不起也, 怒甚 (yú jiàn qí bù qǐ yě, nù shèn)	When I saw that he had not stood up, I was very angry.
請卿視之 (qǐng qīng shì zhī)	Please take a look at it.
吾友之視其肉也, 則狗亡矣 (wú yǒu zhī shì qí ròu yě, zé gǒu wáng yǐ)	By the time my friend saw the meat, the dog had disappeared.

Note: (1) The lack of specific markers for subject, number, tense, etc. may produce many possible translation permutations.

(IV) Demonstratives *(this, that, etc.)*

Demonstratives indicate which entities a speaker refers to and distinguishes those entities from others, e.g. 'this', 'that', 'these', 'those'. We split these into two categories, adjectival and pronominal, for ease of reference.

i) *Adjectival*: (i.e. followed by a noun): 此 (cǐ) 'this', 'these', 'such [a]'; 彼 (bǐ) 'that', 'those'; 是 (shì) 'this'; 其 (qí) 'the', 'that', 'those', 'the ... in question', 'the right (for the job)'; 一 (yī) 'a', 'an' (also 'one'); 夫 (fú) 'the', 'now the'; 人 (rén) 'someone's', 'a', 他 (tā) 'another', 'other'; 何 (hé) 'what?', 'what sort of?'; 各 (gè) 'each'; 眾 (zhòng) / 群 (qún) / 諸 (zhū) / 列 (liè) 'all the', 'the

various' - this may also expressed by large numerals such as 百 (bǎi) '100', 千 (qiān) '1,000' or 萬 (wàn) '10,000'.

ii) *Pronominal*: (similar, but used alone): 此 (cǐ) 'this', 'these'; 'here'; 是 (shì) 'this', 'these', 'in such a case', 'at such a time'; 彼 (bǐ) 'that', 'those'; 'there'; 斯 (sī) and 茲 (zī) 'this' (both rare); 或 (huò) 'somebody', 莫 (mò) 'nobody' and 物莫 (wù mò) 'nothing' - all as subject; 其餘 [者] (qí yú [zhě]) 'the rest'; 其一 (qí yī) 'one of them', 'the other of them', 其一人 (qí yī rén) 'one of them (people)'; 誰 (shuí) 'who?'; 孰 (shú) 'who?', 'which?'; 眾 (zhòng) 'they all'; 各 (gè) 'each (one)' etc.

14

Figure 3: **Examples involving Demonstratives** [1]

此牛 (*cǐ niú*)	this cow
各人 (*gè rén*)	each person
此二牛 (*cǐ èr niú*)	these two cows / both these cows
是物 (*shì wù*)	this thing
彼馬 (*bǐ mǎ*)	that horse
此牛乎？(*cǐ niú hū?*)	Is this a cow?
彼三馬 (*bǐ sān mǎ*)	those three horses
子視彼二馬！(*zǐ shì bǐ èr mǎ!*)	Look at those two horses!
得其人 (*dé qí rén*)	caught the man / get the right person
請他人為之 (*qǐng tā rén wéi zhī*)	asked someone else to do it
之他鄉 (*zhī tā xiāng*)	went to another village
不知何人為之 (*bù zhī hé rén wéi zhī*)	did not know who did it.
至一屋 (*zhì yì wū*)	arrived at a house
吾逢一馬賈 (*wú féng yì mǎ gǔ*)	I met a horse trader.
何馬？(*hé mǎ?*)	Which horse?
我識其人，不識其弟 (*wǒ shì qí rén, bú shì qí dì*)	I know him, [but] not his younger brother.
眾山 (*zhòng shān*)	the hills / all of the hills
各人得其所 (*gè rén dé qí suǒ*)	Each person found his place.
羣臣 (*qún chén*)	the ministers / all the ministers
損己以利眾友 (*sǔn jǐ yǐ lì zhòng yǒu*)	harm oneself to benefit one's friends
諸物 (*zhū wù*)	all things / everything
人臣 (*rén chén*)	a minister / a subject
列國 (*liè guó*)	every country / various countries
人子 (*rén zǐ*)	(someone else's) son

Note: (1) The lack of specific markers for subject, number, tense, etc. may produce many possible translation permutations.

(V) Numerals

Numerals are the same as in Modern Chinese. When numbers are consecutive, such as 八九 (bā jiǔ), the relationship is likely to be 'or', i.e. 'eight or nine'. Where the second of the two numbers is 十 (shí) '10', 百 (bǎi) '100', 千 (qiān) '1,000' or 萬 (wàn) '10,000', the first number acts as an attributive to the second, e.g. in 三十 (sān shí) '30', the 三 (sān) '3' qualifies the 十 (shí) '10'. Finally, where a number follows 10, 100, 1,000, 10,000, the relationship is likely to be 'plus', e.g. 十五 (shí wǔ) '10 + 5', i.e. '15' or 三十五 (sān shí wǔ) '3 x 10 + 5', i.e. '35'.

There are certain exceptions to the above in Classical Chinese. 兩 (liǎng) is usually 'a pair', sometimes 'two' (also a weight, 50g, and a tael of silver). In compound numerals above ten, 有 (read yòu here not yǒu), may be used as a character variant for 又 (yòu) 'also', e.g. 四十有五 (sì shí yòu wǔ) '4 x 10 and 5', i.e. '45'. 百 (bǎi), '100', 千 (qiān) '1,000', and 萬 (wàn) '10,000' etc. do not need 一 (yī) 'one' before them. 數 (shuò alt. pr. shù) 'several' replaces Modern Chinese 幾 (jǐ) 'several', whereas 幾 (jǐ) meaning 'how many?', replaces both Modern Chinese 幾 (jǐ) 'how many? (up to ten)' and 多少 (duō shǎo) 'how many?' 幾何 (jǐ hé) means the same and is used when no measure-word or noun follows. (NB 幾, when read jī, means 'almost'.) Both 餘 (yú) '-odd' (used like Modern Chinese 多, duō, '-odd') and 許 (xǔ) 'approximately' are used as suffixes. Examples: 數日 (shuò rì) 'several days', 幾日 (jǐ rì) 'how many days?'; 馬幾何 (mǎ jǐ hé) 'how many horses?', and; 二十餘日 (èr shí yú rì) 'twenty-odd days'.

/Numeral + Noun/ more often corresponds to the English 'the numeral + noun', e.g. 三馬皆至 (sān mǎ jiē zhì) 'the three horses all arrived'. /Noun + Numeral/ (with or without measure-word)' usually corresponds to English /Numeral + Noun/, e.g. 有馬三[匹]至 (yǒu mǎ sān [pǐ] zhì) 'there were three horses arrived' = 'three horses arrived'; 我買馬三[匹] (wǒ mǎi mǎ sān [pǐ]) 'I bought three horses'. Strictly speaking the two word orders represent quite different structures: in 三馬 (sān mǎ) 'the three horses', the numeral 三 (sān) is qualifying the noun 馬 (mǎ) just as the demonstrative does in 此馬 (cǐ mǎ) 'this horse' or indeed 此三馬 (cǐ sān mǎ) 'these three horses', whereas in 我買馬三 (wǒ mǎi mǎ sān) 'I bought three horses' we have two statements telescoped into one, viz. 我買馬 (wǒ mǎi mǎ) 'I bought some horses' plus 三 (sān) '[there were] three [of them]'. It is important to realise this, since adverbs qualifying the number will come into the second statement, not the first, e.g. 有牛馬各七 (yǒu niú mǎ gè qī) 'there were cattle and horses: of each there were seven' = 'there were seven cows and seven horses'; 公年且八十 (gōng nián qiě bā shí) 'the old gentleman's years are almost eighty', i.e. 'the old gentleman is almost eighty years old'.

The presence or absence of a measure-word is of lesser importance. Measure-words are less used than in Modern Chinese, except of course for weights and measures. It is important to realise that certain nouns (as in Modern Chinese) are quasi-measures, such as 人 (rén) 'person' and 日 (rì) 'day', so one says 三人 (sān rén) 'three people' and 三日 (sān rì) 'three days', not 人三 (rén sān) and not 日三 (rì sān). However,

人 (*rén*) may be used twice in the same phrase, the first time as a noun and the second time as a true measure-word, e.g. 有宋人三人 (*yǒu sòng rén sān rén*) lit. 'there are Sòng people three units' = 'there are three people from Sòng', just like 過友三人 (*guò yǒu sān rén*) 'visited friends three units' = 'visited three friends'. Unlike Modern Chinese, Classical Chinese sometimes omits 一 (*yī*) 'one', 'a' before measure-words for weights and measures where these precede the noun, e.g. 斤肉 (*jīn ròu*) but 肉一斤 (*ròu yì jīn*) both 'a catty of meat'. 一 (*yī*) may also be used in the sense of 'whole', as in 一民 (*yī mín*) 'the whole people'.

In Classical Chinese, ordinals, e.g. 六 (*liù*) 'six', are usually identical with cardinals (六, *liù* also means 'the sixth'). The exceptions are 首 (*shǒu*) 'first' and 次 (*cì*) 'second', 'next', e.g. 二日 (*èr rì*) 'two days', but 次日 (*cì rì*) 'the next / second day'; 三日 (*sān rì*) 'three days' or 'the third day'.

'One of them' is either 其一 (*qí yī*) or 一焉 (*yì yán*). 'One ..., the other ...' is 其一 ..., 其一 ... (*qí yī ..., qí yī ...*) . 'The three of them' is 三者 (*sān zhě*). 四 (*sì*), 'four', may be used with the meaning of 'on all four sides'.

'X times' (referring to occasions) is expressed in one of three ways:

i) By 'X' being used adverbially and being placed between subject (if there is one specified) and verb, e.g. 三視之 (*sān shì zhī*) '[he] thrice looked at it'. 'Twice' is usually expressed as 再 (*zài*) in the same way, e.g. 再拜 (*zài bài*) 'he bowed twice';

ii) By 'X 次 (*cì*)' being placed after the object (in a /S V O/ sentence structure), e.g. 一日視之三次 (*yī rì shì zhī sān cì*) 'looked at it three times a day', and;

iii) By '者 (*zhě*) X', where X is placed in the final position of the sentence. This form is restricted in use, e.g. 如此者三 (*rú cǐ zhě sān*) '[he did] this three times'.

Figure 4: Examples involving Numerals [1]

逢賊數人 (*féng zéi shuò rén*)	met several thieves
內有齊人四人 (*nèi yǒu qí rén sì rén*)	Inside, there were four men from Qí.
得錢幾枚 (*dé qián jǐ méi*)	obtained several coins
買李一斤 (*mǎi lǐ yì jīn*)	bought a catty of plums (1 catty = 0.5 kg)
出錢幾何？出錢一 (*chū qián jǐ hé? chū qián yī*)	How much did he pay? He paid one copper coin.
二人皆知之 (*èr rén jiē zhī zhī*)	Both men knew it.
逢幾人？逢三人 (*féng jǐ rén? féng sān rén*)	How many people did he meet? He met three.
逢賈人十餘人 (*féng gǔ rén shí yú rén*)	met over ten traders/met a dozen merchants

汝買肉幾何？我買肉二斤 (*rǔ mǎi ròu jǐ hé? wǒ mǎi ròu èr jīn*)	How much meat did you buy? I bought two catties.
一與二為三 (*yī yǔ èr wéi sān*)	One plus two equals three.
梨價幾何？三錢一枚 (*lí jià jǐ hé? sān qián yì méi*)	How much are the pears? Three coppers per pear.
此梨甚美，我買二三枚 (*cǐ lí shèn měi, wǒ mǎi èr sān méi*)	These pears are very beautiful, I will buy two or three.
其弟年三十許 (*qí dì nián sān shí xǔ*)	His younger brother is around thirty years old.
首年買屋，次年娶妻，三年買妾 (*shǒu nián mǎi wū, cì nián qǔ qī, sān nián mǎi qiè*)	In the first year, he bought a house, in the second year, he took a wife and in the third year, he bought a concubine.
此十者，我取一焉而舍其餘 (*cǐ shí zhě, wǒ qǔ yì yán ér shě qí yú*)	Of these ten (things), I will take one and leave the rest.
一年三過二者 (*yì nián sān guò èr zhě*)	Each year he visited the two of them three times.
天雨三日始止，四日大晴 (*tiān yù sān rì shǐ zhǐ, sì rì dà qíng*)	It rained for three days and then stopped, on the fourth day, it was fine.

Note: (1) The lack of specific markers for subject, number, tense, etc. may produce many possible translation permutations.

(VI) Copula ('to be')

By copula, we mean here the verb 為 (*wéi*) 'to be' and its negative counterpart 非 (*fēi*) 'not to be', together with their equivalents, including zero, when used for equating or classifying nouns or pronouns, e.g. 爾為爾，我為我 (*ěr wéi ěr, wǒ wéi wǒ*) 'you are you and I am me'; 我非爾也 (*wǒ fēi ěr yě*) 'I am not you'.

為 (*wéi*) is more often used in the sense of 'to be temporarily', 'to act in the capacity of', 'to pretend to be' etc., e.g. 彼且為嬰兒，亦與之為嬰兒 (*bǐ qiě wéi yīng ér, yì yǔ zhī wéi yīng ér*) 'if he wants to be (i.e. act like) a child, be a child with him' or 昔者莊周夢為胡蝶 (*xī zhě zhuāng zhōu mèng wéi hú dié*) 'once upon a time, Zhuāngzǐ dreamt he was (i.e. temporarily) a butterfly'.

為 (*wéi*) may be replaced by 曰 (*yuē*), the old verb 'to be' in certain cases, e.g. to introduce a name, [其]名為 or 曰伯夷 (*[qí] míng wéi* or *yuē bó yí*) 'his name is Bóyí' or before each item on a list. In the case of [其言]曰：不然！ (*[qí yán] yuē: "bù rán!"*) '[his words] were: "Not so!"', i.e. 'he said: "Not so!"', the first part is usually omitted leaving simply 曰：不然！ (*yuē: "bù rán!"*) '[his words] were: "Not so!"' = 'he said: "Not so!"', with the result that this old copula 曰 (*yuē*) has come to be regarded as a defective verb 'said' (like English 'quoth'). In fact,

曰 (*yuē*) is not used to mean 'say' except before direct speech (quotations); elsewhere 言 is used, e.g. 子何言？ (*zǐ hé yán*) 'what did you say?'

為 (*wéi*) also means 'begin', 'to be', 'become', especially after a verb of change, with or without an intervening 而 (*ér*), where it corresponds to the English 'into', e.g. 化而為鳥 (*huà ér wéi niǎo*) 'it changed and became a bird', i.e. 'it changed into a bird'.

為 (*wéi*) is commonly used as a putative verb 'consider to be', 'treat as being', 'regard as', 'use as', 'have as one's ...' etc., usually in conjunction with 以 (*yǐ*) which here is an object-marker like a Modern Chinese 把 (*bǎ*), e.g. 子以我為何如人？ (*zǐ yǐ wǒ wéi hé rú rén*) 'what sort of a person do you consider me to be / think I am / take me for?'

For definitions (equations), 為 (*wéi*) is usually omitted (or, if you prefer, replaced by a zero-copula) and the relationship between the subject and complement of the absent verb is typically clarified by the addition of the clause-final particle 也 (*yě*) 'you see', sometimes with the addition of the topic marker 者 (*zhě*) after the subject, e.g. 此 [ ] 馬也，非牛也 (*cǐ [ ] mǎ yě, fēi niú yě*) 'this is a horse, not a cow'; 其趨 [ ] 一也。一者 [ ] 何也？曰： [ ] 仁也 (*qí qū [ ] yě. yì zhě [ ] hé yě? yuē: [ ] rén yě*) 'Their goals [are] one. What [is] this "one"? Answer: [it is] benevolence.'

It should be noted that the negative counterpart of this zero-copula is 非 (*fēi*), not 不 (*bù*), and that a final 也 (*yě*) is usual with

非 (*fēi*). In addition, an initial clause with 非 (*fēi*) may be used as the protasis in a conditional sentence, e.g. 非彼，無我 (*fēi bǐ, wú wǒ*) 'if it were not for them, we should not exist'.

Be careful of the the two different uses of 者 (*zhě*) in this connection. In 'A者B也' (A *zhě* B *yě*), i.e. 'A is B', the 者 (*zhě*) is a topic marker, e.g. 雛者雞之子也 (*chú zhě jī zhī zǐ yě*) 'a chick is the young of a fowl'. However, in /Verb [Object] 者 (*zhě*) Noun 也 *yě*/' the 者 (*zhě*) is a pronoun meaning 'the one who' or 'that which', e.g. 走者我弟也 (*zǒu zhě wǒ dì yě*) 'the one who is running is my younger brother'. This can lead to ambiguity or at least can be confusing. Compare the following two sentences, which look very similar: (i) 死者，生之終也 (*sǐ zhě, shēng zhī zhōng yě*) 'death (= noun) is the end of life', and (ii) 死者，我之先人也 (*sǐ zhě, wǒ zhī xiān rén yě*) 'those who have died (= verb) are our predecessors'. There is no formal difference between the subjects of these two sentences: the structure can be determined only by reference to their meaning. In addition, both halves of an equation may contain the pronoun 者 (*zhě*), e.g. 今之隱机者非昔之隱机者也 (*jīn zhī yìn jī zhě fēi xī zhī yìn jī zhě yě*) 'the person who is leaning on the table now is not the person who was leaning on the table a while ago'.

Further, the adverbs 乃 (*nǎi*) and 即 (*jí*), which both mean 'in fact' (cf. Modern Chinese 就是, *jiù shi*), are often used as the link words in copula sentences of the 'not X but Y' type, e.g. 此非牛 [也] ，乃馬也 (*cǐ fēi niú [yě], nǎi mǎ yě*) 'this is not a cow, but a horse'.

Classical Chinese Grammar

A final 也 (*yě*) plus 乎 (*hū*) is the sign of a question in Classical Chinese and this is similar to a Modern Chinese 嗎 (*ma*), 呢 (*ne*) or 吧 (*ba*); they may sometimes merge to become 與 or 歟 (both read *yú*), e.g. 此馬與？然，馬也 (*yú cǐ mǎ yú? rán, mǎ yě*) 'is this a horse? Yes, it is a horse.' In questions of choice, e.g. 'is X a Y or a Z?', Classical Chinese expresses the question as: 'X is a Y, is a Z?' Sometimes a word for 'or' such as 其 (*qí*), 抑 (*yì*), or 將 (*jiāng*), may be inserted, e.g. 子人與，其獸與？ (*zǐ rén yú, qí shòu yú?*) 'are you a man, or an animal?' Note also: 非馬而何 [也] ？ (*fēi mǎ ér hé [yě]*) 'if it is not a horse, what is it?' Interrogatives are dealt with in more detail in Section XIV, see pp 48-50.

Figure 5: **Examples involving the Copula** [1]

我人也，非馬也 (*wǒ rén yě, fēi mǎ yě*)	I am a man, not a horse.
我非馬，乃人也 (*wǒ fēi mǎ, nǎi rén yě*)	I am not a horse, but a man.
馬者，獸也乎？ (*mǎ zhě, shòu yě hū?*)	Is a horse an animal?
人者，亦獸歟？非也 or：否，非獸也 (*rén zhě, yì shòu yú? fēi yě*) or (*fǒu, fēi shòu yě*)	Is man also an animal? No. (Or: 'No, he is not an animal.')
非獸而何也？ (*fēi shòu ér hé yě?*)	If it is not an animal, what is it?
我即汝師 (*wǒ jí rǔ shī*)	I am your teacher.
此吾弟也 (*cǐ wú dì yě*)	This is my younger brother.
我問其為誰 (*wǒ wèn qí wéi shuí*)	I asked him who he was.
子非李氏之友與？ (*zǐ fēi lǐ shì zhī yǒu yú?*)	Are you not Mr Lǐ's friend?
白馬非馬也 (*bái mǎ fēi mǎ yě*)	A white horse is not a horse.
其餘者乃吾友之馬也 (*qí yú zhě nǎi wú yǒu zhī mǎ yě*)	The rest are my friend's horses.
仁者，人也 (*rén zhě, rén yě*)	Benevolence is being human.
狐者獸與？然 (*hú zhě shòu yú? rán*)	Are foxes animals? Yes.
雲化而為雨 (*yún huà ér wéi yǔ*)	Clouds turn to rain.
嬰兒為馬而遊 (*yīng ér wéi mǎ ér yóu*)	The child played at being a horse.

以「無有」為「有」 (*yǐ 'wú yǒu' wéi 'yǒu'*)	consider nothing(ness) as something.
非子，則我奈何？ (*fēi zǐ, zé wǒ nài hé?*)	If it were not for you, then what would I do?
問曰：此跡狐與其狼與？ 曰：二者皆非，乃狗也 (*wèn yuē: cǐ jì hú yú qí láng yú? yuē: èr zhě jiē fēi, nǎi gǒu yě*)	[Someone] asked: "Are these tracks those of a fox or a wolf? [Someone else] answered: "They are neither of these, but [those of] a dog.

Note: (1) The lack of specific markers for subject, number, tense, etc. may produce many possible translation permutations.

(VII) Tenses

There are no tenses in Classical Chinese in the strict definition of variant forms of a verb such as 'go', 'gone', 'went', which indicate the location of an event in absolute time, e.g. present or past. However, Classical Chinese does have aspect, in which relative time is indicated by particles and other words or phrases, such as time expressions. The following tense descriptions are based on the typical tense system of European languages and are purely for comparative purposes.

Perfect and pluperfect

In Classical Chinese, the perfect ('has done') and pluperfect ('had done') are expressed by either 已 (*yǐ*) 'already', 既 [已] (*jì [yǐ]*) 'already', or 嘗 (*cháng*) 'once', 'before now', with these being placed before the verb; there may also be an optional function particle, 矣 (*yǐ*), cf. Modern Chinese 了 (*le*), at the end of the sentence. The corresponding negative form ('has not done, had not done') has 未 (*wèi*) before the verb and sometimes 也 (*yě*) at the end of the sentence. When 未 is combined with 嘗

(*cháng*), the force is 'never [yet]', cf. 馬 [已] 亡 [矣] (*mǎ [yǐ] wáng [yǐ]*) 'the horses have / had disappeared'; 馬未亡也 (*mǎ wèi wáng yě*) 'the horses have / had not (yet) disappeared', and 馬未嘗亡也 (*mǎ wèi cháng wáng yě*) 'the horses have / had never yet disappeared'.

Past and present progressive

In Classical Chinese, past progressive ('was doing') and present progressive ('is doing') are not usually marked, though 方 (*fāng*) 'just at this / that moment' before the verb may be used for emphasis, e.g. 馬方食草 (*mǎ fāng shí cǎo*) 'the horse is / was grazing'. For 'just about to', 方且 (*fāng qiě*) or 方欲 (*fāng yù*) are used. 方將 (*fāng jiāng*), it should be noted, can also mean 'is / was doing'.

Two other characters with similar meanings are: 甫 (*fǔ*), which is sometimes used in later texts for 'has just done' or 'was just doing', e.g 我甫見之 (*wǒ fǔ jiàn zhī*) 'I've just seen him', and 適 (*shì*) 'just happened to', 'as it so happens', 'as it so happened', e.g. 至市，適遇吾友 (*zhì shì, shì yù wú yǒu*) 'when I got to the market,

I happened to meet my friend'. In later texts 適 (*shì*) is sometimes used like 方 (*fāng*) and 甫 (*fǔ*). We may also include here 昔 [者] (*xī [zhě]*) 'earlier', 'a while ago', 'the other day', 'once upon a time', which is a vague time-indicator used to mark a contrast with the present.

Future

For the future ('will do', 'is going to do' etc.) and future-in-past ('was going to do', 'was about to do'), Classical Chinese uses either: 將 (*jiāng*), 且 (*qiě*), 欲 (*yù*), or 當 (*dāng*) before the verb. 將 (*jiāng*) is sometimes reinforced with 必 (*bì*) 'definitely', 'certainly', 'inevitably', 'for sure' which precedes it; a final 矣 (*yǐ*) (cf. Modern Chinese 了 *le*, in this sense) is optional. Examples: 我 且 食 之 (*wǒ qiě shí zhī*) 'I'm going to eat it'; 必 將 死 矣 (*bì jiāng sǐ yǐ*) 'he will surely die'.

Preterite, past / present habitual

Preterite ('did'), past habitual ('used to do', 'did'), present habitual ('does'), as well as the progressive and future tenses above, use nothing in the affirmative, 不 (*bù*) in the negative, e.g. 我 食 之 (*wǒ shí zhī*) 'I ate it', 'I used to eat it', 'I eat it' as well as 'I was eating it', 'I am eating it', 'I shall eat it', 'I was going to eat it'; 我 不 食 [之] (*wǒ bù shí zhī*) or 我 不 之 食 (*wǒ bù zhī shí*) or 我 弗 食 (*wǒ fú shí*) are the corresponding negative forms for these tenses. It is important, though, to distinguish 不 食 (*bù shí*) 'did not eat' and 未 食 也 (*wèi shí yě*) 'has not eaten' (both would be translated as 沒 吃, *méi chī*, in Modern Chinese).

Imperative

For the imperative ('do!', 'let's do!'), Classical Chinese uses either nothing (zero) or 可 (*kě*) 'you may', 'we may' or 盍 (*hé*) 'why not', or 且 (*qiě*) 'just' or 其 (*qí*) 'should' or 當 (*dāng*) 'should'. These are placed directly before the verb; there may or may not be an 矣 (*yǐ*) at the end of the sentence to clarify the imperative. Examples: 子 且 待 之 (*zǐ qiě dāi zhī*) 'just wait for him'; 我 可 去 矣 (*wǒ kě qù yǐ*) 'let's go!' The imperative can also be expressed by using the verbs 願 (*yuàn*) '[I] wish that', 請 (*qǐng*) and 求 (*qiú*) both 'I request that', and 望 (*wàng*) 'I hope that'; the pronoun for 'you' may follow these verbs, e.g. 願 子 相 助 (*yuàn zǐ xiāng zhù*) 'help me!' 'Let's', in the sense of '[we] had best ...' can also be expressed as 不 如 (*bù rú*), 莫 若 (*mò ruò*) etc. Sometimes 偕 (*xié*) 'together' or 與 我 (*yǔ wǒ*) 'with me' are used, e.g. 偕 往 矣 (*xié wǎng yǐ*) 'let's go!' Negative imperatives, on the other hand, ('don't! let's not!') use 無 (*wú*), 毋 (*wú*), or 勿 (*wù*) before the verb (a 也 *yě* is optional at the end of the sentence), e.g. 勿 視 也 (*wù shì yě*) 'Don't look [at it]'. Verbs such as 願 (*yuàn*) '[I] wish that' etc. may also be combined with the above negatives, e.g. 望 毋 我 負 (*wàng wú wǒ fù*) 'Don't let me down!'

Figure 6: **Examples involving Tense** [1]

子已見之乎?見之矣／未之見也 (zǐ yǐ jiàn zhī hū? jiàn zhī yǐ / wèi zhī jiàn yě)	Have you seen it? I have seen it. / I have not seen it / I did not see it.
子知之乎?知之／弗知 (zǐ zhī zhī hū? zhī zhī / fú zhī)	Do you know about it? I do. / I do not.
子將見之乎?［將］見之／弗見 (zǐ jiāng jiàn zhī hū? [jiāng] jiàn zhī / fú jiàn)	Will you see it? Yes, I will. / No, I will not.
我五日當復來 (wǒ wǔ rì dāng fù lái)	I will return in five days.
客來乎?來矣 (kè lái hū? lái yǐ)	Has the guest arrived? He has.
君三日當死 (jūn sān rì dāng sǐ)	You will die in three days.
馬已死乎?未［死］也 (mǎ yǐ sǐ hū? wèi [sǐ] yě)	Has the horse already died? No, it has not.
且涉水而見弟趨至 (qiě shè shuǐ ér jiàn dì qū zhì)	He was about to cross the river when he saw his younger brother hurrying up.
時我日一過之 (shí wǒ rì yī guò zhī)	At that time, I visited him once a day.
問曰:已至乎?曰:未也 (wèn yuē: yǐ zhì hū? yuē: wèi yě)	[Someone] asked: "Have they already arrived?" [Someone else] answered: "No, they have not."
勿復為之 (wù fù wéi zhī)	Do not do it again!
子可歸矣 (zǐ kě guī yǐ)	Go home!
未雨而去 (wèi yù ér qù)	He went off before it rained.
無忘其恩也 (wú wàng qí ēn yě)	Do not forget his kindnesses!
師必將問之矣 (shī bì jiāng wèn zhī yǐ)	The teacher will certainly ask about it.
子甫至乃去乎? (zǐ fǔ zhì nǎi qù hū?)	Surely you're not leaving - you've just arrived!
子何不姑試之? (zǐ hé bù gū shì zhī?)	Try it! (lit. 'Why not try it?')
汝既得之,何不持歸 (rǔ jì dé zhī, hé bù chí guī)	When you have found it, take it back with you. (lit. '..., why not take it back with you?')

Note: (1) The lack of specific markers for subject, number, tense, etc. may produce many possible translation permutations.

(VIII) Adverbs and Modal Verbs

In English, the position of adverbs is relatively free. In Classical Chinese prose, though, they almost always occur as A2-type, i.e. they are placed before the verb. Examples include: 獨行 (*dú xíng*) 'walk <u>alone</u>'; 東行 (*dōng xíng*) 'travel <u>eastwards</u>'; 復至 (*fù zhì*) 'come <u>again</u>'; 先至 (*xiān zhì*) 'arrive <u>first</u>'; 全解 (*quán jiě*) 'understand <u>completely</u>'; 立去 (*lì qù*) 'go <u>at once</u>'; 亦買此 (*yì mǎi cǐ*) 'buy this <u>too</u>'; 革食此 (*gé shí cǐ*) 'eat this <u>instead</u>'; 尚居焉 (*shàng jū yán*) '<u>still</u> lives there'; 數見之 (*shuò jiàn zhī*) '<u>often</u> see him'; 徒欲此 (*tú yù cǐ*) '<u>only</u> want this'.

A3-type adverbs in Classical Chinese prose are unusual and often turn out to be predicative adjectives. For example the 久 (*jiǔ*) in 我待之久矣 (*wǒ dāi zhī jiǔ yǐ*) 'I've been waiting for him a long time' is a qualitative verb meaning 'be long', so that the whole sentence is literally 'My waiting for him has been long'; in 我不能久待之 (*wǒ bù néng jiǔ dāi zhī*) 'I cannot wait long for him', 久 (*jiǔ*) is used as an A2-type adverb. 甚 (*shèn*) 'be intense' is used in a similar way in 怒甚 (*nù shèn*) and 甚怒 (*shèn nù*), which both mean 'be very angry', The first, though, would be analysed as /Noun + Predicate/, i.e. 'anger is extreme' and the second as /A2 + Verb/, i.e. 'extremely angry'.

Some adverbs tend to have particular final particles associated with them. For example, 安 (*ān*), 焉 (*yān*), 何 (*hé*), 惡 (*wū*), 烏 (*wū*) and 豈 (*qǐ*) all mean 'how' (implying 'surely not!') and tend to have the exclamatory-interrogative particles 哉 (*zāi*) or 乎 (*hū*) at the end of the clause, e.g. 我焉能知之哉 (*wǒ yān néng zhī zhī zāi*) 'how could I possibly know that?', i.e. 'of course I don't know that!' In addition, 徒 (*tú*), 但 (*dàn*), 止 (*zhǐ*), 特 (*tè*) etc. meaning 'only' tend to have the final particles 而已 [矣] (*ér yǐ [yǐ]*) or 耳 [矣] (*ěr [yǐ]*) 'and that's all', e.g. 我姑止取此耳 (*wǒ gū zhǐ qǔ cǐ ěr*) 'I'll just take this for the time being'.

Modal verbs (auxiliary verbs) also occur between subject and verb, like A2-type adverbials. The most common are 能 (*néng*) 'can'; 可 (*kě*) 'may', 'can', (especially in the passive 'can be X-ed', 'is X-able'), also 'ought', 'must'; 可以 (*kě yǐ*) 'may', 'can'; 得 (*dé*) 'can'; 足 (*zú*) 'is worth X-ing', 'is X-able'; 足以 (*zú yǐ*) 'is up to X-ing'; 不如 (*bù rú*) 'had best'; 敢 (*gǎn*) 'dare'; 宜 (*yí*) 'ought'; as well as 將 (*jiāng*), 且 (*qiě*), 欲 (*yù*) or 當 (*dāng*), which are used to show the future or future-in-past (see Section VII on *Tenses*). It should be noted that the relative order of adverbs and modal verbs in Classical Chinese is not necessarily the same as in English, e.g. 彼蓋將買之 (*bǐ gài jiāng mǎi zhī*) 'he <u>will</u> probably buy it'; 我亦將取彼 (*wǒ yì jiāng qǔ bǐ*) 'I <u>shall</u> also choose that'.

Figure 7: **Examples involving Adverbs and Modal Verbs** (1)

明日我將西行 (*míng rì wǒ jiāng xī xíng*)	Tomorrow, I will travel west.
眾客皆大喜 (*zhòng kè jiē dà xǐ*)	All the guests were delighted.
其弟大怒 (*qí dì dà nù*)	His younger brother was very angry.

夫子待我甚善 (*fū zǐ dài wǒ shèn shàn*)	You treat me very well.
二山皆甚高 (*èr shān jiē shèn gāo*)	Both mountains are very tall.
二人並行 (*èr rén bìng xíng*)	The two men walked side by side.
汝能盡食之乎？ (*rǔ néng jìn shí zhī hū?*)	Can you eat it all?
大毀其城而盡殺其民 (*dà huǐ qí chéng ér jìn shā qí mín*)	largely destroyed the city and killed all of the people
其人有病而未必將死也 (*qí rén yǒu bìng ér wèi bì jiāng sǐ yě*)	The man is ill but will not necessarily die.
兔與狐焉能同居哉！ (*tù yǔ hú yān néng tóng jū zāi!*)	How can foxes and rabbits live together?
次日其病小愈 (*cì rì qí bìng xiǎo yù*)	The next day, his illness was slightly better.
子何舍此而革用彼？ (*zǐ hé shě cǐ ér gé yòng bǐ?*)	Why did you leave this and instead use that?
兔多居而狐則獨居 (*tù duō jū ér hú zé dú jū*)	Rabbits live together, but foxes live alone.
久病始愈 (*jiǔ bìng shǐ yù*)	After a long illness, he is now recovering.
李氏行將歸，盍姑待之？ (*lǐ shì xíng jiāng guī, hé gū dāi zhī?*)	Mr Lǐ will come back soon, why not wait for him a while?
豈徒欲此哉！(*qǐ tú yù cǐ zāi!*)	Surely he wants more than just this!
水太深，安得涉哉！ (*shuǐ tài shēn, ān dé shè zāi!*)	The water is too deep, how on earth can we cross?
眾友亦數過之 (*zhòng yǒu yì shuò guò zhī*)	His friends also visited him often.
久求之而終弗得 (*jiǔ qiú zhī ér zhōng fú dé*)	He sought it for a long time, but never got it.
徒出三錢耳矣 (*tú chū sān qián ěr yǐ*)	He only paid three coppers.
爾何不先盡食之乃去？ (*ěr hé bù xiān jìn shí zhī nǎi qù?*)	Why do you not finish eating it all before leaving?
猶未得之歟？(*yóu wèi dé zhī yú?*)	Have you still not received it?

25

何不立去？ (*hé bú lì qù?*)	Why not leave right away?
何必立去？ (*hé bì lì qù?*)	Why must you leave right away?
其言全不足信 (*qí yán quán bù zú xìn*)	Nothing he says can be believed.
既食三焉，惡能更食其餘哉？ (*jì shí sān yān, wū néng gèng shí qí yú zāi?*)	You have already eaten three of them, how can you still eat the rest?
此鄉之山水不亦美乎？ (*cǐ xiāng zhī shān shuǐ bú yì měi hū?*)	The scenery here is indeed beautiful, is it not?
蓋欲復為之 (*gài yù fù wéi zhī*)	He will probably want to do it again.
安得立毀之哉！ (*ān dé lì huǐ zhī zāi!*)	Surely they cannot destroy it right away?
子之病行當全愈 (*zǐ zhī bìng xíng dāng quán yù*)	You will soon see a full recovery from your illness.
此物必不可食乎！ (*cǐ wù bì bù kě shí hū!*)	Surely this thing is not edible!
此人之言豈足信哉？ (*cǐ rén zhī yán qǐ zú xìn zāi?*)	Surely you cannot consider this man's words trustworthy?
我姑且食此二梨耳 (*wǒ gū qiě shí cǐ èr lí ěr*)	I shall only eat these two pears for now.
子宜數往視之 (*zǐ yí shuò wǎng shì zhī*)	You should go to see him often.
豈敢不立為之哉？ (*qǐ gǎn bú lì wéi zhī zāi?*)	How can you dare not to do it immediately?
君不如姑舍之 (*jūn bù rú gū shě zhī*)	You would be better to leave it a while.
特買此二者乎？ (*tè mǎi cǐ èr zhě hū?*)	Are you only buying these two?
爾焉能浼我哉！ (*ěr yān néng měi wǒ zāi!*)	How can you defile me? (i.e. 'Surely you cannot defile me!')
人皆好之，子獨惡之乎？ (*rén jiē hào zhī, zǐ dú wù zhī hū?*)	Everybody liked it, how come only you hated it?

Note: (1) The lack of specific markers for subject, number, tense, etc. may produce many possible translation permutations.

(IX) Some, All, None as Adverbs

Distributive adverbs such as 'some', 'all', 'none', and 'in no case' are placed before the verb. These A₂-type adverbs are typically expressed in English as adjectives. Thus, 或 (*huò*) 'in some cases', 'in one case', e.g. 馬或食草 (*mǎ huò shí cǎo*) 'some horses eat grass' (but others do not). 莫

(*mò*) 'in no case(s)', e.g. 馬莫食草 (*mǎ mò shí cǎo*) 'no horse(s) eat(s) grass'. 皆 (*jiē*) 'in all/both cases', e.g. 馬皆食草 (*mǎ jiē shí cǎo*) 'all horses eat grass'. 孰 (*shú*) 'in which case(s)?', e.g. 馬孰食草？ (*mǎ shú shí cǎo?*) 'which horse(s) eat(s) grass?' All may be followed by a negative, e.g. 莫不 (*mò bù*) 'none not', i.e. 'all'.

Figure 8: **Examples involving Some, All, None using Adverbs** [1]

馬孰大？ (*mǎ shú dà?*)	Which horse is big?
齊人或食之 (*qí rén huò shí zhī*)	Some people from Qí eat it.
宋人莫智乎？ (*sòng rén mò zhì hū?*)	Are no people from Sòng wise?
我友皆知之 (*wǒ yǒu jiē zhī zhī*)	All my friends know about it.
此二人孰智？ (*cǐ èr rén shú zhì?*)	Of these two people, which is the wiser?
牛莫之食 (*niú mò zhī shí*)	No cow eats it.
梨與李，君孰取孰舍？ (*lí yǔ lǐ, jūn shú qǔ shú shě?*)	Which will you choose, the pear or the plum? (lit. 'Pear and plum, you which choose, which leave?')
是屋或大或小 (*shì wū huò dà huò xiǎo*)	Some of these houses are big and some are small.
此梨皆甚美 (*cǐ lí jiē shèn měi*)	All of these pears are very delicious.
梨與李皆不可 (*lí yǔ lǐ jiē bù kě*)	Neither the pears nor plums will do.
牛莫不食草 (*niú mò bù shí cǎo*)	All cows eat grass. (lit. 'Of cows, there are none which do not eat grass.')
人或說秦昭王曰： (*rén huò shuì qín zhāo wáng yuē:*)	Someone tried to persuade King Zhāo of Qín saying: (lit. 'People, in one case …')
人莫之知 (*rén mò zhī zhī*)	Nobody knew it. (lit. 'People, in no cases …')
鄉人或不好之 (*xiāng rén huò bú hào zhī*)	Some of the villagers do not like it.
宋人孰弗知？ (*sòng rén shú fú zhī?*)	Of the people from Sòng, who does not know about it?

Note: (1) The lack of specific markers for subject, number, tense, etc. may produce many possible translation permutations.

(X) Relative Clauses (which, who, etc.)

In Classical Chinese, the relative clause precedes the noun which it modifies. Thus, from the basic statement 人飲酒 (*rén yǐn jiǔ*) 'the person (*Subject*) drinks (*Verb*) wine (*Object*)' we may extract either the subject or the object to become the head /H/ of the substantival group. To make it into 'the person (H) who drinks (V) wine (O)', Classical Chinese uses the word order:

/V O 之 (*zhī*) H/

i.e. 飲酒之人 (*yǐn jiǔ zhī rén*). However, for 'the wine (H) which the person (S) drinks (V)', the word order becomes:

/[S] [之] 所 V 之 H/

/[S] [*zhī*] *suǒ* V *zhī* H/

i.e. 人 [之] 所飲之酒 (*rén [zhī] suǒ yǐn zhī jiǔ*). Note that 所 (*suǒ*) here means 'that which' and the 之 (*zhī*) indicates subordination.

Where the head is 'what', 'the one', 'he', 'those', 'that', etc. we shall call it a 'pronoun head'; where a noun, a 'noun head'. Combining the two types of extraction (subject or object) with these two head-types makes for four combinations:

i)   *Noun subject head*: 'the person who drinks wine';

ii) *Pronoun subject head*: 'the one who / he who / whoever drinks wine';

iii) *Noun object head*: 'the wine which / that / [zero] the person drinks';

iv) *Pronoun object head*: 'that which / what / whatever the person drinks'.

The attribute may also contain either a noun or a pronoun: '... who drinks the wine', '... who drinks it', '... which the person drinks' or '... which he drinks'. This gives eight possibilities from the four underlying statements (see Figure 9).

Figure 9: Deriving Relative Clauses from an Underlying Statement

Underlying statement	Derived relative subject head	Derived relative object head
the person drinks wine 人飲酒 (*rén yǐn jiǔ*)	the person who drinks wine 飲酒之人 (*yǐn jiǔ zhī rén*)	the wine which the person drinks 人 [之] 所飲之酒 (*rén [zhī] suǒ yǐn zhī jiǔ*)
the person drinks it 人飲之 (*rén yǐn zhī*)	the person who drinks it 飲之之人 (*yǐn zhī zhī rén*)	that which the person drinks 人 [之] 所飲 [者] (*rén [zhī] suǒ yǐn [zhě]*)
he/she drinks wine 飲酒 (*yǐn jiǔ*)	one who drinks wine 飲酒者 (*yǐn jiǔ zhě*)	the wine which he/she drinks [其] 所飲之酒 (*[qí] suǒ yǐn zhī jiǔ*)
he/she drinks it 飲之 (*yǐn zhī*)	one who drinks it 飲之者 (*yǐn zhī zhě*)	that which he/she drinks [其] 所飲 [者] (*[qí] suǒ yǐn [zhě]*)

Figure 10: **Examples involving Relative Clauses** [1]

無居之人 (wú jū zhī rén)	people without homes / homeless people
食人之虎 (shí rén zhī hǔ)	man-eating tigers
學之之人 (xué zhī zhī rén)	people who are studying it
食之之鳥 (shí zhī zhī niǎo)	birds which are eating it
食鼠之鳥 (shí shǔ zhī niǎo)	birds which eat mice
捕魚之人 (bǔ yú zhī rén)	people who catch fish
捕之者 (bǔ zhī zhě)	the one who caught it / arrested him
畫馬者 (huà mǎ zhě)	horse painter
學畫者 (xué huà zhě)	one who studies painting
客所啟之門 (kè suǒ qǐ zhī mén)	the door which the guest opened
其所捕之魚 (qí suǒ bǔ zhī yú)	the fish which he caught
鼠所為之穴 (shǔ suǒ wéi zhī xué)	the hole made by the mouse
其所買之舟 (qí suǒ mǎi zhī zhōu)	the boat which he bought
所見之山 (suǒ jiàn zhī shān)	the mountains which they saw
虎所食 (hǔ suǒ shí)	what tigers eat
子所決者 (zǐ suǒ jué zhě)	what you decided
其所捕 (qí suǒ bǔ)	what he caught
我所啟者 (wǒ suǒ qǐ zhě)	what I opened
所食者 (suǒ shí zhě)	what was eaten
食之者 (shí zhī zhě)	the ones who ate it
虎所食者 (hǔ suǒ shí zhě)	the one which the tiger ate / things which tigers eat
捕魚者 (bǔ yú zhě)	fishermen / fisherwomen
所知者 (suǒ zhī zhě)	what is known
所為之穴 (suǒ wéi zhī xué)	the hole which had been made
所食 (suǒ shí)	what has been eaten
為之之人 (wéi zhī zhī rén)	the man who did it.

子所見之馬 (*zǐ suǒ jiàn zhī mǎ*)	the horse which you saw
客所畫之鳥 (*kè suǒ huà zhī niǎo*)	the bird which the guest had drawn
其所決者 (*qí suǒ jué zhě*)	what they decided
為穴之鳥 (*wéi xué zhī niǎo*)	birds which make holes
客所為 (*kè suǒ wéi*)	what the guest did
其所畫 (*qí suǒ huà*)	what he painted
子所答非我所問也 (*zǐ suǒ dá fēi wǒ suǒ wèn yě*)	What you answered was not what I asked. (i.e. you did not reply to my question)
兒即歸，以所聞告其母 (*ér jí guī, yǐ suǒ wén gào qí mǔ*)	When the son returned home, he told his mother what he had heard.
見之者皆笑之 (*jiàn zhī zhě jiē xiào zhī*)	Everyone who saw them laughed at them.
子無與為之者交也！ (*zǐ wú yú wéi zhī zhě jiāo yě!*)	Don't go around with people who do it.
此豈非彼虎所居之穴哉！ (*cǐ qǐ fēi bǐ hǔ suǒ jū zhī xué zāi!*)	Is this not the cave where that tiger lives? (i.e. 'This must surely be that tiger's lair.')
杜鵑所生卵之巢非己所營也 (*dù juān suǒ shēng luǎn zhī cháo fēi jǐ suǒ yíng yě*)	The nest in which the cuckoo lays its eggs is not one which it builds itself.
昔與捕蛇者遊 (*xī yú bǔ shé zhě yóu*)	In the past, he was friends with a snake-catcher.
所食所飲止此耳 (*suǒ shí suǒ yǐn zhǐ cǐ ěr*)	This is all we have to eat and drink.
勿以我所為為為己而為者也！ (*wù yǐ wǒ suǒ wéi wéi wèi jǐ ér wéi zhě yě!*)	Do not take what I did as just being for myself!

Note: (1) The lack of specific markers for subject, number, tense, etc. may produce many possible translation permutations.

Reversed relative clauses

食人之虎 (*shí rén zhī hǔ*) 'tigers which eat people', i.e. 'man-eating tigers' can also be expressed as 虎之食人者 (*hǔ zhī shí rén zhě*) 'of tigers, those which eat people' or 'the man-eaters among the tigers'. We refer to this construction as a 'reversed relative'. Another example would be 鳥之小者 (*niǎo zhī xiǎo zhě*) 'the small ones among birds', or 'small birds'.

Figure 11: **Examples involving Reversed Relatives** [1]

鳥之南飛者 (*niǎo zhī nán fēi zhě*)	birds which fly south
人之無手者 (*rén zhī wú shǒu zhě*)	people who have no hands
鳥之居穴者 (*niǎo zhī jū xué zhě*)	birds which live in holes
鳥之食鼠者 (*niǎo zhī shí shǔ zhě*)	birds which eat mice
臣之侍王者 (*chén zhī shì wáng zhě*)	ministers who attend the king
國之強於齊者 (*guó zhī qiáng yú qí zhě*)	states which are stronger than Qí
宋人之畫馬者 (*sòng rén zhī huà mǎ zhě*)	horse painters from Sòng
我所知之畫馬者 (*wǒ suǒ zhī zhī huà mǎ zhě*)	horse painters I know

Note: (1) *The lack of specific markers for subject, number, tense, etc. may produce many possible translation permutations.*

(XI) Relative Clauses (*some, all, none*)

'Some', 'all' and 'none' are sometimes expressed by means of A₂-type adverbs such as 或 (*huò*), 皆 (*jiē*), and 莫 (*mò*) (please refer to Section IX). However, they can also (and sometimes must) be expressed by means of the relative construction; sometimes other devices may also be used. It is convenient to deal with these in four groups, depending upon whether it is the subject or the object that is being qualified and upon whether the subject and object are nouns or pronouns. Constructions with 或 (*huò*), 皆 (*jiē*), and 莫 (*mò*) are included here for completeness.

Qualifying a noun subject

i) 'Some people drink wine' becomes 'people include those who drink wine' 人有飲酒者 (*rén yǒu yǐn jiǔ zhě*) or 'people in some cases drink wine' 人或飲酒 (*rén huò yǐn jiǔ*). 'Some people drink it' equals 人有飲之者 (*rén yǒu yǐn zhī zhě*) or 人或飲之 (*rén huò yǐn zhī*).

ii) 'No people drink wine' becomes 'people do not include those who drink wine' 人無飲酒者 (*rén wú yǐn jiǔ zhě*) or 'people in no case drink wine' 人莫飲酒 (*rén mò yǐn jiǔ*). 'No people drink it' equals 人無飲之者 (*rén wú yǐn zhī zhě*) or 人莫飲之 (*rén mò yǐn zhī*).

iii) 'Not all people drink wine' / 'some people do not drink wine' becomes 'people include those who do not drink wine' 人有不飲酒者 (*rén yǒu bù yǐn jiǔ zhě*) or 'people in some cases do not drink wine' 人或不飲酒 (*rén huò bù yǐn jiǔ*). 'Some people do not drink it' equals 人有不飲之者 (*rén yǒu bù yǐn zhī zhě*) or 人或不飲之 (*rén huò bù yǐn zhī*).

iv) 'All people drink wine' becomes 'people do not include any who do not drink wine' 人無不飲酒者 (*rén wú bù yǐn jiǔ zhě*) or 'people in no cases do not drink wine' 人莫不飲酒 (*rén mò bù yǐn jiǔ*) or 'people in all cases drink wine' 人皆飲酒 (*rén jiē yǐn jiǔ*). 'All people drink it' equals 人無不飲之者 (*rén wú bù yǐn zhī zhě*) or 人莫不飲之 (*rén mò bù yǐn zhī*) or 人皆飲之 (*rén jiē yǐn zhī*).

Figure 12: Relative Clauses involving Some, All or None qualifying a Noun Subject [1]

牛無不食草者 (*niú wú bù shí cǎo zhě*)	All cows eat grass. (lit. 'Of cows, there are not ones which do not eat grass.')
鳥有居穴者 (*niǎo yǒu jū xué zhě*)	Some birds live in holes. (lit. 'Of birds, there are ones which live in holes.')
宋人無善捕魚者乎？ (*sòng rén wú shàn bǔ yú zhě hū?*)	Is nobody good at fishing in Sòng? (lit. 'Of Sòng people, are there not ones who are good at fishing?')
鳥有不食肉者 (*niǎo yǒu bù shí ròu zhě*)	Some birds do not eat meat. (lit. 'Of birds, there are ones which do not eat meat.')
人無不之知者 (*rén wú bù zhī zhī zhě*)	Everyone knows it. (lit. 'Of people, there are not ones who do not know [it].')
客有問之者 (*kè yǒu wèn zhī zhě*)	Some guests asked. (lit. 'Of guests, there were those who asked.')
邑人豈有不我知者乎？ (*yì rén qǐ yǒu bù wǒ zhī zhě hū?*)	Everyone knows me in this town. (lit. 'Of the town's people, how could there be ones who do not know me!')
宋人亦無知之者 (*sòng rén yì wú zhī zhī zhě*)	Nobody from Sòng knows it either. (lit. 'Of Sòng people, also there are not ones who know it.')

Note: (1) The lack of specific markers for subject, number, tense, etc. may produce many possible translation permutations.

Qualifying a pronoun subject

i) 'Some of them drink wine' becomes 'there are those who drink wine' 有飲酒者 (*yǒu yǐn jiǔ zhě*) or 'some drink wine' 或飲酒 (*huò yǐn jiǔ*). 'Some of them drink it' equals 有飲之者 (*yǒu yǐn zhī zhě*) or 或飲之 (*huò yǐn zhī*).

ii) 'None of them drinks wine' becomes 'there are not any who drink wine' 無飲酒者 (*wú yǐn jiǔ zhě*) or 'none drinks wine' 莫飲酒 (*mò yǐn jiǔ*). 'None of them drinks it' equals 無飲之者 (*wú yǐn zhī zhě*) or 莫飲之 (*mò yǐn zhī*).

iii) 'Not all of them drink wine' / 'some of them do not drink wine' becomes 'there are those who do not drink wine' 有不飲酒者 (*yǒu bù yǐn jiǔ zhě*) or 'some do not drink wine' 或不飲酒 (*huò bù yǐn jiǔ*). 'Some of them do not drink it' / 'not all of them drink it' equals 有不飲之者 (*yǒu bù yǐn zhī zhě*) or 或不飲之 (*huò bù yǐn zhī*).

iv) 'All of them (or: they all) drink wine' becomes 'there are not any who do not drink

wine' 無不飲酒者 (*wú bù yǐn jiǔ zhě*) or 'none does not drink wine' 莫不飲酒 (*mò bù yǐn jiǔ*) or 'all drink wine' 皆飲酒 (*jiē yǐn jiǔ*). 'They all drink it' equals 無不飲之者 (*wú bù yǐn zhī zhě*) or 莫不飲之 (*mò bù yǐn zhī*) or 皆飲之 (*jiē yǐn zhī*). See the following figure for more examples.

Figure 13: **Relative Clauses involving Some, All or None qualifying a Pronoun Subject** [1]

有不食肉者 (*yǒu bù shí ròu zhě*)	There are ones who do not eat meat.
無不知之者 (*wú bù zhī zhī zhě*)	Everyone knows it. (lit. 'There are not ones who do not know it.')
無問之者乎？ (*wú wèn zhī zhě hū?*)	Does no one ask about it? (lit. 'Are there not ones who ask about it?')
無不知其名者 (*wú bù zhī qí míng zhě*)	Everyone knew his name. (lit. 'There are not ones who did not know his name.')
有好其畫者，亦有弗好者也 (*yǒu hào qí huà zhě, yì yǒu fú hào zhě yě*)	There are those who like his paintings, there are also some who do not like them.

Note: (1) *The lack of specific markers for subject, number, tense, etc. may produce many possible translation permutations.*

Qualifying a pronoun object

i) 'The person drinks something / some of it' becomes 'the person has that which he drinks' 人有 [所] 飲 (*rén yǒu [suǒ] yǐn*).

ii) 'The person drinks nothing / none of it' becomes 'the person has not that which he drinks' 人無 [所] 飲 (*rén wú [suǒ] yǐn*).

iii) 'There are some things that the person does not drink' / 'the person does not drink everything / all of it' becomes 'the person has that which he does not drink' 人有 [所] 不飲 (*rén yǒu [suǒ] bù yǐn*) or 'the person does not completely drink it' 人不

盡飲之 (*rén bú jìn yǐn zhī*).

iv) 'The person drinks everything / all of it' becomes 'the person has not that which he does not drink' 人無 [所] 不飲 (*rén wú [suǒ] bù yǐn*) or 'the person completely drinks it' 人盡飲之 (*rén jìn yǐn zhī*).

It should be noted that in this construction, 不 + 有 (*bù + yǒu*) is not replaced by 無 (*wú*), e.g. 無所不有 (*wú suǒ bù yǒu*) 'has everything' (not 無所無, *wú suǒ wú*). As an aside, although the negative of 有 (*yǒu*) 'exist', 'have', 'there is' is 無 (*wú*), sometimes 不有 (*bù yǒu*) or 無有 (*wú yǒu*) is used.

Figure 14: Relative Clauses involving Some, All or None qualifying a Pronoun Object [1]

無為 (*wú wéi*)	do nothing; inaction (a Daoist term)
子有所未決乎？ (*zǐ yǒu suǒ wèi jué hū?*)	Is there something you have not decided?
子無所不能乎？ (*zǐ wú suǒ bù néng hū?*)	Is there anything you cannot do?
我有所見 (*wǒ yǒu suǒ jiàn*)	I saw something.
此人無所不為 (*cǐ rén wú suǒ bù wéi*)	There is nothing this man will not do.
我無所問 (*wǒ wú suǒ wèn*)	I have nothing to ask.
子無答乎？ (*zǐ wú dá hū?*)	Do you have no answer?
鳥盡食之矣 (*niǎo jìn shí zhī yǐ*)	The birds ate it all.
我未之盡見也 (*wǒ wèi zhī jìn jiàn yě*)	I have not seen it all yet.

Note: (1) *The lack of specific markers for subject, number, tense, etc. may produce many possible translation permutations.*

Qualifying a noun object

There are four ways to qualify a noun object with 'some', 'all' or 'none' in Classical Chinese.

i) ***Exposing both subject and object***: 'The person drinks some (of the) wine' becomes 'what the person does to the wine is to drink some of it' 人 [之] 於 酒 [也]，有 [所] 飲 (*rén [zhī] yú jiǔ [yě], yǒu [suǒ] yǐn*). Alternatively, an adverb or indeterminate numeral meaning 'some' can be used, thus: 'the person to a small extent drinks the wine' 人少飲酒 (*rén shǎo yǐn jiǔ*) or 'the person drinks a little wine' 人飲酒少許 (*rén yǐn jiǔ shǎo xǔ*).

ii) ***Using 於 (yú)***: This is translatable as 'behaviour towards', 'attitude towards', and is similar to the Modern Chinese use of 對於 (*duì yú*). 'The person drinks no (none of the) wine' becomes 'what the person does to the wine is to drink none of it' 人 [之] 於 酒 [也]，無 [所] 飲 (*rén [zhī] yú jiǔ [yě], wú [suǒ] yǐn*). Alternatively, an adverb meaning 'at all' can be used, thus: 'the person does not drink the wine at all' 人全不飲酒 (*rén quán bù yǐn jiǔ*).

iii) ***Mark the topic with 之 ... 也 (zhī...yě)***: This is optional. 'the person does not drink all of the wine' becomes 'what the person does to the wine is not to drink some of it' 人 [之] 於 酒 [也]，有 [所] 不飲 (*rén [zhī] yú jiǔ [yě], yǒu [suǒ] bù yǐn*). An adverb, e.g. 'completely' may also be used, i.e. 'the person does not completely drink the wine' 人不盡飲酒 (*rén bú jìn yǐn jiǔ*).

iv) ***Using a relative construction***: Here, the verb is placed in one of the relative constructions used above, i.e.

/[S] [之] 於 (*[zhī] yú*) O [也] (*yě*)，有 [所] (*yǒu [suǒ]*) V/

For ease, the simplest permutation would be:

/[S] 於 (*yú*) O 有 (*yǒu*) V/

i.e. 'what *Subject* does to *Object* is to *Verb* some of it'. Thus, 'the person drinks all the wine' = 'what the person does to the wine is to drink all of it' 人 [之] 於 酒 [也]，無 [所] 不 飲 (*rén [zhī] yú jiǔ [yě], wú [suǒ] bù yǐn*). Again, an adverb 'completely' may be used, : 'the person completely drinks the wine' 人 盡 飲 酒 (*rén jìn yǐn jiǔ*).

Figure 15: Relative Clauses involving Some, All or None qualifying a Noun Object [1]

其 於 人 也，有 所 好，亦 有 所 惡 (*qí yú rén yě, yǒu suǒ hào, yì yǒu suǒ wù*)	He likes some people, but not others.
於 客 有 不 信，而 於 邑 人 則 無 所 不 信 也 (*yú kè yǒu bù xìn, ér yú yì rén zé wú suǒ bù xìn yě*)	not entirely trust strangers, but completely trust the townspeople
終 得 其 巢 而 盡 取 其 卵 (*zhōng dé qí cháo ér jìn qǔ qí luǎn*)	finally found the nest and took all of the eggs
其 於 馬 畫，未 必 盡 好 之 也 (*qí yú mǎ huà, wèi bì jìn hào zhī yě*)	He would not necessarily like all of the horse paintings.

Note: (1) The lack of specific markers for subject, number, tense, etc. may produce many possible translation permutations.

(XII) Relative Clauses (*where, that which*)

'Where' with verbs indicating location or movement is expressed by means of 所 (*suǒ*) before the verb and it functions like 'that which' as a pronoun object. Compare the following:

i) 鼠 所 為 之 穴 (*shǔ suǒ wéi zhī xué*) 'the hole which the mouse made'; and 鼠 所 居 之 穴 (*shǔ suǒ jū zhī xué*) 'the hole which the mouse inhabits', i.e. 'the hole where the mouse lives';

ii) 虎 所 食 (*hǔ suǒ shí*) 'what the tiger eats'; 虎 所 伏 (*hǔ suǒ fú*) 'where the tiger lies hidden' and 其 所 伏 (*qí suǒ fú*) 'where it lies hidden'.

'Where from' or 'where through' is expressed by means of 所 從 (*suǒ cóng*), 所 自 (*suǒ zì*), 所 由 (*suǒ yóu*) before the verb. For example: 客 所 從 入 邑 之 門 (*kè suǒ cóng rù yì zhī mén*) 'the gate through which the strangers entered the town', and 問 其 所 自 來 (*wèn qí suǒ zì lái*) 'asked where he came from'. It should be noted that 'where from' is sometimes 所 (*suǒ*) alone, e.g. 無 忝 爾 所 生 (*wú tiǎn ěr suǒ sheng*) 'do not disgrace those from whom you were born (i.e. your parents)'.

'How' (the means by which) and 'why' are expressed by means of 所 以 (*suǒ yǐ*) 'that by means of which', 'that because of which' (NB 所

以 , *suǒ yǐ*, does not mean 'therefore' as it does in Modern Chinese). Thus:

i) 庖 以 刀 切 肉 (*páo yǐ dāo qiē ròu*) 'the cook slices the meat with a knife';

ii) 庖 所 以 切 肉 之 刀 (*páo suǒ yǐ qiē ròu zhī dāo*) 'the knife with which the cook slices the meat';

iii) 庖 所 以 切 肉 [者] (*páo suǒ yǐ qiē ròu [zhě]*) 'what the cook slices the meat with';

And:

i) 問 其 所 以 為 此 (*wèn qí suǒ yǐ wéi cǐ*) 'asked why he had done this';

ii) 不 知 其 所 以 然 (*bù zhī qí suǒ yǐ rán*) 'not know why it is so'.

Figure 16: Examples of 所 (*suǒ*) **Relative Clauses** (*contrasting 'where' and 'that which'*) [1]

至 虎 所 伏 (*zhì hǔ suǒ fú*)	arrive at the spot where the tiger was hiding
問 其 所 以 知 之 (*wèn qí suǒ yǐ zhī zhī*)	asked how he knew it
以 其 所 居 告 之 (*yǐ qí suǒ jū gào zhī*)	told them where he lived
不 知 鼠 之 所 由 出 (*bù zhī shǔ zhī suǒ yóu chū*)	did not know where the mouse had come out from
不 知 所 之 (*bù zhī suǒ zhī*)	not know where he was going
至 其 鳥 所 巢 之 林 (*zhì qí niǎo suǒ cháo zhī lín*)	arrive at the forest where the bird had made its nest
指 其 所 從 出 邑 之 門 (*zhǐ qí suǒ cóng chū yì zhī mén*)	pointed out the gate through which he had left the town
求 鳥 所 巢 之 木 , 以 得 其 卵 (*qiú niǎo suǒ cháo zhī mù, yǐ dé qí luǎn*)	looked for the tree where the bird had made its nest in order to take its eggs
此 其 所 由 出 入 之 穴 也 (*cǐ qí suǒ yóu chū rù zhī xué yě*)	This is the hole through which it goes in and out.
不 知 其 所 在 則 奈 何 ？ (*bù zhī qí suǒ zài zé nài hé?*)	If we do not know where he is, what do we do?
以 我 所 知 求 子 所 欲 則 必 得 之 矣 (*yǐ wǒ suǒ zhī qiú zǐ suǒ yù zé bì dé zhī yǐ*)	If we use what I know to look for what you want, then we will certainly find it.
其 所 以 為 之 者 徒 木 耳 (*qí suǒ yǐ wéi zhī zhě tú mù ěr*)	They made it from just wood.

Note: (1) The lack of specific markers for subject, number, tense, etc. may produce many possible translation permutations.

The 為...所 (*wéi ... suǒ*) passive

One common way of indicating the passive in Classical Chinese is by use of the 為 ... 所 (*wéi... suǒ*) relative passive construction.

/[S] 為 (*wéi*) Agent 所 (*suǒ*) V/

For example, 'the mouse was caught by the cat' = 'the mouse was that which (or what) the cat caught', i.e. 鼠為貓所捕 (*shǔ wéi māo suǒ bǔ*). Another way to express the passive is introduced on p 42.

Figure 17: **Examples showing the 為...所 (*wéi...suǒ*) Passive** [1]

其子為虎所食 (*qí zǐ wéi hǔ suǒ shí*)	His son was eaten by a tiger.
戰不利, 為賊所傷 (*zhàn bú lì, wéi zéi suǒ shāng*)	The battle was unsuccessful [and] I was wounded by the rebels.
見一黃雀為鴟梟所搏墜於樹下 (*jiàn yì huáng què wéi chī xiāo suǒ bó zhuì yú shù xià*)	saw a canary pounced upon by an owl and fall from a tree
木穴多為鳥所巢 (*mù xué duō wéi niǎo suǒ cháo*)	Holes in trees are mostly nested in by birds.
昔有女人為鬼所魅羸瘦將死 (*xī yǒu nǔ rén wéi guǐ suǒ mèi léi shòu jiāng sǐ*)	Formerly, there was a woman who was possessed by a demon; she was weak and emaciated and on the point of death.
軍敗於壇邱, 為徐龕所殺 (*jūn bài yú tán qiū, wéi xú kān suǒ shā*)	The army was defeated at Tánqiū and he was killed by Xú Kān.

Note: (1) The lack of specific markers for subject, number, tense, etc. may produce many possible translation permutations.

(XIII) Adverbials and Prepositions

Adverbials, as mentioned earlier, are major non- /S V O/ elements. Sometimes, they are connected by prepositions such as 於 (*yú*), 以 (*yǐ*) or 自 (*zì*) etc. We shall deal here with the principal types that occur before the verb (A₂-types) and after the object at the end of the sentence (A₃-types); this excludes prepositions in the topic position. The treatment is by no means exhaustive, of course. It is in the position of adverbials that we find some of the major syntactic differences between Classical Chinese and Modern Chinese.

The first four categories of adverbials involve 'expressions of place'. To save repetition, here is an explanation of this term. An expression of place (or place-phrase) may consist of:

i) *Place-name*: e.g. 京 (*jīng*) 'the capital', 楚 (*chǔ*) '[the state of] Chǔ', with or without a postposition (see below);

ii) *Noun / pronoun (no postposition)*: this is a restricted category because of the dangers of ambiguity by confusion with subject or object, an ambiguity often removed by placing the preposition 於 (*yú*) in front;

iii) ***Noun / pronoun (with postposition)***: e.g. 案上 (*àn shàng*) 'on the table', 二村間 (*èr cūn jiān*) 'between the two villages';

iv) ***The pronoun 其 (*qí*) plus a postposition***: e.g. 其中 (*qí zhōng*) 'in it';

v) ***Zero plus a postposition***: restricted because of the dangers of ambiguity, see (ii) above.

Postpositions include: 上 (*shàng*) 'on', 'above'; 下 (*xià*) 'under', 'below'; 中 (*zhōng*) 'in'; 內 (*nèi*) 'inside' (中, *zhōng*, and 內, *nèi*, are often, but not always, interchangeable); 外 (*wài*) and 表 (*biǎo*) both meaning 'outside', 'beyond'; 前 (*qián*) 'in front of'; 後 (*hòu*) 'behind'; 左 (*zuǒ*) 'to the left of'; 右 (*yòu*) 'to the right of'; 東 (*dōng*) / 西 (*xī*) / 南 (*nán*) / 北 (*běi*) 'to the east / west / south / north of'; 間 (*jiān*) 'between', 'in'; 處 (*chù*) 'at' (cf. Modern Chinese 那兒, *nà'r*); and 側 (*cè*), 邊, (*biān*), 旁 (*páng*), 畔 (*pàn*) all meaning 'beside', etc.

It should be noted that the preposition 於 (*yú*) will be met here in a wide variety of meanings, viz. 'at', 'to', 'from', 'by' and 'than'. In actual practice this causes little difficulty since the meaning of the main verb and the structure of the sentence usually make it clear which translation of 於 (*yú*) is appropriate:

i) /於 (*yú*) + Place/
= 'at';

This usually translates as 'at', but cf. 夫鵷 鶵發於南海而飛於北海 (*fú yuān chú fā yú nán hǎi ér fēi yú běi hǎi*) 'Now when the yuān-chú bird sets off from the Southern Sea and flies to the Northern Sea', where only 'common sense' can distinguish the two meanings of 於 (*yú*);

ii) /Transfer Noun + 於 (*yú*) + Person/
= 'to';

iii) /Receive Noun + 於 (*yú*) + Person/
= 'from';

iv) /Passive Verb + 於 (*yú*) + Noun/
= 'by';

v) /Verb or Adjective + 於 (*yú*) + Noun/
= 'than'.

An analysis of 於 (*yú*) can also be found in *Classical Chinese Function Characters* (pp 79-80).

Adverbials of place (A₃-type)

In Classsical Chinese, adverbials of place are usually A₃-type placed after the object.

$$/[S] \text{ V O } [於] \text{ (}yú\text{) A}_3/$$

This is unlike Modern Chinese, which would, as a general rule, put such adverbials of place before the verb (i.e. A₂-type). Thus, 'the horse is grazing at the roadside' would be rendered in Classical Chinese as follows: 馬食草[於]路側 (*mǎ shí cǎo [yú] lù cè*), but in Modern Chinese, this would be 馬在路旁邊吃草 (*mǎ zài lù pángbiān chī cǎo*). There is a tendency in Classical Chinese to use either the preposition 於 (*yú*) or a postposition. It is much less common to use both together, e.g. 'then he put it on the table' may thus be rendered in three ways in Classical Chinese, the first two being the more common: 乃置於案 (*nǎi zhì yú àn*), 乃置案上 (*nǎi zhì àn shàng*) or 乃置於案上 (*nǎi zhì yú àn shàng*). The preference here for either preposition or postposition is explicable partly in terms of rhythm (the first two have a normal 4-syllable rhythm whereas the third has 5 syllables) and partly in terms of semantics, since 於 (*yú*) and 上 (*shàng*) both make it clear individually that the table is the place of the action, not its object.

Figure 19: **Examples involving A₃-type Adverbials of Place** [1]

母坐東牖下，子坐其側 (*mǔ zuò dōng yǒu xià, zǐ zuò qí cè*)	His mother sat by the east window with her son at her side.
虎伏叢莽中 (*hǔ fú cóng mǎng zhōng*)	The tiger lay hidden in the thicket.
見一馬臥露草間 (*jiàn yì mǎ wò lù cǎo jiān*)	He saw a horse lying down on the dewy grass.
母抱嬰兒於懷 (*mǔ bào yīng ér yú huái*)	The mother held her child to her bosom.
久探穴中而無所得焉 (*jiǔ tàn xué zhōng ér wú suǒ dé yán*)	searched in the cave for a long while, but found nothing there
汝且視門內 (*rǔ qiě shì mén nèi*)	Take a look inside!

Note: (1) The lack of specific markers for subject, number, tense, etc. may produce many possible translation permutations.

Adverbials of place (A₂-type)

/[S] [於] (*yú*) A₂ V O/

Occasionally 在 (*zài*) may be used instead of 於 (*yú*), but this is less common than in Modern Chinese. The more common place for adverbials of place with 於 (*yú*) is after the object at the end of the sentence (i.e. A₃-type). An A₂-type may be regarded as an alternative chosen for rhythm or clarity. Compare the following two sentences in Modern Chinese and Classical Chinese:

i) 'The child throws the ball (while he is) in the water' in Modern Chinese would be: 小孩子在水裏扔球 (*xiǎo háizi zài shuǐ li rēng qiú*). In Classical Chinese, this would be likely rendered as: 兒於 (or 在) 水中擲毬 (*ér yú (or zài) shuǐ zhōng zhì qiú*).

ii) 'The child throws the ball in(to) the water' in Modern Chinese would be: 小孩子把球扔到水裏 (*xiǎo háizi bǎ qiú rēng dào shuǐ li*), but in Classical Chinese would be rendered as: 兒以毬擲 [於] 水 [中] (*ér yǐ qiú zhì [yú] shuǐ [zhōng]*).

The choice of an A₂-type adverbial in (i) makes it clear that 'in the water' refers to the position of the thrower not the destination of the ball.

Figure 20: **Examples involving A₂-type Adverbials of Place** [1]

夜叉在水中推行如矢 (*yè chā zài shuǐ zhōng tuī xíng rú shǐ*)	The *yaksha* was [swimming] in the river and pushed [the boat] like a [speeding] arrow.

好事者於臨路店索得沸瀋 (*hào shì zhě yú lín lù diàn suǒ dé fèi shěn*)	The onlookers obtained some hot water from a shop by the roadside.
刑於南座對叟休止 (*xíng yú nán zuò duì sǒu xiū zhǐ*)	Xíng rested on the southern seat opposite the old man.

Note: (1) The lack of specific markers for subject, number, tense, etc. may produce many possible translation permutations.

Adverbials of source & route

These may use the following prepositions: 自 (*zì*), 從 (*cóng*), 由 (*yóu*) 'from', 'through' and 於 (*yú*) 'from' only. These are A₂-type adverbials put before the verb and are dealt with together since they have the same form, e.g.:

/[S] 自 (*zì*) A₂ V O/

i) 'From' using 自 (*zì*), 從 (*cóng*), 由 (*yóu*) and 於 (*yú*), e.g. 自林中出 (*zì lín zhōng chū*) 'emerged from the wood'; 自外至 (*zì wài zhì*) 'arrived from outside'; 何自知之？ (*hé zì zhī zhī*) literally 'where from know it?', i.e. 'where did you hear that?';

ii) 'From' with 於 (*yú*), e.g. 叟於案上取刀 (*sǒu yú àn shàng qǔ dāo*) 'the old man took a knife from the table'; 乃於囊中出一錢 (*nǎi yú náng zhōng chū yì qián*) 'then he took a copper out of the bag'.

iii) 'Through' with 自 (*zì*), 從 (*cóng*) and 由 (*yóu*), e.g. 盜自窗入室 (*dào zì chuāng rù shì*) 'the thief entered the room by / through the window'; 我自門縫中外窺 (*wǒ zì mén fèng zhōng wài kuī*) 'I peeped out through the crack of the door'.

iv) 隔 (*gé*) 'separated by', 'across the barrier of', 'on the other side of', 'through', e.g. 隔窗而窺 (*gé chuāng ér kuī*) 'he peeped through the window'; 隔戶與語 (*gé hù yǔ yǔ*) 'I talked to him through the [closed] door'.

Figure 21: Examples involving Adverbials of Place and Route (1)

遂於指上脫環 (*suì yú zhǐ shàng tuō huán*)	Then, she took the jade ring off her finger.
不知其所自來 (*bù zhī qí suǒ zì lái*)	I don't know where he comes from.
其劍自舟中墜於水 (*qí jiàn zì zhōu zhōng zhuì yú shuǐ*)	His sword fell out of the boat into the river.
隔簾聞笑聲 (*gé lián wén xiào shēng*)	He heard laughter from behind the curtain.
於洞深處取流水 (*yú dòng shēn chù qǔ liú shuǐ*)	He obtained running water from the depths of the cave.

次日自竹葉中窺其鄰所為 (*cì rì zì zhú yè zhōng kuī qí lín suǒ wéi*)	The next day, from amongst the bamboo leaves, he sneaked a look at what his neighbour was doing.
於彼有竇，於此有室 (*yú bǐ yǒu dòu, yú cǐ yǒu shì*)	There's a hole over there, there's a room here.

Note: (1) The lack of specific markers for subject, number, tense, etc. may produce many possible translation permutations.

Adverbials showing destination (*A₃-type*)

Adverbials showing destination can be split into three categories:

i) *Simple verb*: In form, this closely resembles A₃-type adverbials of place, i.e.

/[S] V O [於] (*yú*) Destination/

e.g. 置梨筐內 (*zhì lí kuāng nèi*) 'put the pears into the basket'; 繫馬於樹 (*jì mǎ yú shù*) 'tie the horse to a tree'; 挂其項 (*guà qí xiàng*) 'hang [it] round her neck'; 投釜 (*tóu fǔ*) 'throw [it] into a saucepan'. It should be noted that /S V O Destination/ where destination is a noun without either 於 (*yú*) or a postposition is not common, though it does occur, e.g. 僧繫驢池樹 (*sēng jì lǘ chí shù*) 'the monk tied the donkey to a tree by the pond'.

ii) *Compound verb*: This may also take the form of two verbs separated by an object, i.e.

/[S] V [O] V Destination/

e.g. 攜妻子至海岸 (*xié qī zǐ zhì hǎi àn*) 'he took his wife and children to the seaside'; 推墜水中 (*tuī zhuì shuǐ zhōng*) 'he pushed it (so that it fell) into the water'; 率出北門 (*shuài chū běi mén*) 'he led him out through the North Gate'; 躍登案上 (*yuè dēng àn shàng*) 'it jumped up on to the table'; 眾扶歸入門 (*zhòng fú guī rù mén*) 'they all helped him back in through the gate'.

iii) *Destination with disposal form of object*. This takes the following form:

/[S] 以 (*yǐ*) O V Destination/

and it is analogous to the Modern Chinese construction which uses 把 (*bǎ*) instead of 以 (*yǐ*), e.g. 兒以石擲鳥 (*ér yǐ shí zhì niǎo*) 'the boy threw a stone at a bird'; 以所洗之箸置盆側 (*yǐ suǒ xǐ zhī zhù zhì pén cè*) 'she put the chopsticks she had washed down beside the bowl'.

Figure 22: Examples showing A₃-type Adverbials involving Destination [1]

鬻布於市 (*yù bù yú shì*)	sold cloth at the market
挂畫壁間 (*guà huà bì jiān*)	hung a picture on the wall
投書滿地 (*tóu shū mǎn dì*)	threw books all over the floor
眾隨上山 (*zhòng suí shàng shān*)	Everyone followed (him) up the mountain.

扑墜牆下 (*pū zhuì qiáng xià*)	knocked it off the wall
宿於逆旅 (*sù yú nì lǚ*)	spent the night at an inn
即趨出迎客 (*jí qū chū yíng kè*)	hurried out to greet the guests
追至屋後而終不及 (*zhuī zhì wū hòu ér zhōng bù jí*)	chased him to the back of the house, but in the end could not catch him
自投入海 (*zì tóu rù hǎi*)	threw himself into the sea
乃以所買之畫粘壁間 (*nǎi yǐ suǒ mǎi zhī huà zhān bì jiān*)	Then he stuck the paintings he had bought onto the wall.
勿以此盆置案上 (*wù yǐ cǐ pén zhì àn shàng*)	Do not put this basin on the table!

Note: (1) *The lack of specific markers for subject, number, tense, etc. may produce many possible translation permutations.*

Adverbials involving the passive agent

Whereas Modern Chinese has /Subject 被 (*bèi*) Agent Verb/, i.e. 'Subject, by Agent, was Verb-ed', the Classical Chinese passive can sometimes be like English, thus:

/[S] 見 (*jiàn*) V 於 (*yú*) Agent/

i.e. 'Subject was Verb-ed by the Agent', e.g. 虎見殺於其弟 (*hǔ jiàn shā yú qí dì*) 'the tiger was killed by his younger brother'. This particular construction seems originally to have been limited to verbs denoting an unpleasant experience such as being killed or injured or hated or insulted, and so may be understood as 'Subject suffered Verb-ing at the hands of Agent', but in later texts it was used more widely. Remember that the more common way of expressing the passive is:

/[S] 為 (*wéi*) Agent 所 (*suǒ*) V/

and this can be used with a wider range of verbs than the 見 (*jiàn*) construction, e.g. 虎為其弟所殺 (*hǔ wéi qí dì suǒ shā*), see p 37. Note that 'by him' etc. are expressed not as 於之 (*yú zhī*) but as 焉 (*yán*), e.g. 虎見殺焉 (*hǔ jiàn shā yán*) 'the tiger was killed by him'.

Figure 23: Examples showing Adverbials involving the Passive Agent [1]

虎為其人所殺 (*hǔ wéi qí rén suǒ shā*)	The tiger was killed by that person.
求助於鄰而見拒焉 (*qiú zhù yú lín ér jiàn jù yán*)	sought help from his neighbour, but was refused by him
盜見笞於官 (*dào jiàn chī yú guān*)	The robber was flogged by the official.
兒攀木摘而為主所叱 (*ér pān mù zhāi ér wéi zhǔ suǒ chì*)	The boy climbed the tree to pick [fruit], but was shouted at by the owner.

Note: (1) *The lack of specific markers for subject, number, tense, etc. may produce many possible translation permutations.*

Adverbials involving 'time-when' (A₂-type)

Adverbials showing 'time-when' with or without the preposition 於 (*yú*), like their Modern Chinese equivalents, are normally A₂-type placed between subject and verb, thus:

/[S] [於] (*yú*) Time-when V O/

For example, 其父果於是日死 (*qí fù guǒ yú shì rì sǐ*) 'his father actually did die on that day (as predicted)'. The question 'when?' 何時 (*hé shí*) is also A₂-type, i.e. placed before the verb.

Figure 24: Examples showing A₂-type Adverbials involving 'Time-when' [1]

子何時歸？ (*zǐ hé shí guī?*)	When will you return home?
我擬於三月五日置酒 (*wǒ nǐ yú sān yuè wǔ rì zhì jiǔ*)	I am planning a party on the fifth of the third month.
相約十日一飲 (*xiāng yuē shí rì yī yǐn*)	They agreed to meet for a drink in ten days.
蘇秦之楚，三日乃得見乎王 (*sū qín zhī chǔ, sān rì nǎi dé jiàn hū wáng*)	Sūqín went to Chǔ and it was three days before he had an audience with the King.
諸從者日益畏之 (*zhū zòng zhě rì yì wèi zhī*)	His followers daily held him in ever greater awe.
他日復見其鄰之子 (*tā rì fù jiàn qí lín zhī zǐ*)	A few days later he saw his neighbour's son again.
我明日去，月餘返 (*wǒ míng rì qù, yuè yú fǎn*)	I will leave tomorrow and return in over a month.

Note: (1) The lack of specific markers for subject, number, tense, etc. may produce many possible translation permutations.

Adverbials - duration of time (A₃-type)

Adverbials involving duration of time in Classical Chinese, unlike 'time-when' adverbials, are A₃-type and are placed after the object, i.e.

/[S] V O Time Duration/

Thus, 我至此已三日矣 (*wǒ zhì cǐ yǐ sān rì yǐ*) 'I've already been here three days'; 我待之久，終不至，乃歸 (*wǒ dāi zhī jiǔ, zhōng bú zhì, nǎi guī*) 'I waited for him a long time, but he never arrived, so I went home'.

Figure 25: Examples showing Adverbials involving Duration of Time [1]

鬻布於市幾半年 (*yù bù yú shì jī bàn nián*)	sold cloth in the market for almost half a year
夫子事孔子數十年 (*fū zǐ shì kǒng zǐ shuò shí nián*)	You, Sir, followed Confucius for several decades.

與語爾許時，猶不知其所欲乎？(*yǔ yǔ ěr xǔ shí, yóu bù zhī qí suǒ yù hū?*)	You spoke with him for so long and you still don't know what he wants?
死且十年，鄉人猶常言之 (*sǐ qiě shí nián, xiāng rén yóu cháng yán zhī*)	Even though he had been dead for close to ten years, the villagers still talk about him constantly.

Note: (1) The lack of specific markers for subject, number, tense, etc. may produce many possible translation permutations.

Adverbials of negative duration *(A₂-type)*

Adverbials involving negative duration of time, unlike their positive counterparts (see above), are A₂-type adverbials and are placed after the subject and before the verb:

/[S] Duration 不 (*bù*) etc. V O/

For example, 兄數日不返，家人皆憫之 (*xiōng shuò rì bù fǎn, jiā rén jiē mǐn zhī*) 'My brother did not return for several days and the family were all worried about him.'

Figure 26: Examples involving Adverbials with Negative Duration of Time [1]

何久不聞其訊？ (*hé jiǔ bù wén qí xùn?*)	How long has it been since you heard news of him?
漁夫終夜不獲一魚 (*yú fū zhōng yè bú huò yī yú*)	The fisherman did not catch a single fish all night.
此宅向空，十年無敢入者 (*cǐ zhái xiàng kōng, shí nián wú gǎn rù zhě*)	This house has been empty for a long while, nobody has dared enter for ten years.
其疾年餘不愈 (*qí jí nián yú bú yù*)	He has not recovered from his illness in over a year.

Note: (1) The lack of specific markers for subject, number, tense, etc. may produce many possible translation permutations.

Adverbials of measures of action *(A₃-type)*

Adverbials involving measures of action are A₃ type. These include frequency (the number of times an action occurs), distance, weight, size etc. The order is as follows:

/[S] V O Numeral + Measure Word/

For example, 行三里 (*xíng sān lǐ*) 'we walked three *lǐ* (1 *lǐ* = ⅓ of a mile); 去此里餘 (*qù cǐ lǐ yú*) 'it is a *lǐ* or so from here', 勉勵之數語 (*miǎn lì zhī shuò yù*) lit. 'encouraged him several words' = 'gave him a few words of encouragement'; 約重二兩 (*yuē zhòng èr liǎng*) lit. 'approximately heavy two ounces' = 'it weighed about two ounces'; 至一大洞，廣闊盈畝 (*zhì yī dà dòng, guǎng kuò yíng mǔ*) 'they came to a large cave, fully one *mǔ* in extent' (1 *mǔ* = ⅙ of an acre).

Figure 27: **Examples showing Adverbials involving Measures of Action** [1]

二村相去三里許 (èr cūn xiāng qù sān lǐ xǔ)	The two villages are about three *lǐ* apart. (i.e. about one mile apart)
更掘四尺有餘 (gèng jué sì chǐ yòu yú)	He dug a further four feet or so.
行數里，醉困臥 (xíng shuò lǐ, zuì kùn wò)	He went on for several *lǐ* until he collapsed [and slept] from drink and weariness.
晏子長不滿六尺 (yàn zǐ cháng bù mǎn liù chǐ)	Yànzǐ's height is less than six foot.
彈琴數聲而輟 (tán qín shuò shēng ér chuò)	She played a few notes on the lute, then stopped.
此池深二尺耳 (cǐ chí shēn èr chǐ ěr)	This pond is only two feet deep.

Note: (1) The lack of specific markers for subject, number, tense, etc. may produce many possible translation permutations.

Adverbials of equal comparison (A₃-type)

In Classical Chinese, adverbials showing equal comparison 'as Adj. as …' are expressed as follows:

either: /[S] Adj. 如 (rú) Noun (or) Time/
or: /[S] V O 如 (rú) Noun (or) Time/

For example, 鼠大如貓 (shǔ dà rú māo) 'the rat was as big as a cat'; 見巨鼠如貓 (jiàn jù shǔ rú māo) 'he saw a huge rat like a cat' = 'he saw a rat as big as a cat'; 返鄉事親如故 (fǎn xiāng shì qīn rú gù) 'he went back to his native place and looked after his parents as before'.

Figure 28: **Examples showing Adverbials involving Equal Comparison** [1]

聞扣聲如雷 (wén kòu shēng rú léi)	heard a knocking noise like thunder
遙見一物如虎狀 (yáo jiàn yī wù rú hǔ zhuàng)	saw something in the distance shaped like a tiger
今夜月圓如鏡 (jīn yè yuè yuán rú jìng)	Tonight, the moon is full like a mirror.
光陰急逝如走馬 (guāng yīn jí shì rú zǒu mǎ)	Time flies like a galloping horse.

Note: (1) The lack of specific markers for subject, number, tense, etc. may produce many possible translation permutations.

Adverbials - superior comparison (A₃-type)

In Classical Chinese, adverbials showing superior comparison 'Adj.-er than ...' take the following form:

/[S] Adj. 於 (*yú*) Noun (or) Time/

/[S] V 於 (*yú*) Noun (or) Time/

i.e. 'Subject is X-er than Noun or Time', e.g. 鼠大於貓 (*shǔ dà yú māo*) 'the rat was bigger than a cat'; 至冬則價倍於常 (*zhì dōng zé jià bèi yú cháng*) 'in winter, the price is double the normal cost'. When the construction uses 'than it' etc., Classical Chinese replaces 於之 (*yú zhī*) with 焉 (*yán*), e.g. 象者，獸莫大焉 (*xiàng zhě, shòu mò dà yán*) 'as for the elephant, no animal is bigger than it', i.e. 'no animal is bigger than the elephant'.

Although more formal Modern Chinese, especially written, may occasionally use the form /Adj. 於 (*yú*) Noun/, the more common structure is /S 比 (*bǐ*) Noun + Adj./.

Figure 29: Examples showing Adverbials involving Superior Comparison [1]

鄉人無智於李氏者 (*xiāng rén wú zhì yú lǐ shì zhě*)	Amongst the villagers, none was cleverer than Mr Lǐ.
水莫深於海 (*shuǐ mò shēn yú hǎi*)	No water is deeper than the sea.
今日風大於昨日 (*jīn rì fēng dà yú zuó rì*)	The wind is stronger today than yesterday.
楚國之食貴於玉，薪貴於桂 (*chǔ guó zhī shí guì yú yù, xīn guì yú guì*)	In Chǔ, the food is more expensive than jade and firewood is more expensive than cassia.
金玉者，物孰貴焉？ (*jīn yù zhě, wù shú guì yán?*)	What is more valuable than gold and jade?

Note: (1) The lack of specific markers for subject, number, tense, etc. may produce many possible translation permutations.

Adverbials showing 'by means of'

This adverbial is the common / 以 (*yǐ*) + Noun/ construction. Normally an A₂-type before the verb, it may also follow the object as A₃-type:

/[S] 以 (*yǐ*) Noun V O/ or

/[S] V O 以 (*yǐ*) Noun/

The English equivalent is: 'Subject Verb Object by means of Noun', e.g. 遙以手招之 (*yáo yǐ shǒu zhāo zhī*) 'he beckoned him from a distance with his hand'; 蹴之以足 (*cù zhī yǐ zú*) 'he kicked him with his foot'; 以重值購之 (*yǐ zhòng zhí gòu zhī*) literally 'by means of a heavy price purchased it' = 'he paid a high price for it'; 覆以土 (*fù yǐ tǔ*) 'he covered [it] with soil'. There may be a difference of emphasis between the two positions of 以 (*yǐ*), with A₃-type more emphatic, but this is not always the case.

Figure 30: Examples involving Adverbials showing 'by means of' [1]

得錢四百，以赤繩貫之 (*dé qián sì bǎi, yǐ chì shéng guàn zhī*)	received 400 coppers and strung them together with a red string
歸國，以百金貨之 (*guī guó, yǐ bǎi jīn huò zhī*)	He returned to his native country and sold it for one hundred pieces of gold.
包之以布，繫之以繩 (*bāo zhī yǐ bù, jì zhī yǐ shéng*)	He wrapped it in cloth and tied it up with string.
遂以劍擊斷之 (*suì yǐ jiàn jī duàn zhī*)	Then he struck it in two with a sword.
何以知其然？(*hé yǐ zhī qí rán?*)	How can we know that it is so?

Note: (1) *The lack of specific markers for subject, number, tense, etc. may produce many possible translation permutations.*

Adverbials involving recipients

In Classical Chinese, there are two very different ways of expressing the idea of 'giving something to someone'.

i) The first is in the form 'Subject provides a Person with a Noun' and this uses 以 (*yǐ*) as an A₂-type or A₃-type adverbial:

(a) *A₂-type*:

/[S] 以 (*yǐ*) Noun give Person/

e.g. 以此贈之 (*yǐ cǐ zèng zhī*) 'present him with this' or:

(b) *A₃-type*:

/[S] give Person 以 (*yǐ*) Noun/

e.g. 數遺之以書 (*shuò wèi zhī yǐ shū*) 'often sent him letters'.

ii) The second is in the form 'Subject gives a Thing to a Person'. The most common way to show this in Classical Chinese is as follows:

/[S] give Noun 於 (*yú*) Person/

e.g. 不如鬻宅於兄 (*bù rú yù zhái yú xiōng*) 'It would be best to sell the house to your elder brother'. Much less common is the form:

/[S] give Person Noun/

e.g. 為之居 (*wèi zhī jū*) 'provided them [with] dwellings'.

Figure 31: Examples showing Adverbials involving Recipients [1]

託妻於其友而他往 (*tuō qī yú qí yǒu ér tā wǎng*)	entrusted his wife to his friend and went off
教其子以齊語 (*jiāo qí zǐ yǐ qí yǔ*)	taught his son the language of Qí
王以千金賜功臣 (*wáng yǐ qiān jīn cì gōng chén*)	The king bestowed one thousand pieces of gold on the meritorious minister.

子何不告以所往？ (*zǐ hé bú gào yǐ suǒ wǎng?*)	Why will you not tell me where he has gone?
乃以半價返之 (*nǎi yǐ bàn jià fǎn zhī*)	then gave him back half of the cost

Note: (1) The lack of specific markers for subject, number, tense, etc. may produce many possible translation permutations.

(XIV) Interrogatives

Asking questions in Classical Chinese is very similar in form to Modern Chinese. However, without punctuation, which is a modern convenience added only recently to classical texts, confusion can quite easily arise for the uninitiated, since the many characters involving questions have a wide variety of alternative meanings. There are essentially three types of question:

i) ***The simple interrogative***: The easiest way to ask a question in Classical Chinese is to present a statement and essentially ask whether it is true or not, by using the character 乎 (*hū*) at the end of the sentence , thus:

/[S] V O 乎 (*hū*)?/

Other characters which are used in this way and with the same function as 乎 (*hū*) are 與 (*yú*), 歟 (*yú*), 耶 (*yé*) and 邪 (*yé*), which are all fusion versions of 也乎 (*yě hū*), which may also be found in its full form. It is also possible to find 諸 (*zhū*) at the end of a sentence, in which case, it is a fusion character for 之乎 (*zhī hū*); 否 (*fǒu*) at the end of a sentence makes for an alternative question, i.e. '[or] not?'

ii) ***Interrogative pronouns / adjectives***: Such a question is frequently formed with 何 (*hé*), which may be translated as 'why', 'what', 'where', 'how' depending on what it replaces.

As the object of the verb, e.g. 子何言？ (*zǐ hé yán*) 'what did you say?', or 子何之 (*zǐ hé zhī*) 'where are you going?', the 何 (*hé*) precedes the verb. As the interrogative adverb 'why?', it is also placed before the verb, e.g. 王何必曰利 (*wáng hé bì yuē lì*) 'why must your Majesty speak of profit?' 何以 (*hé yǐ*) 'by what means?' is used adverbially in the same way, as are 何自 (*hé zì*), 何由 (*hé yóu*), 何從 (*hé cóng*) 'from where?', 'through where?' and 何時 (*hé shí*) 'when?'

何 (*hé*) may also be the predicate of a question, in which case, it has the force of 'why is it that ...?' In 如何 (*rú hé*), later 何如 (*hé rú*), it acts as the object of the verb and means 'be like what?', e.g. 德何如則可以王矣？ (*dé hé rú zé kě yǐ wàng yǐ*) 'what kind of virtue [does one need] to be able to be a [true] king?'

何 (*hé*) may also be used attributively to a noun such as 何人 (*hé rén*) 'what man?' (with the idea of 'what kind of man?') or 何故 (*hé gù*) 'what reason?', 'why?'

Alternatives to 何 (*hé*), which carry the same meanings and are used in the same way include: 奚 (*xī*) and 胡 (*hú*); 曷 (*hé*), which can also mean 'when'; 焉 (*yān*), 安 (*ān*), 惡乎 (*wū hū*), 惡 (*wū*), and 烏 (*wū*), which are all mostly used in the sense of 'how?' or 'where?'

The negative 'why not ...?' is often rendered by 何不 (*hé bù*), but sometimes the fusion character 盍 (*hé*) is used, which is taken to be either a contraction of 何不 (*hé bù*) or 胡不 (*hú bù*).

誰 (*shuí*) 'who?' can be used in either subject or object position and also as an attributive, e.g. 子以為誰？ (*zǐ yǐ wéi shuí*) 'who do you think it is?' or 是誰之過歟 (*shì shuí zhī guò yú*) 'whose fault is this?'

孰 (*shú*) is used for 'which?' and is usually found in the adverb position, i.e. before the verb. It almost always refers back to the subject, which is usually a larger group, but this is not always the case, e.g. 孰是孰非邪 (*shú shì shú fēi yé*) 'which is right and which is wrong?' or 此二人孰智 (*cǐ èr rén shú zhì*) 'who is the wiser of the two?' Occasionally, 孰 (*shú*) acts like 誰 (*shuí*) in the subject position, i.e. 'who?'

iii) **Rhetorical questions**: The most common indication of a rhetorical question in Classical Chinese is the use of the exclamatory-interrogative particle 哉 (*zāi*) at the end of a question or statement. It is often combined with the following interrogative particles: 安 (*ān*), 焉 (*yān*), 何 (*hé*), 惡 (*wū*), 烏 (*wū*) and 豈 (*qǐ*), all of which with 哉 (*zāi*) mean 'how' (implying 'surely not!'), e.g. 我焉能知之哉 (*wǒ yān néng zhī zhī zāi*) 'how could I possibly know that?', ie. 'of course I don't know that!' Sometimes, the final clause particle is 乎 (*hū*) or 也哉 (*yě zāi*) or 乎哉 (*hū zāi*).

When the predicate in a rhetorical question is an adjective 'is it not Adj. to / that ...?', the usual form is /不亦 Adj. 乎/ (*bú yì* adj. *hū*), e.g. 求劍若此，不亦惑乎 (*qiú jiàn ruò cǐ, bú yì huò hū*) 'how stupid to seek a sword in this way!' or 'is it not stupid to ...?'

Figure 32: Examples involving Question Formation (1)

孔子為人何如？ (*kǒng zǐ wéi rén hé rú?*)	What sort of a man is Confucius?
如此則動心否乎？ (*rú cǐ zé dòng xīn fǒu hū?*)	If it were like this, would it move you or not?
飲而棄酒，於禮可乎？ (*yìn ér qì jiǔ, yú lǐ kě hū?*)	Is it polite to throw away the wine you have been given?
何不炳燭乎？ (*hé bù bǐng zhú hū?*)	Why not carry a candle?
觀百獸之見我而敢不走乎？ (*guān bǎi shòu zhī jiàn wǒ ér gǎn bù zǒu hū?*)	watch whether all the animals dare not to run away when they see me
君曰：何也？ (*jūn yuē hé yě?*)	The ruler said: "Why?"

鮒魚來，子何為者邪？ (*fù yú lái, zǐ hé wéi zhě yé?*)	Hey, there, golden carp, what's the matter with you?
子何故出死不疑如是？ (*zǐ hé gù chū sǐ bù yí rú shì?*)	Why do you risk death without hesitation in this way?
不賢而能之與？ (*bù xián ér néng zhī yú?*)	Could he have done it if he had not been a worthy man?
先生將何處？(*xiān shēng jiāng hé chǔ?*)	Which position would you adopt, Master?
君豈私臣哉！(*jūn qǐ sī chén zāi!*)	How could you have shown favouritism to me?
趙王豈以一璧之故欺秦邪！ (*zhào wáng qǐ yǐ yī bì zhī gù qī qín yé!*)	Is it conceivable that the King of Zhào would cheat Qín just for one jade *bì*?
盍亦返其本矣？(*hé yì fǎn qí běn yǐ?*)	Why not return to the basics?
今公子安在？(*jīn gōng zǐ ān zài?*)	Where is the prince now?
王曰：誰可使者？ (*wáng yuē: shuí kě shǐ zhě?*)	The King said: "Who can be sent as our envoy?"
勸齊伐燕，有諸？ (*quàn qí fá yān, yǒu zhū?*)	Did you urge Qí to attack Yān?
何功之有哉？ (*hé gōng zhī yǒu zāi?*)	What merit is there in that?

Note: (1) The lack of specific markers for subject, number, tense, etc. may produce many possible translation permutations.

(XV) Exposure

We have noted earlier that for either rhetorical or stylistic effect, Classical Chinese will move certain elements of a clause, which would more normally occur in medial or final position, and place them in the initial position. The exposed text, particularly when it is a whole clause encompassing an idea, becomes the topic of the sentence. There is a tendency to see exposure as emphasis, but it is not the topic which is being emphasised, it is the following comment. The exposed topic might be a simple expression of time or place; it might be the object of the main verb; or it might even be the grammatical subject itself. Although it might only be the unusual positioning of the text which marks it as a topic, e.g. 五畝之宅樹之以桑 (*wǔ mǔ zhī zhái, shù zhī yǐ sāng*) 'let them plant their five *mǔ* plots of land with mulberries', Classical Chinese does employ various function particles which offer clearer signposts for the reader that certain characters are being exposed in this way.

i) 也 (*yě*): One of the functions of 也 is to mark a nominalised phrase, cf. the 之 ... 也

(*zhī...yě*) and 其 **...** 也 (*qí..yě*) constructions introduced on page 13. A similar structure is /X 之 於 (*zhī yú*) Y ［也］ (*yě*)/ meaning 'as for X's [attitude, etc.] to Y', e.g. 寡 人 之 於 國 也 (*guǎ rén zhī yú guó yě*) 'as for my [attitude] to my state, ...'. As a topic marker, 也 (*yě*) is also found highlighting time expressions, sometimes with a contrastive emphasis, e.g. 今 也 (*jīn yě*) 'nowadays'. It may also be found after the names of people.

ii) 者 (*zhě*): One of the functions of 者 (*zhě*) is to act as a position marker for an exposed topic. The topic which 者 (*zhě*) highlights is often a proper noun or a proper name or a time expression, e.g. 古 者 (*gǔ zhě*) 'in ancient times', 昔 者 (*xī zhě*) 'formerly' or even 今 者 (*jīn zhě*) 'nowadays'. Since this particle is also used to create a nominalised verb phrase, i.e. /Verb 者 (*zhě*)/ 'one who Verbs', the fact that the nominalised phrase is put in the topic position is usually the only marker. It should be noted, too, that in the

structure /A 者 (*zhě*) B 也 (*yě*)/, i.e. 'A is B', the 者 (*zhě*) is effectively acting as a topic marker.

iii) 則 (*zé*): One of the main functions of 則 (*zé*) is to introduce the apodosis in a conditional sentence, where it translates as 'then'. However, when this particle is placed immediately after the subject, it exposes the subject with a contrastive force. It may properly be viewed as an abbreviated condition, thus 'X 則 (*zé*) Y' means '[if it is] X [that we are talking about], then Y ...', e.g. 此 則 寡 人 之 罪 也 (*cǐ zé guǎ rén zhī zuì yě*) '*this* is my fault'.

iv) 夫 (*fú*): At the beginning of a sentence, 夫 (*fú*) acts as an introductory topic particle, e.g 夫 戰 ，勇 氣 也 (*fú zhàn, yǒng qì yě*) 'fighting - it's a matter of courage'. At the beginning of a question, 夫 (*fú*) emphasises the interrogative, giving it a rhetorical quality, e.g. 夫 誰 與 王 敵 ？ (*fú shuí yǔ wáng dí*) 'who on earth will oppose Your Majesty?'

Figure 33: Examples involving Exposure and Function Particles [1]

君子之於禽獸也，見其生，不忍其死 (*jūn zǐ zhī yú qín shòu yě, jiàn qí shēng, bù rěn qí sǐ*)	The superior man's attitude towards animals [is this]: having seen them alive, he cannot bear to see them die.
夫子之求之也，其諸異乎人之求之與 (*fū zǐ zhī qiú zhī yě, qí zhū yì hū rén zhī qiú zhī yú*)	The way the Master seeks it (i.e. information) is it not, perhaps, different from the way other men seek it?
子曰：聽訟，吾猶人也，必也，使無訟乎 (*zǐ yuē: tīng sòng, wú yóu rén yě, bì yě, shǐ wú sòng hū*)	Confucius said: "When hearing litigations, I am like any other person. What is needed, though, is to make it so that there are no litigations."

於趙則有功矣，於魏則未為忠臣也 (*yú zhào zé yǒu gōng yǐ, yú wèi zé wèi wéi zhōng chén yě*)	So far as Zhào was concerned you performed a meritorious deed, but so far as Wèi was concerned you were not a loyal subject.
夫豫讓之君亦何如哉！ (*fú yù ràng zhī jūn yì hé rú zāi!*)	Now, ask yourself, what was Yùràng's ruler like!
賜則奚足以識之！ (*cì zé xī zú yǐ shì zhī!*)	How could I be qualified to judge him! (賜, *cì*, is the name of Confucius' disciple, here = I)
其子趨而往視之，苗則槁矣 (*qí zǐ qū ér wǎng shì zhī, miáo zé gǎo yǐ*)	His son went in a great hurry to look at them, and found that the seedlings had wilted.
此龜者寧其死為留骨而貴乎 ... (*cǐ guī zhě nìng qí sǐ wéi liú gǔ ér guì hū ...*)	Now would this turtle prefer to be dead and have his bones preserved and honoured ...
嚮者，使汝狗白而往，黑而來 ⋯ (*xiàng zhě, shǐ rǔ gǒu bái ér wǎng, hēi ér lái ...*)	if just now your dog had gone out white and come back black ...

Note: (1) The lack of specific markers for subject, number, tense, etc. may produce many possible translation permutations.

Classical Chinese
Function Characters

Classical Chinese Function Characters

Classical Chinese, like Modern Chinese, is heavily dependent on 虛詞 (*xūcí*). These so-called function characters (lit. 'empty words') can sometimes be extremely difficult to pin down in translation, since the same 虛詞 (*xūcí*) may take on a wide variety of functions: as adverb, as conjunction, as preposition or as modifier. They may also act as grammar particles or just add to the mood or act as stylistic fillers or be simple pause markers. This all means that translations into English can differ significantly and still be technically correct; Modern Chinese translations may offer even further shades of interpretation.

We attempt here to indicate the wide variety of uses and functions of some of the more common 虛詞 (*xūcí*); there are over 60 in the following pages, arranged in alphabetical order by pīnyīn romanisation. As the reader becomes more aware of the nuances and flavour of Classical Chinese and more accustomed to its rhythm, it will be easier to appreciate how a certain character or phrase functions in a particular sentence. Functions, though, do overlap and sometimes the lack of clear grammatical signposts, and a tendency in Classical Chinese towards 'optional precision' means that the reader must rely on experience, common sense and technical knowledge of Chinese culture to resolve some of the inevitable ambiguities which may arise. Context often provides the best clue, but even then, it is best that the reader does not assume that there is one perfect, all-encompassing translation from Classical Chinese.

The uses and functions of 而 (*ér*)

When not being used to mean 'you' or 'your', 而 (*ér*) is principally a clause-initial adverb, which connects the second clause of a sentence to the first. It essentially links verbal units, i.e. what comes either side of 而 (*ér*) is verbal in intent, even though there may be no actual verb. The connection is a vague one corresponding to English 'and', 'whereas', 'but', 'and then', 'and only then', 'and so', 'moreover', 'furthermore', 'still', 'yet' etc. Context will usually provide a clue as to how best to translate 而 (*ér*). This means that the same simple phrase can be given a wide variety of differently textured meanings in translation; the preference for a particular translation will depend upon how the text as a whole is being interpreted by the reader. The second use of 而 (*ér*) outlined here is as a final particle.

i) **Linking verbal units**: Here, 而 (*ér*) either links two main clauses, or it links a main clause which follows 而 (*ér*) to the subordinate clause which precedes it.

a) **Between main clauses**: When 而 (*ér*) acts as the link between two main clauses, its translation may be 'and', 'but', 'yet', etc. We provide here a few examples of how context pushes the translation towards one particular version: 北救趙而西卻秦 (*běi jiù zhào ér xī què qín*) 'rescue Zhào in the North and repel Qín in the West'; 舟已行矣而劍不行 (*zhōu yǐ xíng yǐ ér jiàn bù xíng*) 'the boat had already moved, but the sword had not'. The link may also be between two predicative adjectives: 宰予之詞雅而文也 (*zǎi yǔ zhī cí yǎ ér wén yě*) 'Zǎiyǔ's utterances are refined and elegant'.

b) ***Between subordinate and main clause***: 而 (*ér*) often connects two clauses, where the first clause is subordinate to the second or where there is an obvious succession or dependence between the clauses. This means that context tends to play a major part in deciding the appropriate shade of meaning to be given in translation. It is important to realise, too, that there may, in fact, be no direct word-for-word translation of a Classical Chinese 而 (*ér*), especially for the more polished translation.

For example, the connection between two clauses in English might be provided by a first-clause or second-clause initial 'when', 'whilst' or 'after' etc. All Classical Chinese needs in the same situation is an 而 (*ér*) between the two clauses, even though 而 (*ér*) does not semantically mean any of these words.

On the other hand, if the 而 (*ér*) is translated into English and maintains its position between the clauses, it is much more likely to follow its Modern Chinese equivalents and meanings: 就 (*jiù*) 'then', 才 (*cái*) 'then and only then', 又 (*yòu*) 'and', 'but', 再 (*zài*) 'again', 'furthermore', 然後 (*ránhòu*) 'and then', 'after that', 因而 (*yīn'ér*)

'and so', 'consequently', 'thereupon', 而且 (*érqiě*) 'and', 'furthermore', 然而 (*rán'ér*) 'even so', 'but', 但是 (*dànshì*) 'but', 'however', 卻 (*què*) 'however', 反倒, (*fǎndào*) 'on the contrary', 竟然 (*jìngrán*) 'yet', 而況 (*érkuàng*) 'still more' etc.

A few examples may serve to show these different uses: 抇其谷而得其鈇 (*jué qí gǔ ér dé qí fū*) 'he found his axe whilst digging in the valley'; 至死而止 (*zhì sǐ ér zhǐ*) 'only stopping when they had died'; 將及華泉，驂絓於木而止 (*jiāng jí huá quán, cān guà yú mù ér zhǐ*) 'as they were about to reach Huáquán, the chariot's horses stumbled over a branch and [then] came to a halt'; 余聞而愈悲 (*yú wén ér yù bēi*) 'after I heard [the news], I became even more despondent'. Sometimes, it may not be necessary to translate directly, e.g. 執策而臨之 (*zhí cè ér lín zhī*) 'stand over him holding a whip'.

At this point, it bears repeating that translations into Modern Chinese or English sometimes demand more of the Classical Chinese than it is actually able to give. Context, familiarity and common sense are often the only salves.

c) ***Used in conditional sentences***: When an 而 (*ér*) comes between subject and verb, it may may impy a conditional 'if', e.g. 管氏而知禮，孰不知禮？(*guǎn shì ér zhī lǐ, shú bù zhī lǐ*) 'if [even] Mr Guǎn knew the rules of propriety, who would not know them?' or 人而無知，與木何異？ (*rén ér wú zhī, yǔ mù hé yì?*) 'if man has no consciousness, how is he different from a tree?' The 而 (*ér*) here introduces a contrastive, unexpected element within the protasis of the conditional sentence: 'to be a person *yet* be without consciousness, how is this different from a tree?"

Moreover, in addition to being used in the protasis ('if' clause) of a conditional sentence, 而 (*ér*) is also sometimes found introducing the apodosis (main clause), where it functions in the same way as 則 (*zé*), i.e. 'then', 'in that case', e.g. 與楚則漢破，與漢而楚破 (*yǔ chǔ zé hàn pò, yǔ hàn ér chǔ pò*) 'if we side with Chǔ, then Hàn will fall; if we side with Hàn, then Chǔ will fall'.

d) **Used in expressions of direction**: 而 (*ér*) can be used before characters indicating direction (either temporal or spatial) such as 前 (*qián*) 'before', 後 (*hòu*) 'after', 來 (*lái*) 'coming', 往 (*wǎng*) 'going' etc. The 而 (*ér*) may combine with a character such as 由 (*yóu*) 'from' (sometimes it is a zero or an implied 'from'); in these cases, 而 (*ér*) has the force of 'to', 'up to' etc., e.g. 由孔子而來 (*yóu kǒng zǐ ér lái*) 'from the time of Confucius onwards'. It can also be combined with the cardinal

directions (north, east, south and west) and other directional indicators such as up or down, e.g. 割鴻沟而西者為漢，鴻沟而東者為楚 (*gē hóng gōu ér xī zhě wéi hàn, hóng gōu ér dōng zhě wéi chǔ*) 'carve out the area to the west of Hónggōu for Hàn and [everything] to the east of Hónggōu for Chǔ'.

e) **Used in time expressions**: 而 (*ér*) often occurs after simple time expressions, such as 'morning', and 'evening', e.g. 朝而往，暮而歸 (*zhāo ér wǎng, mù ér guī*) 'he left in the morning and returned in the evening'. Here the characters for 'morning' and 'evening' are both being used verbally, i.e. the 而 (*ér*) acts as the link between the main clause 'he left' and the subordinate clause '[when it was] morning'. It is the same for indefinite time expressions such as 俄而 (*é ér*) 'after a while, presently' and 忽而 (*hū ér*) 'suddenly'.

ii) **As a final particle**:

a) **Exclamatory use**: 而 (*ér*) can be used at the end of an exclamation, in which case, it has the force of a Modern Chinese 啊 (*a*), e.g. 唐棣之華，偏其反而！ (*táng dì zhī huā, piān qí fǎn ér!*) 'the flowers of the aspen-plum, how gracefully they sway!' (NB 偏, *piān*, here is understood as 翩, *piān*, i.e. 'lightly', 'elegantly', 'gracefully' - it is used to describe a fluttering action).

b) ***Interrogative use***: At the end of a question, it is not unlike the Modern Chinese use of 嗎 (*ma*), i.e. it can be treated like a question mark; it is often used with 其 (*qí*) to form a rhetorical question, e.g. 鬼擾求食，若敖氏之鬼不其餒而？(*guǐ rǎo qiú shí, ruò áo shì zhī guǐ bù qí něi ér?*) 'ghosts cause trouble when they are looking for food, isn't Mr Ruòáo's spirit just likely to be hungry?'

c) ***Used in commands***: 而 (*ér*) tends to give a softening edge to a command rather like a Modern Chinese 吧 (ba), e.g. 已而，已而！今之從政者殆而 (*yǐ ér, yǐ ér! jīn zhī cóng zhèng zhě dài ér*) 'Give up, give up! Perilous is the lot of those in office today'.

d) ***Used to show finality***: As can be seen in the very last 而 (*ér*) of the above example in (c), it can also be found at the end of a sentence where it will add a note of finality to the meaning, not unlike the Modern Chinese use of 了 (*le*). It is not necessary to translate the 而 (*ér*) into English when it is used in this way.

Combinations of 而 (*ér*)

Combinations of 而 (*ér*) are often used in the same form and with the same meaning in more formal Modern Chinese. Thus we have the conjunctions 而後 (*ér hòu*) 'then', 'and then', 'after that', 'only then', 而且 (*ér qiě*) 'and', 'furthermore', 'moreover', and 而況 (*ér kuàng*) 'still more', 'with still stronger reason'. In addition, we have the final particle set 而已 (*ér yǐ*) 'only',

'that's all', which is still very common in Taiwanese spoken Mandarin. 而 (*ér*) can also be found in the classical final particle set 而已乎 (*ér yǐ hū*), where it emphasises the rhetorical mood, e.g. 梁王安得晏然而已乎 (*liáng wáng ān dé yàn rán ér yǐ hū*) 'how could King Liáng possibly [sleep] peacefully [at night]!'

The uses and functions of 乎 (*hū*)

乎 (*hū*) is very common in Classical Chinese both as a particle (described below) and as a preposition, where it is the equivalent of 於 (*yú*) (see p 79 for more details of this usage).

i) ***As a final particle***:

a) ***Used in interrogatives***: 乎 (*hū*) is the main indicator of a yes-or-no question. It is directly equivalent to a Modern Chinese 嗎 (*ma*), e.g. 汝亦知射乎？(*rǔ yì zhī shè hū?*) 'do you know archery, too?' When it is used as a final particle in questions involving 誰 (*shuí*) 'who' or 安 (*ān*) 'where' etc., it is equivalent to a Modern Chinese 呢 (*ne*). In questions involving 何 (*hé*) 'what', 'why', 'how' etc., 孰 (*shú*) 'who, which', 況 (*kuàng*) 'not to mention ...!', 寧 (*nìng*) 'how could ...!', 庸 (*yōng*) 'how could ...!', 豈 (*qǐ*) 'how could ...!' and the negatives 不 (*bù*) and 非 (*fēi*), the force of the 乎 (*hū*) as a final particle is to emphasise the rhetorical effect. In such cases, its Modern Chinese equivalent is a 呢 (*ne*) or 嗎 (*ma*). See Section XIV on *Interrogatives* for examples (pp 48-50).

b) ***Used in exclamations***: 乎 (*hū*) is also found at the end of an exclamation, where it acts like a Modern Chinese 啊 (*a*), e.g. 天<u>乎</u>，無罪！ (*tiān hū, wú zuì!*) 'My God! I'm innocent!' or 神<u>乎</u>！神<u>乎</u>！ (*shén hū! shén hū!*) 'It's a miracle! A miracle!'

c) ***Used in imperatives***: In this usage, the 乎 (*hū*) adds a softening, Modern Chinese 吧 (*ba*) element to the command or plea, e.g. 左右曰：夫人少辟火<u>乎</u>！ (*zuǒ yòu yuē: fū rén shǎo bì huǒ hū!*) 'the servants said: "Lady, do keep clear of the fire!"' or 默默<u>乎</u>，河伯！ (*mò mò hū, hé bó!*) 'Be silent, River God!'

d) ***Used in conjectures***: 乎 (*hū*) is often used with 殆 (*dài*) 'probably', 其 (*qí*) 'probably' or 或 (*huò*) 'perhaps' etc., e.g. 吾聞聖人不相，殆先生<u>乎</u>? (*wú wén shèng rén bú xiàng, dài xiān shēng hū?*) 'I have heard it said that one cannot tell a wise man from his looks, [they would] probably [have been talking about] you!'

ii) ***As pause marker or filler***: 乎 (*hū*) can work as a pause marker between two clauses in a sentence. This is not common; the 乎 (*hū*) does not need to be translated, e.g. 故翟以為雖不耕織<u>乎</u>，而功賢于耕織也 (*gù dí yǐ wéi suī bù gēng zhī hū, ér gōng xián yú gēng zhī yě*) 'and so, I think that even though I may not till or weave, my accomplishments are more worthy than tilling or weaving' (NB 翟, *dí*, is short

for 墨翟, Mò Dí, i.e. Mòzǐ, 墨子, the fifth century BCE philosopher - it is used pronominally here).

As a filler, 乎 (*hū*) can be used to slow down the flow of a sentence, providing for slight emphasis. Modern Chinese would translate with a 呢 (*ne*), e.g. 仕非為貧也，而有時<u>乎</u>為貧 (*shì fēi wèi pín yě, ér yǒu shí hū wèi pín*) 'People should not seek office because of poverty, but sometimes that is the reason'.

Occasionally, 乎 (*hū*) follows an adjective or adverb. Chinese commentators see this 乎 (*hū*) as an adverb suffix, i.e. it functions like 然 (*rán*) and works like the suffix ~ly in English. However, some still prefer to view it as a pause marker (usually for descriptive words), which allows for a more dramatic re-ordering of the sentence, e.g. 巍巍<u>乎</u>其有成功也 (*wēi wēi hū qí yǒu chéng gōng yě*) 'magnificent indeed were his accomplishments!' or 確<u>乎</u>其不可拔 (*què hū qí bù kě bá*) 'steadfast, he could not be moved.'

iii) ***As general preposition***: 乎 (*hū*), like 於 (*yú*), corresponds variously to the English 'at', 'in', 'on', 'to', 'from', 'by', 'than', etc. e.g. 俄則束<u>乎</u>有司而戮<u>乎</u>大市 (*é zé shù hū yǒu sī ér lù hū dà shì*) 'after a short while, he was trussed up by the officers and executed in the market place' or 是故知命者不立<u>乎</u>岩牆之下 (*shì gù zhī mìng zhě bú lì hū yán qiáng zhī xià*) 'Hence someone who understands fate does not stand under a dangerous wall'.

Combinations of 乎 *(hū)*

When 乎 *(hū)* appears in a 乎哉 *(hū zāi)* combination, it either emphasises the question or adds to the rhetorical effect, e.g 子曰：吾有知乎哉？無知也 *(zǐ yuē: wú yǒu zhī hū? wú zhī yě)* 'The Master said: "Am I a learned person? I am not." 乎 *(hū)* also appears in the combination 乎爾 *(hū ěr)*, where it emphasises the affirmation, e.g. 然而無有乎爾 ，則亦無有乎爾 *(rán ér wú yǒu hū ěr, zé yì wú yǒu hū ěr)* 'in these circumstances, if there is no one [to transmit the sage's doctrines], then that is how it is'. It is worth noting here that although the negative of 有 *(yǒu)* 'exist', 'have', 'there is' is 無 *(wú)*, sometimes 不有 *(bù yǒu)* or 無有 *(wú yǒu)* is used.

The uses and functions of 其 *(qí)*

其 *(qí)* in Classical Chinese has two main areas of meaning. The first is as a possessive pronoun or demonstrative: 'his', 'hers', 'its', 'that' etc.; the second is as a modal particle indicating the speaker's exhortation, command or assessment of probability. As with other function characters, 其 *(qí)* has a variety of meanings beyond these two areas:

i) *Possessive pronoun / demonstrative*: The most common use of 其 *(qí)* is as a possessive pronoun or as a demonstrative meaning variously 'his', 'her', 'its', 'their', 'ones' and also 'the ... in question', 'the appropriate ...', e.g. 盡其材 *(jìn qí cái)* 'maximise his potential', 得其人 *(dé qí rén)* 'find the right person (for the job)'. With the tendency for the speaker to speak in the third person in Classical Chinese and also for the person

addressed to be referred to in the third person, it may well be necessary to translate 其 *(qí)* as 'my', 'our' or indeed 'you', 'your'. In addition, since Modern Chinese does not have a definite article like the English 'the', 其 *(qí)* is often translated into the Modern Chinese equivalents of 'this' (這個, *zhège*), 'that' (那個, *nàge*), 'these' (這些, *zhèxie*) and 'those' (那些, *nàxie*).

ii) *Nominalisation*: 其 *(qí)* is also used to create a noun-phrase, in a similar way to 之 *(zhī)* (see pp 84-86). As with noun-phrases with 之 *(zhī)*, 其 *(qí)* noun phrases are commonly found in both topic and object functions. In the topic position, it is common to end the phrase with a 也 *(yě)* particle:

/ 其 *(qí)* V [O] 也 *(yě)*, .../

and this construction means 'as for his Verb-ing [O], ...', or 'if (or when) he Verb-ed [O], ...', e.g. 其為人也 ，仁義人也 *(qí wéi rén yě, rén yì rén yě)* 'as for his being a person, he was a good and just man', or simply 'as a person, he was a good and just man'.

其 *(qí)* may also mark the start of a phrase which is the object of a verb such as 知 *(zhī)* 'know'. In such cases, the 其 *(qí)* usually corresponds, in English, to a noun clause '[knew] that he + Verb'. The 也 *(yě)* at the end of such a clause is optional, e.g. 叔魚之生也 ，其母視之 ，知其必以賄死 *(shū yú zhī shēng yě, qí mǔ shì zhī, zhī qí bì yǐ huì sǐ)* 'when Shūyú was born, his mother looked at him and knew that he would certainly die as a result of venality'. Other verbs such as 患 *(huàn)* 'be upset about', 見 (*jiàn*) 'see', 聽 (*tīng*) 'allow', and 恐 (*kǒng*) 'fear' are also commonly used in this construction, e.g. 尚恐<u>其</u>不我欲也 (*shàng kǒng qí bù wǒ yù yě*) 'still afraid that they might not want me'.

iii) ***Reducing attribution markers***: 其 (*qí*) can be used to avoid a clumsy succession of attribution markers such as /N 之 (*zhī*) N 之 (*zhī*) N/. This would be simplified as:

/N 之 (*zhī*) N, 其 (*qí*) N/

e.g. 古之聖人，<u>其</u>出人也遠矣 (*gǔ zhī shèng rén, qí chū rén yě yuǎn yǐ*) literally 'as for the wise rulers of antiquity, their surpassing other people was indeed far!', i.e. 'the degree to which the wise rulers of antiquity surpassed other people was indeed great!' Without the 其 (*qí*) construction, the sentence would be a more unwieldy 古之聖人之出人也遠矣 (*gǔ zhī shèng rén zhī chū rén yě yuǎn yǐ*).

其 (*qí*) may be used in disjunctive questions, i.e. those involving 'or', e.g. 子以秦為將救韓乎？<u>其</u>不乎？ (*zǐ yǐ qín wéi jiāng jiù hán hū? qí bù hū?*) 'do you think that Qín will save Hán or not?' Some commentators see this use of 其 (*qí*) as a reduction in attribution markers with the 'or' implied by the double question. Chinese commentators, though, view one of the meanings of 其 (*qí*) as a disjunctive 'or'.

iv) ***Conditional usage***: When 其 (*qí*) starts a sentence or appears between an explicit subject and verb, its meaning may be understood as 'if', e.g. 湯<u>其</u>無郼，武<u>其</u>無岐，賢雖十全，不

能成功 (*tāng qí wú yī, wǔ qí wú qí, xián suī shí quán, bù néng chéng gōng*) 'if King Tāng had not held [the land of] Yī and if King Wǔ had not held [Mount] Qí, although they would still have been perfectly virtuous, they would not have been successful' or <u>其</u>濟，君之靈也 (*qí jì, jūn zhī líng yě*) 'if successful, it is thanks to you'. For some commentators, this last 其 (*qí*) could also be understood as 'its' or 'the', i.e. 'its success will be down to you'. Chinese commentators, though, offer 'if' as one of the Classical Chinese meanings of 其 (*qí*).

v) ***The modal*** 其 (*qí*): Its use indicates hope or expectation on the part of the speaker.

a) ***To indicate the future***: 其 (*qí*) may be used as an indicator of the future, i.e. 'will'. It equates to a Modern Chinese 將 (*jiāng*) or 將要 (*jiāngyào*), e.g. 今殷<u>其</u>淪喪 (*jīn yīn qí lún sàng*) 'now the Yīn [dynasty] will be destroyed' or 喪田不懲，禍亂<u>其</u>興 (*sàng tián bù chéng, huò luàn qí xīng*) 'if arable land is lost and no-one is punished, turmoil will flourish'.

b) ***To indicate supposition***: This usage may be related to the character 期 (*qī*) 'to expect'. Here, 其 (*qí*) indicates supposition. especially about the future (e.g. 'I expect that ...'), or it suggests a course of action (e.g. 'let him ...'); it also has the force of 'probably', 'I expect', 'I imagine', 'perhaps', 'could it be that ...?' etc., e.g. 通於此說者，<u>其</u>知所以為天下乎 (*tōng yú cǐ shuō* *zhě, qí zhī suǒ yǐ wèi tiān xià hū)* 'one who understands this theory would, I think, know how to rule the Empire' or 始作俑者，其無後乎 (*shǐ zuò yǒng zhě, qí wú hòu hū*) 'The person who first made sacrificial grave dolls probably [died] childless!'

When the 其 (*qí*) is followed by a negative (as in the last example above), it may also be interpreted as a rhetorical question requiring an affirmative answer: '... was he not without posterity?"

c) *To indicate the imperative*: In this usage, 其 (*qí*) is placed directly before the verb and normally follows a noun or pronoun indicating the person or people being commanded. Examples include: 爾其無忘乃父之志！ (*ěr qí wú wàng nǎi fù zhī zhì!*) 'Do not forget your father's ideals!'; 諸君其籌之！ (*zhū jūn qí chóu zhī!*) 'Gentleman, please consider it carefully!' Occasionally, there is a final particle at the end of the imperative; this would be either 矣 (*yǐ*) or 也 (*yě*), e.g. 吾其還也 (*wú qí huán yě*) 'Let's go back!'

vi) *As an attributive*: When 其 (*qí*) is found between a modifier and a head-word, it shows attribution like a a Classical Chinese 之 (*zhī*) or a Modern Chinese 的 (*de*), e.g. 朕其弟 (*zhèn qí dì*) 'Our [royal] brother' or 君其祀 (*jūn qí sì*) 'your ancestral sacrifices'.

vii) *As final particle (pronounced jī)*: Like other function characters we meet in this section, 其 can also be found at the end of interrogatives. In this position, the character is pronounced *jī*. It acts like a Modern Chinese 呢 (*ne*) or 了 (*le*), e.g. 若之何其？ (*ruò zhī hé jī?*) 'what can we do?' This phrase equates to the Modern Chinese 怎麼辦呢！ (*zěnme bàn ne!*) 'what's to be done?' etc.

Combinations of 其 (qí)

There are three common combinations of 其 (*qí*): 其殆 (*qí dài*), 其庸 (*qí yōng*) and 其諸 (*qí zhū*). All have the force of 'probably', 'I expect', 'perhaps' etc., e.g. 夫子之求之也，其諸異乎人之求之與？ (*fū zǐ zhī qiú zhī yě, qí zhū yì hū rén zhí qiú zhī yú?*) 'the way the Master seeks it (i.e. information) is it not, perhaps, different from the way other men seek it?'

The uses and functions of 然 (rán)

然 (*rán*) in Classical Chinese is equivalent to 如此 (*rú cǐ*) in the sense of '[be] like this', 'thus', 'so'. It can be found in the following situations:

i) *The affirmative answer (yes)*: In Classical Chinese, 然 (*rán*) was used to affirm a statement: 'yes', e.g. 非罪歟？皆曰：然 (*fēi zuì yú? jiē yuē: rán*) '"was it not a crime?" They all said: "Yes"'. Its negative is 否 (*fǒu*) 'no'. 不然 (*bù rán*) means either 'no, it is not so' or else 'if it is not so', i.e. 'otherwise', 'or else'.

ii) *Reinforcement*: 然 (*rán*) is sometimes used to reinforce a preceding element; it adds nothing to the actual meaning. The preceding element may be a comparison:

61

/X [若] (*ruò*) O 然 (*rán*)/

literally 'X like O, like this' or simply 'X like O', e.g. 無若宋人然 (*wú ruò sòng rén rán*) 'Don't be like the man from Sòng!' or 夫子若有不豫色然 (*fū zǐ ruò yǒu bú yù sè rán*) 'you seem to have an unhappy look on your face, Master'

iii) *Adjective to adverb*: Another use of 然 (*rán*) is to make an adjective into an A₂-type adverb (i.e. one which precedes the verb) like the ~ly suffix in English, e.g. 天油然作雲，沛然下雨 (*tiān yóu rán zuò yún, pèi rán xià yǔ*) 'heaven abundantly produced clouds and rain copiously fell' or 君愀然不乐 (*jūn qiǎo rán bú lè*) 'you were miserable and depressed'.

Combinations of 然 (*rán*)

There are four 然 (*rán*) combinations with the following meanings and uses, some of which may appear at first glance to be close to their Modern Chinese uses:

i) 雖然 (*suī rán*): In Classical Chinese, the force of 雖然 (*suī rán*), which in Modern Chinese means 'although', is more correctly read as 'though it is so, ...'.

ii) 然而 (*rán ér*) in Modern Chinese means 'however'. In classical texts, it is better rendered as 'this being so, yet ...'.

iii) 然後 (*rán hòu*): means in Classical Chinese 'then and only then' not 'after', which is its Modern Chinese meaning. Examples include: 傳諸人，得大聖，然後人莫敢爭 (*chuán zhū rén, dé dà shèng, rán hòu rén mò gǎn zhēng*) 'if one

bequeaths it to someone else (i.e. other than one's son) and [in so doing] gets a great sage, only then will no one dare fight over it' and 禹之後四百年，然後得桀 (*yǔ zhī hòu sì bǎi nián, rán hòu dé jié*) 'it was not until four hundred years after Yǔ that we got [the tyrant] Jié'.

iv) 然則 (*rán zé*): means 'if it is so, then ...' or 'this being so, then', e.g. 然則廢釁鐘與？ (*rán zé fèi xìn zhōng yú*) 'in that case, shall we abandon the consecration of the bell?'

Uses and functions of 所 (*suǒ*)

Apart from its role as a noun meaning 'place', 所 (*suǒ*) is the Classical Chinese function word used to create a relative clause. 所 (*suǒ*) has no equivalent in Modern Chinese, where it still continues to be used in more formal language contexts.

A relative clause is a subordinate clause modifying a noun. In English, relative clauses follow the noun they refer to and are often introduced by the relative pronouns 'that', 'which', 'whom', etc. (these may be omitted). For example: 'The shoes (which) his brother bought were very expensive', where '(which) his brother bought' is a relative clause modifying 'shoes'. In Chinese, the modifying phrase comes before the noun headword; this is like an adjective in English, e.g. 'expensive shoes'. This rule applies to both Classical Chinese and Modern Chinese word order. However, whereas Modern Chinese uses 的 (*de*) between the modifying phrase and the noun headword, Classical Chinese uses 所 (*suǒ*) before the verb in the modifying phrase, with an optional 之 (*zhī*), the Classical Chinese equivalent of 的 (*de*), before the noun headword. This gives the grammar formula:

/S₂ 所 (*suǒ*) V₂ [之 (*zhī*)] S₁ V₁/

Thus, the above example 'The shoes (which) his brother bought were very expensive.' would be rendered in Classical Chinese as S₂其弟所 V₂買 (之)S₁履V₁貴甚 (*qí dì suǒ mǎi zhī lǚ guì shèn*), where S₁ (shoes) is the main subject, V₁ (be expensive) the main verb / adjective, and S₂ (the brother) and V₂ (bought) are the subject and verb of the relative clause modifying the main subject.

i) ***Used with a noun headword***: This is the 所 (*suǒ*) pattern above. i.e. 人 所 飲 (之) 水 (*rén suǒ yǐn zhī shuǐ*) 'water (that) people drink'. Other examples include: 取 所 獻 狐 白 裘 至 (*qǔ suǒ xiàn bái qiú zhì*) '[the cat burglar] arrived having retrieved the white fox fur (that) [Mèng Chángjūn] had presented [to the King]' or 仲 子 所 居 之 室 , 伯 夷 之 所 築 與 ? (*zhòng zǐ suǒ jū zhī shì, bó yí zhī suǒ zhù yú?*) 'The house that Zhòngzǐ lived in, was it built by Bó Yí?' Note that where the noun headword is omitted, as in the second phrase 伯 夷 之 所 築 (*bó yí zhī suǒ zhù*), the 所 築 (*suǒ zhù*) becomes a noun phrase (see iii) below) hence the 之 (*zhī*). The basic construction of this latter sentence is /A, B也 (*yě*)/, i.e. an 'A is B' construction, in which both A and B need to be nouns or noun phrases.

ii) 所 (*suǒ*) ***used with*** 者 (*zhě*) ***headword***: The noun headword may be substituted by

the generic 者 (*zhě*) to make the pattern:

/(N) 所 (*suǒ*) V 者 (*zhě*)/

i.e. 'what the (N) V'. This nominal phrase can be used as the topic, subject or object of the sentence. Examples include: 所 欲 者 不 成 , 所 求 者 不 得 (*suǒ yù zhě bù chéng, suǒ qiú zhě bù dé*) '(You) will not succeed in what (you) desire, (you) will not attain what (you) seek.' Here the subjects of the verbs 欲 (*yù*) and 求 (*qiú*) are omitted, as commonly occurs when the second person ('you') is being addressed.

A second example is: 臣 見 其 所 持 者 狹 而 所 欲 者 奢 , 故 笑 之 (*chén jiàn qí suǒ chí zhě xiá ér suǒ yù zhě shē gù xiào zhī*) 'I saw what he was carrying (as an offering to the gods) was stingy, and what he wanted was extravagant, so I laughed at him.' Here the noun phrases 其 所 持 者 (*qí suǒ chí zhě*) 'what he was carrying' and [其] 所 欲 者 (*[qí] suǒ yù zhě*) 'what he wanted' are pivotal, being the object of the verb 見 (*jiàn*) 'saw' and the subjects of the adjectives 狹 (*xiá*) 'stingy' and 奢 (*shē*) 'extravagant'.

Compare also: 人 之 所 不 學 而 能 者 , 其 良 能 也 , 所 不 慮 而 知 者 , 其 良 知 也 (*rén zhī suǒ bù xué ér néng zhě, qí liáng néng yě, suǒ bù lù ér zhī zhě, qí liáng zhī yě*) 'What a person can do without learning is their innate ability; what a person knows without thinking is their innate knowledge.' The 之 (*zhī*) following 人 (*rén*) is clearly signalling in both cases that the /所 (*suǒ*)...者 (*zhě*)/ is a noun phrase, paralleled by the 其 (*qí*) in the following clause denoting that the 能 (*néng*) and the 知 (*zhī*) are both being used as nouns , i.e. 'ability and 'knowledge' respectively.

iii) ***Used alone in a noun phrase***: 所 (*suǒ*) is very commonly used in the pattern

/所 (*suǒ*) V/

to create a noun phrase. For example: 所欲 (*suǒ yù*) 'what (you) desire', 所言 (*suǒ yán*) 'what you speak of'. This is similar to the situation with 的 (*de*) in Modern Chinese, where 吃的 (*chīde*) means 'what is eaten'. Examples of this usage in Classical Chinese include the following: 是非爾所知也 (*shì fēi ěr suǒ zhī yě*) 'this is not something you know about'; 就之而不見所畏焉 (*jiù zhī ér bú jiàn suǒ wèi yán*) 'when you approach him you don't see anything to be in awe of there'; 姑舍女所學而從我 (*gū shè rǔ suǒ xué ér cóng wǒ*) 'for now put aside what you have learnt and follow me'; 所欲有甚於生者 (*suǒ yù yǒu shèn yú shēng zhě*) 'there are things we desire more than life itself'; 諸子所言，皆人生之累也，死則無此矣 (*zhū zǐ suǒ yán, jiē rén shēng zhī léi yě, sǐ zé wú cǐ yǐ*), 'All that you speak of is just the trammels of human existence; when you are dead there is none of this.'

Combinations of 所 (*suǒ*)

所以 (*suǒ yǐ*) is very common in Classical Chinese, where it is not a single word in the Modern Chinese sense of 'therefore' but rather 'that by which' i.e. 'the reason why'. In Classical Chinese, we can see clearly the 所 (*suǒ*) functioning as

the relative pronoun 'which' and the 以 (*yǐ*) used as a postposition 'by'. (Note that although 以 (*yǐ*) is normally a preposition, it is typically used as a postposition after pronouns such as 所 (*suǒ*) 'which', 何 (*hé*) 'what' and 是 (*shì*) 'this' becoming 所以 (*suǒ yǐ*) 'by which', 何以 (*hé yǐ*) 'why' and 是以 (*shì yǐ*) 'hence').

Examples of the use of 所以 (*suǒ yǐ*) include: 所以然者何？水土異也 (*suǒ yǐ rán zhě hé? shuǐ tǔ yì yě*) 'What is the reason this is so? It is because the environment is different'; 此吾所以悲也 (*cǐ wú suǒ yǐ bēi yě*) 'This is why I am sad.'; 古之人所以大過人者⋯ (*gǔ zhī rén suǒ yǐ dà guò rén zhě ...*) 'The way in which the ancients greatly surpassed other people is ....'; 君子不以其所以養人者害人 (*jūn zǐ bù yǐ qí suǒ yǐ yǎng rén zhě hài rén*) 'The superior man does not use his means of supporting people in order to harm them'.

所為 (*suǒ wéi*) is sometimes used in the same sense as 所以 (*suǒ yǐ*), i.e. 'the reason why', e.g. 上所為數問君者，畏君傾動關中 (*shàng suǒ wéi shuò wèn jūn zhě, wèi jūn qīng dòng guān zhōng*) 'The reason the emperor (Hàn Gāozǔ) has repeatedly asked you is because he is afraid you will cause trouble in Guānzhōng'. Note however, in the vast majority of instances 所為 (*suó wéi*) falls into the /X 所為 (*suǒ wéi*)/ pattern, i.e. 'what X did'.

所謂 (*suǒ wèi*) is likewise common in Modern Chinese, in the sense of 'so-called', but in Classical Chinese the characters should be read individually in the sense of 'what is called'. Examples include: 非所謂踰也貧富

不同也 (*fēi suǒ wèi yú yě; pín fù bù tóng yě*) 'it cannot be described as surpassing; it was due to a difference in wealth'; 所謂故國者，非謂有喬木之謂也，有世臣之謂也 (*suǒ wèi gù guó zhě, fēi wèi yǒu qiáo mù zhī wèi yě, yǒu shì chén zhī wèi yě*) 'what is meant by an "established state" refers not to the fact that it has lofty trees in it, but rather to the fact that it has ministers [which have been noted in it] for generations.'

為 ··· 所 (*wéi...suǒ*) is common in Classical Chinese as a passive construction in the form:

/ 為 (*wéi*) X 所 (*suǒ*) V/

'be V-ed by X', with 為 (*wéi*) introducing the agent ('by'). Examples include: 吾聞先即制人，後則為人所制 (*wú wén xiān jí zhì rén, hòu zé wéi rén suǒ zhì*) 'I have heard that if [you do it] first, then you control others, but if [you do it] later, you are controlled by others'; 布為人所略，賣為奴于燕 (*bù wéi rén lüè mài wéi nú yú yān*) 'Bù was abducted (by people) and sold into slavery in Yān'; 不為利祿所誘 (*bù wéi lì lù suǒ yòu*) 'not be enticed by profit and salary'. More examples on this usage can be found on p 42.

Uses and functions of 為 (*wéi / wèi*)

為 (*wéi*) is the Classical Chinese copula, i.e. the verb 'to be'. These and associated meanings are dealt with in Section VI, *Copula*, (see pp 18-21). As a full verb, 為 (*wéi*) also means 'to do', 'make', 'become', 'act', 'think', and in certain texts, it may have other meanings such as 'administer', 'study', plant', 'establish', 'let', etc. We deal here mainly with the non-verbal functions of 為 (*wéi / wèi*).

i) *As preposition* (*wèi / wéi*):

a) '*on behalf of*', '*for the benefit of*': The use of 為 (*wèi*) in this sense is similar to a Modern Chinese 給 (*gěi*), e.g. 為天下興利除害 (*wèi tiān xià xing lì chú hài*) 'create benefits and eliminate harm for the empire'.

b) '*because of*': The use of 為 (*wèi*) in this sense is similar to a Modern Chinese 因為 (*yīnwèi*) 'because', e.g. 君子不為小人之匈匈而易其行 (*jūn zǐ bú wèi xiǎo rén xiōng xiōng ér yì qí xíng*) 'The superior man does not change his behaviour because of the clamour of petty people.'

c) '*for*', '*for the sake of*': The use of 為 (*wèi*) in this sense is similar to 為了 (*wèile*) in Modern Chinese, e.g. 天下熙熙，皆為利來，天下壤壤，皆為利往 (*tiān xià xī xī, jiē wèi lì lái, tiān xià rǎng rǎng, jiē wèi lì wǎng*) 'when the empire is at peace, everyone comes for the benefits; when the empire is in turmoil, everyone leaves for the benefits [elsewhere]'.

d) '*with*', '*to*': 為 (*wèi*) can be used with verbs of speech to indicate the person spoken to / with, cf. 對 (*duì*) in Modern Chinese, e.g. 不足為外人道也 (*bù zú wèi wài rén dào yě*) 'not worth discussing with other people'.

e) *Used in the passive (pron. wéi)*: 為 (*wéi*) is often used with 所 (*suǒ*); it introduces the agent like the Modern Chinese 被 (*bèi*) 'by', e.g. 其子為

65

虎所食 (*qí zǐ wéi hǔ suǒ shí*) 'his son was eaten by a tiger' and 為水神所責 (*wéi shuǐ shén suǒ zé*) 'upbraided by the River God'; the 所 (*suǒ*) may also be omitted, e.g. 身為宋國笑 (*shēn wéi sòng guó xiào*) 'he himself was laughed at by (all) the land of Sòng'.

ii) **As conjunction** ('if', 'when', 'because', 'and'):

a) **'if', 'when'**: Second tone 為 (*wéi*) can be used to indicate conditionality, e.g. 王甚喜人之掩口也，為近王，必掩口 (*wáng shèn xǐ rén zhī yǎn kǒu yě, wéi jìn wáng, bì yǎn kǒu*) 'the king very much liked people to cover their mouths; if (or when) anyone approached the king, they had to cover their mouth'.

In addition, fourth tone 為 (*wèi*) may also translate as a Modern Chinese 當 (*dāng*) 'when', e.g. 為其來也 (*wèi qí lái yě*) 'when he comes'.

b) **'because'**: A fourth tone 為 (*wèi*) can also function as the subordinating conjunction 'because' (cf. Modern Chinese 因為, *yīnwèi*, 'because'), e.g. 為其老，強忍，下取履 (*wèi qí lǎo, qiáng rěn, xià qǔ lǚ*) 'because [the man] was old, [Zhāng Liáng] kept his temper, went down [under the bridge] and fetched [the old man's] shoe'.

c) **'and'**: 為 (*wéi*) can occasionally join two words or short phrases, in which case it has the force of 'and'. This is unusual, e.g. 得之為有財，古之人皆用之 (*dé zhī wéi yǒu cái, gǔ zhī rén jiē yòng zhī*) 'when they could obtain it and they had the wealth, people in ancient times all used it [i.e. high-grade wood for coffin-making]'.

iii) **As adverbial modifier** (*wéi*): 為 (*wéi*) may be translated as a Modern Chinese 就 (*jiù*) 'then', e.g. 同於己為是之，異於己為非之 (*tóng yú jǐ wéi shì zhī, yì yú jǐ wéi fēi zhī*) 'those [views] which agree with their own they hold to be right, and those which do not so agree they hold to be wrong'. When combined with 惟 / 唯 (*wéi*) 'only', the 為 (*wéi*) has the force of a Modern Chinese 才 (*cái*) 'then and only then', e.g 惟助為有公田 (*wéi zhù wéi yǒu gōng tián*) 'it is only in the system of mutual aid that there is a public field'.

iv) **As a particle**:

a) **Used with 之** (*zhī*): The 之為 (*zhī wéi*) construction is often used in combination with 惟 / 唯 (*wéi*) in order to expose the object for emphatic effect. 之為 (*zhī wéi*) has a syntactical function, but no separate semantic meaning when used in this way, e.g. 使弈秋悔二人弈，其一人專心致志，惟弈秋之為聽⋯ (*shǐ yì qiū huǐ èr rén yì, qí yì rén zhuān xīn zhì zhì, wéi yì qiū zhī wéi tīng ...*) 'supposing Chess Qiū was teaching two people to play chess and one of them was totally dedicated and only listened to Chess Qiū ...'.

b) **As final exclamatory particle** (*wéi*): 為 (*wéi*) can be used at the end of an exclamatory sentence either on its own or in the combination 為也 (*wéi yě*) as a means to emphasise the statement. Modern Chinese would translate with an 啊 (*a*), e.g. 予無所用天下為！(*yú wú suǒ yòng tiān xià wéi!*) 'I have no use for the world!'

c) *As final interrogative particle (wéi)*: 為 (*wéi*) is used in interrogatives both with 何 (*hé*) and as a final interrogative particle. With 何 (*hé*) 'what', it is used as a preposition and becomes 何為 (*hé wèi*) 'for what' = 'why'. In this case, the 為 is fourth tone (wèi), e.g.: 何為獨釋牛而取羊？(*hé wèi dú shì niú ér qǔ yáng?*) 'Why did you just release the ox and choose a sheep?' Used as a final interrogative particle, 為 is read in the second tone (*wéi*) and is typically used with 何以 (*hé yǐ*) 'how', 'why'. It often has a rhetorical sense, e.g.: 何以伐為？(*hé yǐ fá wéi?*) 'Why attack him?' The 為 (*wéi*) in this usage can be followed by an interrogative particle such as 乎 (*hū*) or 哉 (*zāi*), e.g.: 今我何以子之千金劍為乎？(*jīn wǒ hé yǐ zǐ zhī qiān jīn jiàn wéi hū?*) 'Now what can I do with your precious sword?' Since 何為 (*hé wèi*) can be split, the function of 為 (*wéi/wèi*) as a final interrogative particle can become ambiguous, e.g.: 天之亡我，我何渡為！(*tiān zhī wáng wǒ, wǒ hé dù wéi/wèi?*) 'Since Heaven has abandoned me, what is the point of crossing (the river)?'

The uses and functions of 焉 (*yán, yān*)

Many modern dictionaries give the character 焉 with only one tone (i.e. *yān*) and this first tone covers all of its variant meanings. Older dictionaries, though, tend to distinguish between first tone *yān*, which is the interrogative particle 'how', 'why', 'where' etc. and second tone *yán*, which is equivalent to 於／于＋之 (*yú + zhī*) as a fusion particle. For ease of differentiation, we have decided to maintain this tonal distinction throughout.

i) *As a contraction of 於之 (yú zhī)*: As a fusion particle, 焉 (*yán*) is functionally equivalent to 於／于＋之 (*yú + zhī*) or 於／于＋是 (*yú + shì*). This fusion principle is similar to Modern Chinese 甭 (*béng*) 'no need to', which is a fusion of the two characters 不＋用 (*bú + yòng*). The combination of 於之 (*yú zhī*) almost never appears in Classical Chinese, the fusion character 焉 (*yán*) being used instead, e.g. 學焉而後臣之 (*xué yán ér hòu chén zhī*) 'learnt from him and afterwards made him a minister'. 於是 (*yú shì*) is used, but usually only in its temporal sense of 'thereupon', 'at this point'; where it refers to a place 'here' or 'there' it is more commonly expressed as 焉 (*yán*), e.g. 他日，又往坐焉 (*tā rì, yòu wǎng zuò yán*) 'on another day, I again went and sat there'.

As a fusion particle equivalent to 於＋之 (*yú + zhī*), it is also common in the passive, where 焉 (*yán*) introduces the agent and means 'by him', 'by her', 'by them' etc., e.g. 昔者吾舅死於虎，吾夫又死

焉，今吾子又死焉 (*xī zhě wú jiù sǐ yú hǔ, wú fū yòu sǐ yán, jīn wú zǐ yòu sǐ yán*) 'some time ago, my uncle was killed by a tiger, then my husband was killed by one, now my son has been killed by one'.

ii) ***As object pronoun***: 焉 (*yán*) is considered in some cases as equivalent to a simple 之 (*zhī*), i.e. the object pronoun, 'it', 'him', 'her', etc. It is restricted in this case to certain types of verb, hence is scarcely distinguishable from (i) above, e.g. 眾惡之必察焉，眾好之必察焉 (*zhòng wù zhī bì chá yán, zhòng hào zhī bì chá yán*) 'if the people hate him, be sure to look into this case; likewise if the people like him, be sure to look into it'.

iii) ***To replace 然 (rán)***: 焉 (*yān*) can be used instead of 然 (*rán*) as a suffix for an expressive adverb, e.g. 徐徐焉實狼其中 (*xú xú yān, shí láng qí zhōng*) 'very slowly and gently, he placed the wolf in it [i.e. the bag]' and 自三代以下者，匈匈焉 (*zì sān dài yǐ xià zhě, xiōng xiōng yān*) 'from the time of the three dynasties onwards, there has been nothing but turmoil and strife'.

iv) ***As interrogative and rhetorical particle***: It should be noted that first tone 焉 (*yān*), of which a variant was 安 (*ān*), is used to mean 'how' both as an exclamation and as a question, usually in the sense of 'surely not', e.g. 未知生，焉知死？ (*wèi zhī shēng, yān zhī sǐ?*) 'you do not know about life, what [on earth] could you know about death?' 焉 (*yān*) often occurs with a final particle, e.g. a 乎 (*hū*) or a 哉 (*zāi*), which tends to emphasise the rhetorical element, e.g. 臧氏之子焉能使予不遇哉！ (*zāng shì zhī zǐ yān néng shǐ yú bú yù zāi!*) 'how could a son of the Zāng family have possibly caused me not to meet [him]?' Apart from 'how', 焉 (*yān*) can also be used to express the other interrogatives 'who', 'what', 'why' and 'where'. As above, there is likely to be a rhetorical element even without a 哉 (*zāi*) or 乎 (*hū*) marker, e.g. 割雞焉用牛刀？ (*gē jī yān yòng niú dāo?*) 'why use an ox-knife to kill a chicken?' or 'surely you don't need to use an ox-knife to kill a chicken!'

v) ***As pause marker***: As a pause marker, 焉 (*yān*) can be used for effect in sentences where it is semantically redundant, e.g. 於是焉河伯欣然自喜 (*yú shì yān hé bó xīn rán zì xǐ*) 'at this point, the River God was delighted with himself' or 至八十焉，九十焉，百年焉，未有不思怛化者矣 (*zhì bā shí yān, jiǔ shí yān, bǎi nián yān, wèi yǒu bù sī dá huà zhě yǐ*) 'by the time you reach 80, 90 or 100 years old, there really is no one who does not think of death'. It is not necessary to translate a 焉 (*yān*) used in this way.

Sometimes, the function of 焉 (*yān*) is not clear-cut, e.g. 南方有鳥焉，名曰蒙鳩 (*nán fāng yǒu niǎo yān, míng yuē méng jiū*) 'in the South, there is a bird called the *méng jiū*'; here, the 焉 could be viewed either as a pause marker, *yān*, or as a 於之 (*yú zhī*) '*yán*', i.e. 'there'.

vi) *As a final particle*:

a) *Mood* (*finality, emphasis*): According to some Chinese commentators, a final particle 焉 (*yān*) can function like a Modern Chinese 呢 (*ne*), giving an air of finality or emphasis to an assertion or affirmation, e.g. 君子之過也，如日月之食<u>焉</u> (*jūn zǐ zhī guò yě, rú rì yuè zhī shí yān*) 'the errors of a gentleman are like a solar or lunar eclipse' (i.e. everyone notices them). This example is also cited: 宅邊有五柳樹，因以為號<u>焉</u> (*zhái biān yǒu wǔ liǔ shù, yīn yǐ wéi hào yān*) 'by the side of his house there were five willow trees and that's why he took that name [i.e. Wǔliǔ / Five Willows]'. This last 焉 (*yān*), though, could be understood as 'from them'.

b) *Interrogative use*: When 焉 (*yān*) is used at the end of a question, especially in conjunction with a 何 (*hé*) 'what', 'why' etc. or a 何如 (*hé rú*) 'how about?', it has an emphatic effect rather like a Modern Chinese 呢 (*ne*), but this is often debatable, e.g. 桀伐蒙山，何所得<u>焉</u>？(*jié fá méng shān, hé suǒ dé yān?*) 'when Jié attacked Mount Méng, what did he get?' This translation assumes that 焉 (*yān*) functions rhetorically. However, it could also be understood as: 'When Jié attacked Mount Méng, what did he get from it?', where the 焉 (*yán*) is equivalent to 於之 (*yú zhī*) or an English 'from it'.

Combinations of 焉 (*yān*)

In combinations, 焉 (*yān*) generally has an emphatic effect. 焉哉 (*yān zāi*), for example, emphasises the rhetorical question; for statements, 焉耳 (*yān ěr*), 焉爾 (*yān ěr*), 焉矣 (*yān yǐ*) and 焉耳矣 (*yān ěr yǐ*) are used.

It is sometimes difficult to pin down with certainty in what sense 焉 is being used. For example, in 寡人之於國也，盡心<u>焉耳矣</u> (*guǎ rén zhī yú guó yě, jìn xīn yān ěr yǐ*), if we take 焉 (*yán*) as being short for 於之 (*yú zhī*) it would be translated as 'as for my [attitude] towards the state, I have completely and utterly devoted myself to it'. However, if we take 焉耳矣 (*yān ěr yǐ*) as purely emphatic, we could translate it more as 'when it comes to [running] the country, I really and truly try my best'.

It is the same for the question particles 焉為 (*yān wéi*) and 焉耳乎 (*yān ěr hū*). Modern Chinese prefers to translate with a simple 呢 (*ne*) or 嗎 (*ma*), whilst English translations might prefer to interpret 焉 (*yān*) as short for 於之 (*yú zhī*).

The uses and functions of 也 (*yě*)

也 (*yě*) does not have its Modern Chinese meaning of 'also' in Classical Chinese, even though it is used in that sense in the vernacular literary Chinese of later periods. In Classical Chinese, the use of 也 (*yě*) falls principally into two main areas: that of pause marker, usually after the topic, and that of final particle.

As a final particle, 也 (*yě*) is extremely common. It may appear at the end of all of the four different types of sentence: declarative (a statement), interrogative, imperative and exclamatory. This makes it one of the most multi-purpose, multi-functional of all the Classical Chinese 虛詞 (*xūcí*). Of course, not all statements, the type of sentence where it is most commonly used, need to end with 也 (*yě*), but certain types of statement such as 'A is B' or the /A 者 (*zhě*) B 也 (*yě*)/ construction almost always do take a final 也 (*yě*) particle. It also tends to appear in declarative sentences which offer a judgement or an explanation. In addition, 也 (*yě*) also plays the same kind of softening, emphasising, affirming or filling role that a 呢 (*ne*), 吧 (*ba*), 麼 (*me*), 了 (*le*), 啦 (*la*), 哩 (*li*), 呀 (*ya*), 啊 (*a*) or 罷了 (*ba le*) etc. does in Modern Chinese. Sometimes, though, 也 (*yě*) simply marks the end of a sentence, a kind of stylistic filler which adds nothing particular to the meaning, as in the basic 'A is B' construction above.

There will often be no direct translation of 也 (*yě*). Furthermore, due to its wide variety of uses and the flexibility allowed by 'optional precision', it may well be difficult to pin down exactly how a 也 (*yě*) is being used in a particular sentence. We offer the following as a guide:

i) *As a pause marker*: 也 (*yě*), in this function, often marks the preceding phrase or words as a topic. The topic may gramatically be the subject or the object of the sentence; it might also be a time phrase or clause. The 也 (*yě*) acts as a pause-marker (rather like a comma). Since topics are often nominalised phrases, they typically include nominalising particles such as 之 (*zhī*) or 其 (*qí*) giving the following grammar formula:

$$/N \ 之 \ (zhī) \ V \ [O] \ 也 \ (yě), ... /$$

This can be translated as 'as for N's Verb-ing of [O], ...' or 'if (or when) N Verb-ed [O] ...' etc., e.g 媼之送燕后也，持其踵為之泣 (*ǎo zhī sòng yān hòu yě, chí qí zhǒng wèi zhī qì*) 'when you send off Yānhòu [to be married], grab hold of her heel and cry for her', or 君子之於禽獸也，見其生，不忍見其死 (*jūn zǐ zhī yú qín shòu yě, jiàn qí shēng, bù rěn jiàn qí sǐ*) 'the superior man's attitude towards animals [is this]: having seen them alive, he cannot bear to see them die'. It is also a feature of the common phrase /X 之為人也/ (X *zhī wéi rén yě*) 'as a person, X' or 'in character, X', e.g. 夫楚王之為人也形尊而嚴 (*fú chǔ wáng zhī wéi rén yě xíng zūn ér yán*) 'now as a person, the King of Chǔ looks dignified and severe'.

When 也 (*yě*) is employed after a time expression in topic position, it acts, like 者 (*zhě*), as a simple pause maker; sometimes there is also an extra contrastive or emphatic dimension, e.g. 今 (*jīn*) means 'now', but in 今也 (*jīn yě*) or 今者 (*jīn zhě*), it may have the extra force of 'nowadays' or 'these days' etc. e.g. 當是時也，五素不得一紫 (*dāng shì shí yě, wǔ sù bù dé yì zǐ*) 'at *that* time you couldn't get one purple [garment] in exchange for five white ones'.

The topic marked by the 也 (*yě*) may also just be a simple subject e.g. 柴也愚，參也魯，師也辟，由也喭

... (*chái yě yú, shēn yě lǔ, shī yě bì, yóu yě yàn* ...) 'Chái is stupid, Shēn is slow, Shī goes to extremes and Yóu is coarse ...' Here the repetition of 也 (*yě*) is contrastive and is used for stylistic effect.

ii) ***As a final particle*** (*declarative sentence*): Simply because a sentence is declarative does not mean that it must end with 也 (*yě*). However, certain types of declarative sentences or statements typically do end with a 也 (*yě*). This is particularly so for the 'A is B' type, i.e.:

/A 者 (*zhě*) B 也 (*yě*)/

The 者 (*zhě*), which here acts as a topic marking or nominalising suffix to the noun, may be omitted, e.g. 孔子吾師之弟子也 (*kǒng zǐ wú shī zhī dì zǐ yě*) 'Confucius was our teacher's disciple'. To be clear, the 也 (*yě*) does not replace the copula, nor is it the copula. Thus, the following four constructions can all mean 'A is B':

/A 者 (*zhě*) B 也 (*yě*)/
/A 者 (*zhě*) B/
/A B 也 (*yě*)/ and
/A B/

As this point, it is probably worth reiterating that the basic copula verb 'to be' is 為 (*wéi*) (see pp 18-21). 為 (*wéi*) is typically omitted except in negative sentences where it appears as 非 (*fēi*) 'is not', e.g. 白馬非馬也 (*bái mǎ fēi mǎ yě*) 'a white horse is not a horse'. Note that the 也 (*yě*) still appears in negative sentences - see (v) below.

iii) ***As a final particle*** (*reasoning / explanation*): Declarative sentences which offer a reason or explanation also tend to end with 也 (*yě*); it has the force of a 'you see?' or 'get it?', e.g. 虎不知獸畏己而走也，以為畏狐也 (*hǔ bù zhī shòu wèi jǐ ér zǒu yě, yǐ wéi wèi hú yě*) 'the tiger did not realise that the animals were running because they were afraid of him (i.e. the tiger), but supposed that they were afraid of the fox'. In sentences involving 是以 (*shì yǐ*), 以是 (*yǐ shì*), 是故 (*shì gù*), or sometimes simply 故 (*gù*), which all mean 'therefore', 'so', 'and so', 'for this reason', a 也 (*yě*) is often found as the final clause particle. Some interpret the 也 (*yě*) used in this way as having an additional emphatic force of 'and that is why ...'. We note the following common constructions:

/是以 (*shì yǐ*) [S] V O 也 (*yě*)/
/是故 (*shì gù*) [S] V O 也 (*yě*)/
/故 (*gù*) [S] V O 也 (*yě*)/

e.g. 敏而好學，不恥下問，是以謂之文也 (*mǐn ér hào xué, bù chǐ xià wèn, shì yǐ wèi zhī wén yě*) 'he is bright and fond of studying, and he is not ashamed to learn from his subordinates; that's why we call him Wén (i.e. 'Cultured')'.

Since Classical Chinese makes full use of 'optional precision', the 也 (*yě*), in the right context, on its own and with no other markers, may well maintain the force of an explanation, e.g. 堯舜之傳賢也，欲天下之得其所也 (*yáo shùn zhī chuán xián yě, yù tiān xià zhī dé qí suǒ yě*) 'The reason why Yáo and Shùn handed on [the throne] to worthy men was that they wanted the world to find its right place' (NB the first 也, *yě*, is the topic marker).

iv) **As a final particle** *(continuing state)*: In a declarative sentence, 也 (*yě*) often appears at the end of a phrase or after a predicate as a mark of 'continuing state'. This puts it in sharp contrast to 矣 (*yǐ*), which shows, like its Modern Chinese counterpart, 了 (*le*), that a change of state has taken place, is taking place or will / might take place. A simple example showing this contrast would be: 臣老矣不可問也 (*chén lǎo yǐ bù kě wèn yě*). 'I am now old and hardly worth consulting'. Indeed, predicates using 可 (*kě*) and a passive verb often end with 也 (*yě*):

/可 (*kě*) + passive V 也 (*yě*)/

and this can often be translated as 'Adj. + ~able', e.g. 'not ask~able', or 殺臣，宋莫能守，可攻也 (*shā chén, sòng mò néng shǒu, kě gōng yě*) 'if I am killed, no one in Sòng will be able to hold [the country] and we can be attacked'. This use of 也 (*yě*) is not unlike the use of 呢 (*ne*) in Modern Chinese.

v) **As a final partice** *(negation)*: The negative statement with copula, i.e. 'A is not B' also involves 也 (*yě*):

/A 非 (*fēi*) B 也 (*yě*)/

非 (*fēi*) is also used to mean 'is not a case of ...'. An example of this usage is 我非愛其財而易之以羊也 (*wǒ fēi ài qí cái ér yì zhī yǐ yáng yě*) 'it is not the case that I exchanged it for a sheep because I begrudged its high value'. When 也 (*yě*) is used in negation, there is typically an element of 'continuing state', e.g. 趙王田獵耳，非為寇也 (*zhào wáng tián liè ěr, fēi wéi kòu yě*) 'the King of Zhào is just hunting, he is not about to invade [us]'.

The negative of the perfect and pluperfect tense in Classical Chinese ('has not done, had not done') uses the following form with an optional 也 (*yě*) at the end of the sentence:

/[S] 未 [嘗] V O [也] /
/[S] *wèi* [*cháng*] V O [*yě*]/

e.g. 故彌子之行未變於初也 (*gù mí zǐ zhī xíng wèi biàn yú chū yě*) 'so in fact, what Mízǐ did had never changed (from the start)'. As above, the use of 也 (*yě*) here can be seen as marking a continuing state. With the same function, it may also be found with 不 (*bù*) 'not', e.g. 平原君之遊，徒豪舉耳，不求士也 (*píng yuán jūn zhī yóu, tú háo jǔ ěr, bù qiú shì yě*) 'Lord Píngyuán, [your] friendships are just show only, you don't seek out knights' or 高祖每過之而令民奉祠不絕也 (*gāo zǔ měi guò zhī ér lìng mín fèng cí bù jué yě*) 'each time Gāozǔ visited, he ordered the people to make sacrifices in perpetuity'.

vi) **As a final particle** *(imperative)*: 也 (*yě*) is very often found at the end of negative imperatives. Negative imperatives (don't!, let's not!) use 無 (*wú*), 毋 (*wú*), or 勿 (*wù*) before the verb, with an optional 也 (*yě*) or sometimes 矣 (*yǐ*) as final particle, e.g. 王

勿異也 (*wáng wù yì yě*) 'Your Majesty, do not think it strange' or 子毋擊也 (*zǐ wú jī yě*) 'don't beat [it]' This usage may also be understood as 'continuing state'.

Although less common, 也 (*yě*) does occur at the end of affirmative imperatives, where it adds a softening element to the command (cf. 吧, *ba*, in Modern Chinese), e.g. 吾其還也! (*wú qí huán yě!*) 'let's go back!' or 民苟利矣，遷也！吉莫如之 (*mín gǒu lì yǐ, qiān yě! jí mò rú zhī*) 'if it benefits the people, then let's move [the capital], there is nothing as auspicious' or 公子有德於人，願公子忘之也 (*gōng zǐ yǒu dé yú rén, yuàn gōng zǐ wàng zhī yě*) 'when you do someone else a kindness, you should forget it'.

vii) *As a final particle (interrogative)*: In simple yes-or-no questions, the 也 (*yě*) can act like a question mark, not unlike 嗎 (*ma*) in Modern Chinese, thus: 子張問：十世可知也？ (*zǐ zhāng wèn: shí shì kě zhī yě*) 'Zǐ Zhāng asked: "Can [the state of affairs] be known ten generations hence?"'; similarly in disjunctive questions: 不識臣之力也，抑君之力也 (*bú shì chén zhī lì yě, yì jūn zhī lì yě*) 'I do not know whether this was my ability or my sovereign's ability'. With specific question markers, like 何 (*hé*) or 誰 (*shuí*), it acts like a Modern Chinese 呢 (*ne*). The following is an example of its use as both a pause marker and a question marker: 斯道也，何道也？ (*sī dào yě, hé dào yě?*) 'what kind of Way is this Way [of yours]?' In sentences using 蓋 (*gài*)

or 殆 (*dài*) etc., both meaning 'probably' in this context, the 也 (*yě*) adds a softening element to the question, like a Modern Chinese 吧 (*ba*): 孔子罕稱命，蓋難言之也 (*kǒng zǐ hǎn chēng mìng, gài nán yán zhī yě*) 'Confucius rarely mentioned fate; did he perhaps find discussing it difficult?'

viii) *As a final particle (surprise, exclamation)*: After predicates which indicate surprise or an exclamation etc., the force of the 也 (*yě*) is not unlike a Modern Chinese 啊 (*a*). It may not be necessary to translate it, e.g. 小子識之，苛政猛於虎也 (*xiǎo zǐ zhì zhī, gǒu zhèng měng yú hǔ yě*) 'Remember, young man, tyranny is more cruel than a tiger!'

Combinations of 也 (*yě*)

There are many combinations of characters in Classical Chinese which include 也 (*yě*); these mostly tend to emphasise the mood aspect.

i) *Emphatic*: The 也 (*yě*) in the following combinations acts as a Modern Chinese 啊 (*a*), emphasising the exclamatory effect: 也哉 (*yě zāi*), 也夫 (*yě fú*), 也且 (*yě jū*) and 也已矣 (*yě yǐ yǐ*). There may be no direct translation, e.g. 說而不繹，從而不改，吾末如之何也已矣 (*yuè ér bú yì, cóng ér bù gǎi, wú mò rú zhī hé yě yǐ yǐ*) 'to be pleased but not analyze, to follow but not reform, what on earth can I do [with people like this]!'

也已 (*yě yǐ*) and 也已矣 (*yě yǐ yǐ*) can also bring the force of a Modern Chinese 了

(le) or 罷了 (ba le) to a sentence, rather like the English 'indeed', thus: 此亦妄人也已矣 (cǐ yì wàng rén yě yǐ yǐ) 'this is just a crazy person' or 可謂好學也已 (kě wèi hào xué yě yǐ) 'he may indeed be said to love to learn'.

In the following combinations, the 也 (yě) helps to emphasise the question, the conjecture, or the rhetorical aspect: 也與 (yě yú), 也耶 (yě yé), 也邪 (yě yé), 也哉 (yě zāi), 也乎 (yě hū) and 也乎哉 (yě hū zāi). Depending on the context, its Modern Chinese translation would be a 吧 (ba), 嗎 (ma) or 呢 (ne) etc., e.g. 吾罪也乎哉！ (wú zuì yě hū zāi), which translates into a rhetorical 'Is it my fault?'

ii) *As topic marker*: This includes 也者 (yě zhě) and 也與 (yě yú), e.g. 鳥獸也者，大別名也 (niǎo shòu yě zhě, dà bié míng yě) 'bird and animals are the major classifications'.

The uses and functions of 以 (yǐ)

以 (yǐ) was originally a verb meaning 'to use' and 'to have as one's reason or purpose'. In Classical Chinese, one of its major functions is as a preposition meaning 'by' or 'with'. In conjunction with 為 (wéi) it means 'take as' or 'consider something to be'. 以 (yǐ) also acts as a conjunction similar to 而 (ér) where it means 'and' or 'in order to'. There are other less common functions and meanings (a study of the use of this character in Mencius gives a total of 30), some of which include 以 (yǐ) being equivalent to other function characters such as 已 (yǐ) 'already'.

i) *As preposition / prepositional verb*: Most of the meanings derive naturally from the use of 以 (yǐ) as a verb 'to use'. With certain verbs, it also acts like a Modern Chinese 把 (bǎ).

a) *'with', 'using' 'by means of'*: The most common use of 以 (yǐ) is as a prepositional verb meaning 'using', 'by means of', 'with' (similar to a Modern Chinese 用, yòng), e.g 許子以釜甑爨，以鐵耕乎？ (xǔ zǐ yǐ fǔ zèng cuàn, yǐ tiě gēng hū?) 'did Master Xǔ use a pot and a steamer for cooking and use iron for ploughing?' Sometimes, 以 (yǐ) is placed after the verb, e.g. 殺人以梃 (shā rén yǐ tǐng) 'kill a man with a club' or 何不試之以足？ (hé bú shì zhī yǐ zú) 'Why did you not try them (i.e. the shoes) on your feet?' In the phrase 以是故 (yǐ shì gù) 'for this reason', 'therefore', 以 (yǐ) is being used in the same way. This phrase is variously abbreviated to 以故 (yǐ gù), 是故 (shì gù) or simply 故 (gù).

The combination of 以之 (yǐ zhī) is rarely used in Classical Chinese, since 以 (yǐ) can actually carry an implied 之 (zhī), i.e. 'using [it]', 'with [it]' etc., e.g. 相如持其璧，睨柱，欲以擊柱 (xiāng rú chí qí bì, nì zhù, yù yǐ jī zhù) 'holding the jade in his hand, Xiāngrú looked sideways at the pillar and was about to strike the pillar with it'. This links to an extended meaning of 以 (yǐ), i.e. 'in order to', 'thereby' etc. (see iii below).

b) **'in', 'according to'**: This usage is similar to a Modern Chinese 依 (*yī*) 'accord with', 'comply with', e.g. 餘船以次俱進 (*yú chuán yǐ cì jù jìn*) 'the rest of the boats all advanced in sequence'.

c) **'in', 'on'**: This usage is similar to a Modern Chinese 在 (*zài*) 'be at'. Examples include: 斧斤以時入山林，材木不可勝用也 (*fǔ jīn yǐ shí rù shān lín, cái mù bù kě shèng yòng yě*) 'if axes [are only allowed] into the mountain forests at the right time, there will be more timber than can be used' and 武安君之死也，以秦昭王五十年十一月 (*wǔ ān jūn zhī sǐ yě, yǐ qín zhāo wáng wǔ shí nián shí yī yuè*) 'the death of Lord Wǔ'ān was in the eleventh month of King Zhāo of Qín's fiftieth year'.

d) **'because of'**: This is similar to a Modern Chinese 因為 (*yīnwèi*), e.g. 宋以其善於晉侯也，叛楚即晉 (*sòng yǐ qí shàn yú jìn hóu yě, pàn chǔ jí jìn*) 'Sòng, because of having made friends with the Marquis of Jìn, revolted against Chǔ and went over to Jìn'. In this usage, it may also appear with 故 (*gù*) 'reason', 'cause', e.g. 今以并國之故 (*jīn yǐ bīng guó zhī gù*) '[and] now, because of the annexation of one state by another'.

e) **Marking a direct object**: A further extension of the use of 以 (*yǐ*) as a prepositional verb is to mark a direct object like a Modern Chinese 把 (*bǎ*).

In Classical Chinese, 以 (*yǐ*) can be placed either before the verb (more common) or after the verb. Typically, the verbs are of 'giving', 'telling, 'teaching' etc., e.g. 堯以天下與舜 (*yáo yǐ tiān xià yǔ shùn*) 'Yáo gave the world to Shùn' or 乃以所乘馬贈之 (*nǎi yǐ suǒ chéng mǎ zèng zhī*) 'then gave him the horse he was riding'. 以 may also refer back to a stated object, e.g. 舜不能以傳禹 (*shùn bù néng yǐ chuán yǔ*) 'Shùn could not bequeath it to Yǔ' or 衣食所安，弗敢專也，必以分人 (*yī shí suǒ ān, fú gǎn zhuān yě, bì yǐ fèn rén*) 'the comfort that food and clothing bring, I do not presume to monopolise, I always share them with others'. This use of 以 (*yǐ*) plus an implied 之 (*zhī*) or 'it' leads to an extended meaning: 'in order to', 'thereby', etc. (see iii below).

ii) **Set construction 以...為** (*yǐ...wéi*): This construction is very common in Classical Chinese and can still be found in more formal, especially written, Modern Chinese:

/以 (*yǐ*) A 為 (wéi) B/

It literally means to 'take A as B'. This appears in two main senses:

a) **'use A as B'**: Examples include: 以鞍為几 (*yǐ ān wéi jī*) 'use a saddle as a table' or 必以長安君為質，兵乃出 (*bì yǐ cháng ān jūn wéi zhì, bīng nǎi chū*) 'certainly, it is only by taking Lord Cháng'ān hostage that the army will be sent out'.

b) *'consider A as B'*: Examples include: 以此為王者之事 (*yǐ cǐ wéi wàng zhě zhī shì*) 'consider this to be a matter for the ruler' and 鮑叔不以我為貪，知我貧也 (*bào shū bù yǐ wǒ wéi tān, zhī wǒ pín yě*) 'Bào Shū did not consider me greedy: he knew that (it was because) I was poor.' In Classical Chinese, 以為 (*yǐ wéi*) may appear together in the 'consider' sense but not in the 'use' sense, e.g. 竊以為捨本逐末終必無成 (*qiè yǐ wéi shě běn zhú mò zhōng bì wú chéng*) 'I believe that if we abandon the essentials to pursue what is peripheral, in the end we will not succeed'. In Classical Chinese, 以為 (*yǐ wéi*) does not have its typical modern connotation of 'mistakenly believe'.

iii) *As a conjunction*: 以 (*yǐ*) is very common in the conjunctive senses of 'in order to', 'yet', 'because' and 'thereby' etc. This use extends from 以 (*yǐ*) carrying an implied 之 (*zhī*) 'it', 'this' etc., hence 'by this'. It is less common in the sense of 'and', where it is limited to linking adjectives and verbs.

a) *'in order to', 'and thereby'*: This links two clauses, e.g. 審樂以知政 (*shěn yuè yǐ zhī zhèng*) 'examine their music in order to know about their government'. It is often used with verbs like 求 (*qiú*) 'seek' or 免 (*miǎn*) 'avoid' in this sense, e.g. 隱居以求其志 (*yǐn jū yǐ qiú qí zhì*) 'living in seclusion to achieve their ambitions'. This usage is essentially

以 (*yǐ*) with 之 (*zhī*) implied, i.e. 'and by this'. It is in this sense used for a mode of action e.g. 傾耳以聽 (*qīng ěr yǐ tīng*) 'incline the ear [in order] to listen'.

b) *'as a result'*: This meaning and usage is very close to (a) above, e.g. 回也聞一以知十，賜也聞一以知二 (*huí yě wén yī yǐ zhī shí, cì yě wén yī yǐ zhī èr*) 'Huí heard one part and (as a result) understood ten, Cì heard one part and understood two'.

c) *'and'* (*between adjectives and verbs*): This usage links two adjectives or verbs; e.g. 其責己也重以周，其待人也輕以約 (*qí zé jǐ yě zhòng yǐ zhōu, qí dài rén yě qīng yǐ yuē*) 'his demands on himself are onerous and comprehensive, his expectations of others are modest and limited'.

iv) *Mark direction, time etc.*: The use of 以 (*yǐ*) in expressions of time and direction is still very common in Modern Chinese, i.e.:

/X 以 (*yǐ*) Time or Direction/

and it means '[from] X to Time or Direction', e.g. 閫以內者，寡人制之；閫以外者，將軍制之 (*kǔn yǐ nèi zhě, guǎ rén zhì zhī; kǔn yǐ wài zhě, jiāng jūn zhì zhī*) 'for affairs within the city walls, We will handle them, for affairs beyond the city gates Our generals will handle them'.

v) *As a demonstrative* (*this, like this*): Using 以 (*yǐ*) to mean 'this' or 'like this' is not common, e.g. 妾唯以一太子一

女奈何棄之匈奴 (*qiè wéi yǐ yī tài zǐ yī nǚ, nài hé qì zhī xiōng nú*) 'I only have this one crown prince and this one daughter, how could I possibly abandon them to the Xiōngnú?' Sometimes commentators differ in their interpretations, e.g. when defamatory remarks were made of Confucius, Zǐgòng said 無以為也！ (*wú yǐ wéi yě!*). This can be translated as: 'don't do that!', i.e. the 以 (*yǐ*) means 'like this'. Some, though, prefer to take the 無以 (*wú yǐ*) as short for 無所以 (*wú suǒ yǐ*) 'not have the means by which', in which case it translates as 'it is of no use doing so' (J. Legge) or even 'he is simply wasting his time' (D.C. Lau). Sometimes it is unclear whether 以 (*yǐ*) is being used as a demonstrative adjective or a demonstrative pronoun, e.g. 以告者過也 (*yǐ gào zhě guò yě*) 'this informant is mistaken' might also be translated as 'this is the informant being mistaken'.

vi) *As adverbial modifier* ('too', 'only', 'already'): The use of 以 (*yǐ*) as an adverb is not common, but it does occur. Thus, 以 (*yǐ*), in context, may be translated as a Modern Chinese 太 (*tài*) 'too', or 只 (*zhǐ*) 'only' or 已 (*yǐ*) 'already', e.g. 子之報仇，其以甚乎！ (*zǐ zhī bào chóu, qí yǐ shèn hū!*) 'your reprisals, aren't they too extreme?' or 今兩侯以出 (*jīn liǎng hóu yǐ chū*) 'now the two marquises have already been demoted'.

vii) *As a noun* ('reason', 'means'): In the Classical Chinese phrases 有以 (*yǒu yǐ*) and 無以 (*wú yǐ*), the 以 (*yǐ*) is used like a noun

meaning 'reason' or 'means', thus 'to have the means to' and 'not have the means to', e.g. 然龍弗得雲，無以神其靈矣 (*rán lóng fú dé yún, wú yǐ shén qí líng yǐ*) 'but if the dragon does not get its cloud, it will not have the means to exert its magical powers'. That said, some commentators prefer to view 有以 (*yǒu yǐ*) as the abbreviated form of 有所以 (*yǒu suǒ yǐ*) 'have the means by which' and 無以 (*wú yǐ*) as short for 無所以 (*wú suǒ yǐ*) 'not have the means by which'.

The uses and functions of 矣 (*yǐ*)

In Classical Chinese, 矣 (*yǐ*) is principally used as a final particle, i.e. it follows the predicate. It is used in dynamic situations to show 'change of state', rather like a Modern Chinese 了 (*le*) and in this respect it is in sharp contrast to 也 (*yě*), which is used in static situations to show 'continuing state'. However, 矣 (*yǐ*) also helps to set the mood and it is here that there is undoubtedly some functional overlap with 也 (*yě*). The Modern Chinese translations of 矣 (*yǐ*) range from 呀 (*ya*), 了 (*le*), 啊 (*a*), 吧 (*ba*), 呢 (*ne*) and even 嗎 (*ma*) depending on context.

i) *Final particle* (*change of state*): Like its Modern Chinese counterpart 了 (*le*), 矣 (*yǐ*) can indicate an actual change of state or it may just point to a change in knowledge about a state. As with 了 (*le*), change is not restricted to the past; indeed 矣 (*yǐ*) may refer to an anticipated future change.

a) *Change of state* (*past*): This is very common, e.g. 其子趨而往視

之，苗則槁矣 (*qí zǐ qū ér wǎng shì zhī, miáo zé gǎo yǐ*) 'his son hurried off to look at them, and found that the seedlings had wilted'. Since the change in state may have happened already, it is commonly used with adverbs such as 已 (*yǐ*) 'already', 嘗 (*cháng*) 'once' or 既 (*jì*) 'already' to show the perfective aspect, e.g. 肉食者已慮之矣 (*ròu shí zhě yǐ lù zhī yǐ*) 'the senior officials have already considered it'.

b) ***Change of state*** *(future)*: 矣 (*yǐ*) also works with an implied future change, e.g. 孔子曰：諾我將仕矣 (*kǒng zǐ yuē: nuò wǒ jiāng shì yǐ*) 'Confucius said: "All right, I shall take up office."'

ii) ***Final particle*** *(exclamatory)*: In a declarative sentence, it may also give an element of affirmation to the statement, rather like an English 'indeed' or 'certainly', e.g. 天下之無道也，久矣 (*tiān xià zhī dào yě, jiǔ yǐ*) 'it is indeed a long time that the world has been without the Way'. It is common for emphatic inversion to be used in such sentences; technically the 矣 (*yǐ*) is no longer a sentence final particle in these cases, though the underlying structure is still of 矣 (*yǐ*) following the predicative verb, e.g. 甚矣吾衰也，久矣吾不復夢見周公 (*shèn yǐ wú shuāi yě, jiǔ yǐ wú bú fù mèng jiàn zhōu gōng*) 'how far I have declined - it is so long since I dreamt of the Duke of Zhōu!'

iii) ***Final particle*** *(imperative, exhortation)*: Some authorities suggest that 矣 (*yǐ*) gives

a softening element to the command etc, rather like 吧 (*ba*) in Modern Chinese. However, many of the examples given to back this up do not obviously reflect this. An example showing the use of 矣 (*yǐ*) with a command is: 往矣，吾將曳尾於塗中 (*wǎng yǐ, wú jiāng yè wěi yú tú zhōng*) 'Go! I will drag my tail in the mud.'

It is not an infallible rule, but there is a tendency for 矣 (*yǐ*) to be used more in positive commands, with the rationale being that an impending change of state is implied. Negative commands, on the other hand, tend to take 也 (*yě*) as the final particle. Thus, we find: 公往矣，毋污我 (*gōng wǎng yǐ, wú wū wǒ*) 'You go and do not defile us!' We also have the simple 子其歸矣 (*zǐ qí guī yǐ*) 'You, go home!' or 已矣，勿言之矣 (*yǐ yǐ, wù yán zhī yǐ*) 'Stop! Don't speak about it!'

iv) ***Final particle*** *(interrogative)*: One leading authority, Lǔ Shūxiāng (呂叔湘), states that 矣 (*yǐ*) is not used interrogatively. It is clearly the case, though, that 矣 (*yǐ*) is used in interrogative sentences. There are many examples, but arguably these do tend to be with interrogatives such as 何 (*hé*) and 何如 (*hé rú*), where the 矣 (*yǐ*) can be seen as equivalent to 了 (*le*) in Modern Chinese, implying some change of state. This can be seen clearly in 年幾何矣？ (*nián jǐ hé yǐ?*) 'how old is he now?', which translates directly into Modern Chinese as 幾歲了 (*jǐ suì le?*). Examples of interrogative sentences with 矣 (*yǐ*) include: 德何如

則可以王矣？(*dé hé rú zé kě yǐ wàng yǐ*) 'what kind of virtue [does one need] to be able to be a [true] king?' and 女何夢矣？(*rǔ hé mèng yǐ?*) 'what did you dream about?'

v) *As pause marker (in compound sentences):* 矣 (*yǐ*) in this usage follows the predicate of the first half of a compound sentence. It acts as a pause marker and is used as a means to slow down and break up the flow of the sentence or phrase, such as 苟志於仁矣，無惡也 (*gǒu zhì yú rén yǐ, wú è yě*) 'if you are really committed to benevolence, you will have no evil [in you]'.

Combinations of 矣 (*yǐ*)

In the following 矣 (*yǐ*) combinations: 矣夫 (*yǐ fú*), 矣哉 (*yǐ zāi*) and 矣乎 (*yǐ hū*), 矣 (*yǐ*) has an emphatic role, adding force to the exclamation, the mood, aspect or question. Examples include the following: 服三年之喪，亦已久矣夫 (*fú sān nián zhī sāng, yì yǐ jiǔ yǐ fú*) 'three years of mourning is certainly a long time', 甚矣哉，為欺也！ (*shèn yǐ zāi, wéi qī yě*) 'it really is too much - such deception!' and 中庸之為德也，其至矣乎！ (*zhōng yōng zhī wéi dé yě, qí zhì yǐ hū!*) 'Perfect, indeed, is virtue which accords with the Constant Mean'. However, as with other 虛詞 (*xūcí*) used as mood indicators, there may well be more than one way to interpret the phrase.

The uses and functions of 於 / 于 (*yú*)

於 (*yú*) is a general preposition with a wide range of uses, corresponding variously to the English 'at', 'in', 'on', 'to', 'from', 'by', 'than' or nothing at all. Especially in older texts, 於 (*yú*) was written 于, a likely dialect variant (NB: this is now the simplified character for 於), e.g. 火于秦 (*huǒ yú qín*) '[there was] fire (= book-burning) in the Qín dynasty'. 乎 (*hū*) was also another dialect variant, e.g. 生乎吾前 (*shēng hū wú qián*) 'born before me'. These may be treated as alternatives in most Classical Chinese texts.

i) *As general preposition:* 於 (*yú*) is extremely versatile; its use as a general preposition is explored at length in Section XIII *Adverbials and Prepositions* (see pp 37-48). The correct preposition to use in English will usually be obvious from context, e.g. 筆之於其書 (*bǐ zhī yú qí shū*) 'they penned it in their writings'; 學於師 (*xué yú shī*) 'study under a teacher', 'learn from a teacher'; 出於此 (*chū yú cǐ*) 'arises from this'; 傷於矢 (*shāng yú shǐ*) 'wounded by an arrow'; 請於人 (*qǐng yú rén*) 'ask a favour of someone'; 富於周公 (*fù yú zhōu gōng*) 'richer than the Duke of Zhōu'; 兵破於陳涉，地奪於劉氏 (*bīng pò yú chén shè, dì duó yú liú shì*) 'his army was destroyed by Chén Shè and his territory was seized by Liú [Bāng]'.

ii) *As conjunction ('and', 'moreover'):* This is not a common use, but 於 (*yú*) is occasionally taken to have the meaning of 'and', 'moreover' e.g. 日食大水則鼓，於用牲於社 (*rì shí dà shuǐ zé gǔ, yú yòng shēng yú shè*) 'for eclipses and floods, we beat the drums and furthermore make sacrifices of livestock to the land god'. In this example, the first 於 (*yú*) has the force of 'moreover', in the second 於 (*yú*), it functions as a general preposition.

iii) ***Used to voice praise (wū)***: This is mostly seen in earlier texts like the 詩經 (*shī jīng*), the *Book of Songs*. It is pronounced *wū* in this usage and is simply a sign of praise like a Modern Chinese 啊 (*a*). In later Classical Chinese, it can be found in compounds such as: 於戲 (*wū xì*), 於乎 (*wū hū*) and 於呼 (*wū hū*), with the same meaning.

Combinations of 於 (*yú*)

There are only three 於 (*yú*) character compounds apart from the *wū* combinations above: 於是 (*yú shì*), 於此 (*yú cǐ*) and 於茲 (*yú zī*). When these are used to join two sentences, the meaning is 'thereupon', 'hence', 'consequently', 'as a result'. 是 (*shì*,), 此, (*cǐ*) and 茲 (*zī*) all mean 'this' in these combinations.

The uses and functions of 與 (*yǔ / yú*)

與 (*yǔ*) is a verb with a range of meanings including 'to give', 'help', 'approve', 'be friendly with', 'follow', 'conform with', 'wait', 'permit', 'pay' and when pronounced *yù* means 'participate in' and 'intefere in'. Like 以 (*yǐ*), though, it has developed a range of functions as a preposition and conjunction. 與 (*yǔ / yú*) has two main uses: prepositional, when it is read *yǔ*, and as a final interrogative particle when it is read *yú*. As the question marker, both 與 (*yú*) and its variant 歟 (*yú*) are commonly taken as fusions of 也乎 (*yě hū*).

i) ***As conjunction ('and')***: 與 (*yǔ*) is very commonly used as the conjunction 'and' between words and phrases, e.g. 富與貴 (*fù yǔ guì*) 'riches and honours' 我與爾 (*wǒ yǔ ěr*) 'you and I (lit. I and you)', 梃與刃 (*tǐng yǔ rèn*) 'a club and a sword'.

ii) ***As preposition / co-verb***: 與 (*yǔ*) has a large number of uses as a preposition/co-verb:

a) ***'with'***: One of the most common meanings of 與 (*yǔ*) is 'with' in the sense of accompanying, e.g. 賢者不樂仕於朝而思與其友歸於農圃 (*xián zhě bú lè shì yú cháo ér sī yǔ qí yǒu guī yú nóng pǔ*) 'worthy men are not happy to serve in court and want to return with their friends to their vegetable gardens'. It should also be noted that 與 (*yǔ*) may also carry an implied object such as 'it', 'him', 'her', 'them' etc., e.g. 客從外來，與坐談 (*kè cóng wài lái, yǔ zuò tán*) 'the guest came from afar and [Zōu Jì] sat down with him to talk'.

b) ***'be at'***: 與 (*yú*) can also act like a Modern Chinese 在 (*zài*) 'be at', e.g. 昔者楚人與越人舟戰與江 (*xī zhě chǔ rén yǔ yuè rén zhōu zhàn yǔ jiāng*) 'in former times, people from Chǔ and people from Yuè engaged in naval battle on the River' (NB the first 與, *yǔ*, means 'and' or 'with').

c) ***'along with'***: 與 (*yú*) can also have the force of an 'along with', e.g. 與時變 (*yǔ shí biàn*) 'change with the seasons'.

d) ***'to' or 'for'***: 與 (*yú*) sometimes acts like a 'to' or a 'for', e.g. 不私與己

(*bù sī yǔ jǐ*) 'did not show favouritisim to himself'.

e) **'by' *(the passive agent)*:** 與 (*yú*) can also on occasion introduce the passive agent meaning 'by' or 'at the hands of', e.g. 遂 與 勾 踐 擒 (*suì yú gōu jiàn qín*) 'then was captured by Gōu Jiàn'.

iii) **Interrogative particle** (*yú*): when 與 (*yú*) and its variant 歟 (*yú*) appear as the final particle in a question, it is equivalent to either a Modern Chinese 嗎 (*ma*) or 呢 (*ne*), e.g. 是 誰 之 過 與？ (*shì shuí zhī guò yú?*) 'whose error is this?' Sometimes the marker appears earlier in the sentence, for emphasis, e.g. 誰 與 哭 者？ (*shuí yú kū zhě?*) 'who is it, that person who is crying?' 與 (*yú*) may be used with other interrogative pronouns.

iv) **Exclamatory / rhetorical particle**: When 與 / 歟 (*yú*) appears as a final particle in conjunction with, for example, 其 (*qí*) used adverbially and in the sense of 'probably', its force is like a Modern Chinese 吧 (*ba*); there may be a rhetorical and / or exclamatory element to the sentence. Examples include: 語 之 而 不 惰 者 ， 其 回 也 與！ (*yǔ zhī ér bú duò zhě, qí huí yě yú!*) 'never flagging when I discuss anything with him - that must be Huí!' and 孝 弟 也 者 ， 其 為 仁 之 本 與！ (*xiào tì yě zhě, qí wéi rén zhī běn yú!*) 'filial and fraternal piety, are these not the basis for benevolence?', i.e. '... surely these must be the basis for benevolence!' The rhetorical element may be reinforced by the use of a negative, e.g. 可 不 慎 與？ (*kě bú shèn yú?*) 'can [one] be

incautious [on this]?' or 'shouldn't we be careful on this?'

v) **Adverb** *('all')*: 與 (*yú*) is occasionally used as an adverb meaning 'all', 'completely', e.g. 故 天 下 之 君 子 與 謂 之 不 祥 者 (*gù tiān xià zhī jūn zǐ yú wèi zhī bù xiáng zhě*) 'then all the gentlemen of the world will call him an unlucky person' or 制 與 在 我 ， 亡 乎 人 (*zhì yú zài wǒ, wáng hū rén*) 'the institutions [of government and kingship] all reside in me, they [can] not be found in others'.

vi) **As connector** *('rather than', 'if')*: Occasionally 與 (*yú*) will start the first half of a sentence when it has the force of a Modern Chinese 與 其 (*yǔ qí*) 'rather than' and is used as follows:

/ 與 (*yǔ*) V1, 寧 (*nìng*) V2 /

The construction means 'rather than Verb 1, it is better to Verb 2' or more fluidly 'rather Verb 2 than Verb 1' (不 如, *bù rú*, may be used instead of 寧, *nìng*, with the same meaning), e.g. 與 人 刃 我 ， 寧 自 刃 (*yǔ rén rèn wǒ, níng zì rèn*) 'I would rather kill myself with a sword than have someone kill me with a sword' (NB English prefers the second verb to be placed first).

Sometimes, 與 (*yú*) will have the force of an 'if', although this is not very common, e.g. 回 與 執 政 ， 則 由 賜 焉 施 其 能 哉？ (*huí yú zhí zhèng, zé yóu cì yān shī qí néng zāi?*) 'if Huí were to take the reins of government, how could Yóu and Cì demonstrate their abilities?'

vii) ***As a pause marker***: 與 (*yǔ*) as a pause marker is not common, but it does occur, e.g. 於予與何誅？ (*yú yǔ yǔ hé zhū?*) 'well, as for Yǔ! - what [is the point in my] reproving [him]?'

The uses and functions of 則 (*zé*)

Although in Classical Chinese 則 (*zé*) is used as a noun, meaning 'rule', 'regulation', and as a verb, meaning 'to model oneself on', it is most often used to link clauses, when it acts as an adverb or conjunction meaning 'then'. It is very similar in function to 就 (*jiù*) in Modern Chinese, though it may differ in position (則, *zé*, is clause initial and precedes the subject).

i) ***Linking two statements***:

a) ***In a sequence of events*** (*'then ...'*): When 則 (*zé*) links two statements which refer to actual events (past time or habitual present), it establishes a sequence of linked events and is not unlike the second half of a 'when' statement, e.g. 每聞琴瑟之聲，則應節而舞 (*měi wén qín sè zhī shēng, zé yìng jié ér wǔ*) 'whenever I hear the lute, I dance in time to the beat'.

b) ***To introduce the apodosis*** (*'then ...'*): When 則 (*zé*) links two statements which refer to possible future events, the link is suppositional or conditional and 則 (*zé*) means 'then'. 'If' may be expressed by 若 (*ruò*), 苟 (*gǒu*), 如 (*rú*), 使 (*shǐ*), or 倘 (*tǎng*) etc., but more often than not this is omitted leaving 則 (*zé*) to imply the conditionality. Context will normally make the conditionality of the sentence clear, e.g. 傳之子，則不爭 (*chuán zhī zǐ, zé bù zhēng*) 'if one bequeaths it to one's son, then it will not be fought over' or 戰則請從 (*zhàn zé qǐng cóng*) 'if you go to war, I beg leave to go with you'.

c) ***'already', 'it turned out that', 'but'***: This is not unlike a Modern Chinese 原來 (*yuánlái*); context usually helps when choosing the most appropriate translation into English, e.g. 及諸河，則在舟矣 (*jí zhū hé, zé zài zhōu yǐ*) 'when he arrived at the river, she was already on the boat'; 至則無可用 (*zhì zé wú kě yòng*) '[the mule] arrived, but could not be used'; 就而視之則赫然死人也 (*jiù ér shì zhī zé hè rán sǐ rén yě*) 'when he approached and looked at him, it turned out he was clearly dead'; 欲見謝，則未知何如 (*yù jiàn xiè, zé wèi zhī hé rú*) 'he wanted to seek an audience to apologise, but was unsure how [to go about it]'.

ii) ***To introduce the protasis*** (*'if ...'*): According to some Chinese commentators, 則 (*zé*) may also introduce the protasis of a conditional sentence, i.e. it can mean 'if'. Examples given often include the following: 項羽曰：謹守成皋，則漢欲挑戰，慎勿與戰 (*xiàng yǔ yuē: jǐn shǒu chéng gāo, zé hàn yù tiǎo zhàn, shèn wù yǔ zhàn*) 'Xiàng Yǔ said: "Guard [the city of] Chénggāo with care, if the Hàn [army] tries to challenge you to a battle, be careful not to fight [with them]' and 今 則 來 ， 沛 公 恐 不 得 有 此 (*jīn zé lái, pèi gōng kǒng bù dé yǒu cǐ*) 'if he (Xiàng Yǔ) should come now, I fear the Duke of Pèi will not be able to take possession of this'.

In both of these examples, though, other less strained translations could be made, e.g. '[if as you] carefully guard Chénggāo, it turns out that the Hàn [army] try to challenge you to battle, take care not to fight with them'. In the second example, the 今 則 來 (*jīn zé lái*) could also be taken as '[if] now then come' - this would make it an abbreviated condition exposing the topic 'now', see (iii) below.

iii) ***To expose the topic***: In this use, 則 (*zé*) can also be regarded as an abbreviated condition. It can be found in the following form:

/S 則 (*zé*) V/

and means '[if it is] S [that we are talking about], then Verb'. Depending on context, the force of the 則 (*zé*) may be translated as 'by contrast', 'however' etc., e.g. 今 之 君 子 則 不 然 (*jīn zhī jūn zǐ zé bù rán*) 'the gentlemen of today, however, are not like this' or 貌 則 人 ， 其 心 則 禽 獸 (*mào zé rén, qí xīn zé qín shòu*) 'they were human beings in their outward appearance, but in their hearts they were beasts'. Sometimes, the 則 (*zé*) does not need to be translated.

iv) ***At the end of a question***: 則 (*zé*) can be found at the end of questions, most commonly with 何 (*hé*) 'why', 'what', 'how' etc. Modern Chinese would translate with a 呢 (*ne*), e.g.

何 則 ？ (*hé zé?*) 'why?' / 'why, then?' or 安 知 民 則 ？ (*ān zhī mín zé?*) 'how can we [possibly] understand the people?'

Combinations of 則 (*zé*)

Apart from 然 則 (*rán zé*) 'if it is so, then ...' and 然 而 (*rán ér*) 'it is so, but ...', which are both dealt with under the sub-section on 然 (*rán*) (see p 62), 則 (*zé*) is found in 則 已 矣 (*zé yǐ yǐ*), where it is equivalent to a Modern Chinese 罷 了 (*ba le*), e.g. 其 視 下 也 ， 亦 若 是 則 已 矣 (*qí shì xià yě, yì ruò shì zé yǐ yǐ*) 'when [the *péng* bird] looks down [from above], [its view] is really very much the same'. It is also found in 則 安 (*zé ān*) and 則 案 (*zé àn*), which would both translate into a Modern Chinese 就 (*jiù*), e.g. 凡 攻 人 者 ， 非 以 為 名 ， 則 案 為 利 (*fán gōng rén zhě, fēi yǐ wèi míng, zé àn wèi lì*) 'whenever an attack is made on others, it is either for fame or fortune'.

The uses and functions of 者 (*zhě*)

The basic meaning of 者 (*zhě*) in Classical Chinese is 'this one'. It often refers to people, but may refer to places, events, times, etc. We note the following situations where 者 (*zhě*) is used:

i) ***As qualifier head*** ('*the one which ...*'): The most common use of 者 (*zhě*) is as the qualifier head of a noun-phrase in the form:

/V [O] 者 (*zhě*)/

and means 'the one who Verbs [O]', e.g. 位 於 朝 者 (*wèi yú cháo zhě*) 'those who have a position at court' or 有 出 於 胥 商 之 族 者 (*yǒu chū yú xū shāng zhī zú zhě*) 'there were some who came from the families of clerks or merchants'.

In addition, it is found in the reversed relative construction:

/N 之 (*zhī*) V 者 (*zhě*)/

which means 'those of the Ns which Verb-ed', e.g. 馬之死者 (*mǎ zhī sǐ zhě*) 'the horses which died', literally, 'of horses, those which died' or 'dead horses', similarly, 萬物之老者 (*wàn wù zhī lǎo zhě*) 'of the myriad creatures, those which are old' or simply 'old creatures'.

ii) ***Topic marking suffix to a noun***: In its second use, 者 (*zhě*) follows a noun or noun-phrase: /N 者 (*zhě*) / and means 'as for N'. In this form, it is also common as the 'A is B' construction:

/A 者 (*zhě*) B 也 (*yě*)/

e.g. 石奢者，楚昭王相也 (*shí shē zhě, chǔ zhāo wáng xiàng yě*) 'Shíshē was Prime Minister to King Zhāo of Chǔ'.

iii) ***As a time marker in the topic position***: Certain time expressions occur almost exclusively in the topic position, in which case, they tend to be marked by a 者 (*zhě*), although sometimes the marker is a 也 (*yě*) or zero. The more common ones are: 昔［者］ (*xī [zhě]*) 'formerly', 'in former times', 'in the past', 'once upon a time'; 古［者］ (*gǔ [zhě]*) 'in ancient times'; 鄉［者］ (*xiàng [zhě]*) 'formerly', 'in the past', 'once upon a time'; 今［者］ (*jīn [zhě]*) 'now', 'nowadays' etc.

The uses and meanings of 之 (*zhī*)

之 (*zhī*) is one of the most common function characters in Classical Chinese. One of its basic meanings is the verb 'go to'. As a function character its main areas of use are as an object pronoun ('it', 'her', 'him', 'them', etc.) and as a subordinating particle used to show attribution. In addition, 之 (*zhī*) has a number of other less common functional uses.

i) ***Attribution***

a) ***Attribution marker (possession)***: One of the most common uses of 之 (*zhī*) is as an attribution marker. It indicates simple subordination or possession etc. and takes the form:

/X 之 (*zhī*) N/

and it literally means 'this N associated with X', e.g. 我之矛 (*wǒ zhī máo*) 'this spear associated with me', i.e. 'my spear'. Here it is identical to its Modern Chinese counterpart 的 (*de*). When X is a noun-phrase, the whole structure usually means 'the N of X' or 'X's N', e.g. 京師之人 (*jīng shī zhī rén*) 'the people of the capital', 今之天下 (*jīn zhī tiān xià*) 'the world of today' or 孔子之徒 (*kǒng zǐ zhī tú*) 'Confucius' disciples'.

b) ***Attribution marker (nominalisation)***: 之 (*zhī*) is also an attribution marker when it is used to create a noun-phrase. This is referred to as nominalising. The noun or nominalised phrase may be either the topic, subject or object of the sentence in Classical Chinese. In the topic position, 也 (*yě*) is often used as a final pause particle in the construction:

/N 之 (*zhī*) V [O] 也 (*yě*), .../

and essentially means 'as for N's Verb-ing [O], ...', i.e. 'if (or when) N Verb-ed [O], ...', e.g. 天之生大聖也不數 (*tiān zhī shēng dà shèng yě bú shuò*) 'heaven's producing a great sage is not frequent', 'heaven does not often produce a great sage' or 先生之選人也已詳 (*xiān shēng zhī xuǎn rén yě yǐ xiáng*) 'your selecting men is too detailed', 'you are too demanding in your personnel-selection'. In the next example we see two examples of this nominalising 之 (*zhī*), the second being as the object of the verb 欲 (*yù*), thus: 堯舜之傳賢也，欲天下之得其所也 (*yáo shùn zhī chuán xián yě, yù tiān xià zhī dé qí suǒ yě*) 'the reason why Yáo and Shùn handed on [the throne] to worthy men was that they wanted the world to find its right place'.

As in the example above, the nominalised phrase with 之 (*zhī*) may appear as the object of the sentence and is particularly common after certain types of verbs such as 知 (*zhī*) 'know', 見 (*jiàn*) 'see', 聽 (*tīng*) 'allow' and 忍 (*rěn*) 'tolerate' etc. Quite often such phrases themselves will be followed by 也 (*yě*), which makes for the following construction:

/[S] (知) X 之 V [O] 也 /
/[S] (*zhī*) X *zhī* V [O] *yě*/

meaning 'S (knew) that X ...', e.g. 臣固知公子之還也 (*chén gù zhī gōng zǐ zhī huán yě*) 'I definitely knew that you

would return' or 吾不忍赤子之不得乳於其母也 (*wú bù rěn chì zǐ zhī bù dé rǔ yú qí mǔ yě*) 'I cannot bear [the thought] that babies may not be able to suckle from their mothers'. It is also common after adjectival verbs, such as 恐 (*kǒng*) 'fear', 患 (*huàn*) 'be upset about' and 怒 (*nù*) 'angry that', e.g. 魏王怒公子之盜其兵符 (*wèi wáng nù gōng zǐ zhī dào qí bīng fú*) 'the King of Wèi was angry that the Prince had stolen his military tally' (cf. the English gerund 'stealing': '... angry at the Prince stealing his military tally').

This 之...也 (*zhī...yě*) construction is also commonly used to introduce a person's character in the form:

/X 之 為人也 .../
/X *zhī wéi rén yě* .../

meaning 'X, as a person, ...', e.g. 回之為人也，擇乎中庸 (*huí zhī wéi rén yě, zé hū zhōng yōng*) '[Yán] Huí, as a person, chose the Constant Mean'. It should be noted that, as always, the 之 (*zhī*) and 也 (*yě*) markers may, due to the demands of phrasing or balance, be implied i.e. they may be omitted. Thus, this phrase may be shortened to a simple /X 為人/ (X *wéi rén*).

c) *Attribution marker (relative clause)*: When 之 (*zhī*) comes between a verbal phrase and a noun, it translates as a relative clause in English, just like 的 (*de*) in Modern Chinese. The form is as follows:

/V O 之 (*zhī*) N/

e.g. 吞舟之魚 (*tūn zhōu zhī yú*) 'fish that swallow ships' or 遊世之樂 (*yóu shì zhī lè*) 'pleasures associated with wandering [freely] in the world'.

d) *Creating a causal clause*: One of the ways of showing causality, 'the reason why ...', is by use of the following structure:

/ [以] [S] V O [之] 故 /

/ [*yǐ*] [S] V O [*zhī*] *gù*/

as in the example: 今以并國之故，萬國有餘皆滅，而四國獨立 (*jīn yǐ bīng guó zhī gù, wàn guó yǒu yú jiē miè, ér sì guó dú lì*) 'and now, because of the annexation of one state by another, a vast number of domains have all disappeared and only four states remain'.

e) *Creating a temporal clause*: As seen in (b) above, the /[S] 之 (*zhī*) V O 也 (*yě*)/ structure can be used for a 'when ...' clause in Classical Chinese. Much more common, particularly in later periods, was to use the following grammatical structure, which can still be found in formal Modern Chinese:

/[S] V O [之] 時 ([*zhī*] *shí*)/

This form is very close to the Modern Chinese:

/[S] V O 的 時候 (*de shíhou*)/

which like Classical Chinese can be simplified to just one character, /[S] V O 時 (*shí*)/. Examples include: 取金之

時不見人徒見金 (*qǔ jīn zhī shí bú jiàn rén tú jiàn jīn*) 'when I took the gold, I didn't see the people, I only saw the gold' and 君子有三戒；少之時，血氣未定，戒之在色… (*jūn zǐ yǒu sān jiè; shào zhī shí, xuè qì wèi dìng, jiè zhī zài sè …*) 'there are three things which a gentleman should guard against: when he is young and emotionally unsettled, he should guard against lust ...' (see ii below for an explanation of the second 之, *zhī*).

ii) *As object pronoun*: One of the basic meanings of 之 (*zhī*) is 'this' or 'this one'. This leads to its use as an object pronoun, e.g. 'him', 'her', 'it', 'them' etc. e.g. 閉門而拒之 (*bì mén ér jù zhī*) 'he shut the door and refused them [entry]' or 禹傳之子 (*yǔ chuán zhī zǐ*) 'Yǔ bequeathed it to his son'. Since in Classical Chinese, the speaker may refer to himself in third person and may address a person in third person, 之 (*zhī*) can also mean 'me', 'us', 'your', e.g. 君將哀而生之乎？ (*jūn jiāng āi ér shēng zhī hū?*) 'will you take pity [on me] and let me live?' This is a direct quote and in context the 之 (*zhī*) has to be understood as 'me' (literally 'this [person]').

之 (*zhī*) may also be used anaphorically to refer back to an exposed topic. 入者，附之 (*rù zhě, fù zhī*) literally 'what one enters, one adheres to it', i.e. 'one adheres to whatever [religion] one joins'. A variation on this can be seen in the above example in (e)

… 戒 之 在 色 (… *jiè zhī zài sè*), which literally means 'guarding against it, lies in lust', i.e. 'what he [should] guard against is lust'.

Like 他 (*tā*) in Modern Chinese, 之 (*zhī*) can also act in a pivotal function where it is both the object of the first verb and the subject of the next, e.g. 助 之 就 学 (*zhù zhī jiù xué*) 'help him to study'.

iii) **A fusion of 於之** (*yú zhī*): In certain cases, 之 (*zhī*) may have the same meaning as 焉 (*yán*), the fusion equivalent of 於 之 (*yú zhī*) 'on it', 'in it', 'there' etc. The 於 (*yú*) is probably dropped for stylistic reasons, e.g. 及其廣大，草木生之，禽獸居 之，寶藏興焉 (*jí qí guǎng dà, cǎo mù shēng zhī, qín shòu jū zhī, bǎo zàng xīng yán*) 'but when [the mountain] is contemplated in all its vastness, we see how the grass and the trees grow on it, birds and animals dwell on it and treasures arise from it'.

iv) **Acting as a dummy object**: In time expressions such as 久之 (*jiǔ zhī*) '[after a] long while' or '[took/be] a long while' and 頃之 (*qǐng zhī*) 'in/after a while' etc., the 之 (*zhī*) effectively acts as a dummy object. In such expressions, there is no direct translation of a 之 (*zhī*) used in this way.

v) **Used in names**: 之 (*zhī*) is occasionally seen in early names. In Mencius, 尹 公 他, Yǐngōng Tuō, is referred to as 尹 公 之 他 (*yǐn gōng zhī tuō*) and 庾 公 斯, Yǔgōng Sī, is referred to as 庾 公 之 斯 (*yǔ gōng zhī sī*) and in the 左 傳 (the *Zuǒ Zhuàn*) 燭武, Zhú Wǔ, is referred to as 燭 之 武

(*zhú zhī wǔ*) etc. This is analogous to *de* in French, *von* in German or *of* in English when used in names. It should not be translated.

vi) **Subsumed into other characters**: As a final point, 之 (*zhī*) is often subsumed into other characters; the most common are.

不 (*bù*) + 之 (*zhī*) = 弗 (*fú*)
如 (*rú*) + 之 (*zhī*) = 然 (*rán*)
毋 (*wú*) + 之 (*zhī*) = 勿 (*wù*)
之 (*zhī*) + 於 (*yú*) = 諸 (*zhū*)
之 (*zhī*) + 乎 (*hū*) = 諸 (*zhū*)
於 (*yú*) + 之 (*zhī*) = 焉 (*yán*)
之 (*zhī*) + 焉 (*yān*) = 旃 (*zhān*)

The uses and functions of 諸 (*zhū*)

Compared to some of the other 虛 詞 (*xūcí*) met in this section, 諸 (*zhū*) is straightforward. It has three separate uses and meanings:

i) **As a pluralising prefix**: In this usage, it is placed before the noun and means 'all the various'. Examples include: 諸侯 (*zhū hóu*) 'the feudal lords'; 諸公子 (*zhū gōng zǐ*) 'the princes', 諸從者 (*zhū zòng zhě*) 'his followers' and 諸 大 夫 皆 曰：賢 ，未 可 也 (*zhū dà fū jiē yuē: xián, wèi kě yě*) '[even when] all of your great officers say that [this man] is virtuous, [you] cannot [accept it]'. Although 諸 (*zhū*) is sometimes translated as 'all', it is not an inclusive 'all'. In most cases, it should simply be considered the mark of a plural.

ii) **A fusion of 之於** (*zhī yú*): When 諸 (*zhū*) is placed between a verb and its object, it is a contraction of 之 於 (*zhī yú*) meaning 'it (etc.) to (etc.)', e.g. 傳諸人 (*chuán zhū* *rén*) 'bequeathed it to someone else' or 置 諸 橐 以 與 之 (*zhì zhū tuó yǐ yǔ zhī*) 'put it into a bag and gave it to him'.

iii) ***Final particle - short for*** 之乎 *(zhī hū)*: When 諸 (*zhū*) is found at the end of a clause, it denotes 之 (*zhī*) plus the interrogative particle 乎 (*hū*); this is like a Modern Chinese 嗎 (*ma*), 呢, (*ne*) etc.,

e.g. 盍 及 其 勞 且 未 定 也 伐 諸? (*hé jí qí láo qiě wèi dìng yě fá zhū?*) 'why do we not attack them when they are tired and unprepared?' Or, it might be a simple 有 諸? (*yǒu zhū?*) at the end of a statement, which being short for 有 之 乎? (*yǒu zhī hū?*) literally means 'have this?' or 'is it true that ...?' etc.

Five
Classical Chinese
Stories

Story 1: 梟逢鳩 (*xiāo féng jiū*) ①

xiāo	féng	jiū	jiū	yuē	zǐ	jiāng	ān	zhī
❶梟	逢	鳩，	鳩	曰②：「	子③	將④	安⑤	之？」⑥
[An] owl	met	[a] pigeon,	[the] pigeon	said:	"You	will	where	go?"

xiāo	yuē	wǒ	jiāng	dōng	xǐ	jiū	yuē	hé	gù
梟	曰：❷「我	將	東	徙。」		鳩	曰：「何⑦	故？」	
[The] owl	said:	"I	will	east	move."	[The] pigeon	said:	"What	reason?"

xiāo	yuē	xiāng	rén	jiē	wù	wǒ	míng	yǐ	gù
梟	曰：❸「鄉	人	皆⑧	惡⑨	我	鳴，	以⑩	故	
[The] owl	said:	"Village	people	all	dislike	my	song,	for	[this] reason

dōng	xǐ	jiū	yuē	zǐ	néng	gēng	míng	kě	yǐ
東	徙。」	鳩	曰：❹「子③	能	更⑪	鳴	可	矣⑫；	
east	move."	[The] pigeon	said:	"[If] you	can	change	song,	[then] acceptable	{c.o.s. fin. part.};

bù	néng	gēng	míng	dōng	xǐ	yóu	wù	zǐ	zhī
不	能⑬	更	鳴，	東	徙，	猶	惡	子	之⑭
[if] not	can	change	song,	[then] east	move,	[people] still	dislike	your	(...'s)

shēng
聲。」
voice.

Notes on numbering: ① *These numbers refer to grammar and textual footnotes which can be found on the lower right-hand page;* ❶ *These numbers are simple text markers allowing the reader to switch more easily between the trot, the English translation and the Chinese text-only versions.*

Notes on underlines: (i) Characters underlined with straight lines, e.g. 宋 *(sòng) are names (people, places, etc.) (ii) Wavy underlines joining characters or words indicate a very close connection, e.g. ...'s time under* 之時 *(zhī shí) followed by 'i.e. when' indicates that* 之時 *(zhī shí) = when.*

Story 1: **The Owl and the Pigeon**

❶An owl met a pigeon. The pigeon said: "Where are you going?" The owl said: ❷"I'm moving east." The pigeon said: "What for?" The owl said: ❸"The locals all dislike my song, that's why I'm moving east." The pigeon said: ❹"If you can change your song, it will be fine; if not, then they'll still dislike your song even if you move east."

Original text (traditional)   *Original text (simplified)*

梟逢鳩(說苑)   ## 梟逢鳩(说苑)

❶梟逢鳩，鳩曰：「子將安 之？」梟曰：❷「我將東徙。」鳩 曰：「何故？」梟曰：❸「鄉人皆 惡我鳴，以故東徙。」鳩曰： ❹「子能更鳴可矣；不能更鳴，東 徙，猶惡子之聲。」

❶梟逢鳩，鳩曰：「子将安 之？」梟曰：❷「我将东徙。」鳩 曰：「何故？」梟曰：❸「乡人皆 恶我鸣，以故东徙。」鳩曰： ❹「子能更鸣可矣；不能更鸣，东 徙，犹恶子之声。」

Grammar and textual footnotes:

① Story taken from the 說苑 **Shuōyuàn** or *Garden of Stories* compiled by Confucianist Liú Xiàng (劉向), 77-6 BCE.   ② 曰 **yuē**: vb 'say'; is usually used to introduce a quote; may also be used with other speech verbs, e.g. 謂曰(*wèi yuē*) 'addressed [him] saying'.   ③ 子 **zǐ**: pron. 'you' (informal) see p 11.   ④ 將 **jiāng**: part. 'about to' 'will'; indicates future aspect.   ⑤ 安 **ān**: interrog. part. 'where' or 'how', see pp 48-50.   ⑥ 之 **zhī**: vb 'go'; see pp 84-87 for other uses.   ⑦ 何 **hé**: interrog. part. 'what', 'how', 'where', 'why'; it is the commonest of the interrogatives and can also be used as an adjective e.g. 何故 (*hé gù*) 'what reason' or a pronoun 何也 (*hé yě*) 'what is it?', see pp 48-50.   ⑧ 皆 **jiē**: adv. 'all'; this is the CC equivalent of 都 (*dōu*) in MC and as with 都 (*dōu*) in modern usage, it must follow the noun it refers to, but precede the verb.   ⑨ 惡 **wù**: vb 'hate'; also pronounced *è* (adj. 'ugly' 'bad') and *wū* (interrog. part. 'how').   ⑩ 以 **yǐ**: prep. 'by', 'with', 'for', 'using'; introduces an instrument e.g. 以故 (*yǐ gù*) 'for [this] reason', see p 74.   ⑪ 更 **gēng**: vb 'change'; not used in CC in the MC derived meaning of 'even more'.   ⑫ 矣 **yǐ**: fin. part.; an important CC final-clause aspect particle; similar to 了 (*le*) in MC. Indicates, as here, a change of state, e.g. 可矣 (*kě yǐ*) 'it will become acceptable', see pp 77-78.   ⑬ 能...不能... **néng ... bù néng ...**: in CC conditional 'if/then' sentences can be marked with 如 (*rú*), 若 (*ruò*), 使 (*shǐ*) etc. before the protasis and/or 則 (*zé*) 'then' before the apodosis, but very commonly the conditional sense is implied, as here, by presenting juxtaposed statements: '[if] you can ...,[then] ..., [if] you cannot ... ..., [then]', see p 82.   ⑭ 之 **zhī**: part.: here used as an attributive, i.e. /...'s/, e.g. 子之 (*zǐ zhī*) 'your', 人之 (*rén zhī*) 'the person's, see p 84.

Story 2: 守株待兔① (*shǒu zhū dài tù*)②

	sòng	rén	yǒu	gēng	zhě		tián	zhōng	yǒu	zhū
❶	宋③	人	有④	耕	者⑤，		田	中⑥	有④	株，
	[Amongst] Sòng	people,	exist	ploughs (i.e. [a]	one who ploughman)		field's (i.e. in [his]	midst field)	exist	[a] stump,

	tù	zǒu	chù	zhū	zhé	jǐng	ér	sǐ		yīn	shì
❷	兔	走⑦	觸	株，	折	頸	而⑧	死。	❸	因⑨	釋
	[a] rabbit	run [and]	collide into	stump,	break	neck	and	die.		Thereupon	[he] abandon

	qí	lěi	ér	shǒu	zhū	jì	fù	dé	tù		tù
	其⑩	耒	而⑧	守	株，	冀	復	得⑪	兔。	❹	兔
	his	plough	and	keep watch over	stump,	hope	additionally	get	rabbit.		Rabbit

bù	kě	fù	dé	ér	shēn	wéi	sòng	guó	xiào
不	可	復	得，	而⑧	身	為⑫	宋	國	笑。
not	can	again	get,	and	self	by	Sòng	country	laugh (at).

Story 2: **The Ploughman from Sòng**

❶A man of Sòng was ploughing. There was a tree stump in the field. ❷A rabbit ran and collided with it, breaking its neck and dying. ❸Whereupon the man left his plough and kept watch over the stump, hoping to get another rabbit. ❹He failed to get another rabbit and he himself was laughed at by (all) the land of Sòng.

Original text (traditional)

守株待兔(韓非子)

❶宋人有耕者，田中有株，❷兔走觸株，折頸而死。❸因釋其耒而守株，冀復得兔。❹兔不可復得，而身為宋國笑。

Original text (simplified)

守株待兔(韩非子)

❶宋人有耕者，田中有株，❷兔走触株，折颈而死。❸因释其耒而守株，冀复得兔。❹兔不可复得，而身为宋国笑。

Grammar and textual footnotes:

① 守株待兔 **shǒu zhū dài tù**: this has become a four-character idiom based on this story - it means 'to wait for something impossible to happen'. ② Story taken from 韓非子 **Hán Fēizǐ** the 55-chapter book written by the philosopher Hán Fēi (韓非), ca. 288-230 BCE, whose legalist doctrines were famously adopted by China's first emperor Qín Shǐhuáng (秦始皇), 259-210 BCE. ③ 宋 **Sòng**: prop. n. Sòng; a state in the Eastern Zhou Spring and Autumn period (東周春秋) *Dōngzhōu Chūnqiū*, 770-476 BCE. The people of Sòng were renowned for their stupidity. ④ 有 **yǒu**: vb 'have', 'exist'; as in MC, 有 (*yǒu*) is used in CC to indicate both possession and existence e.g. 有株 (*yǒu zhū*) 'there was a tree-stump'. ⑤ 者 **zhě**: pron. 'one who ...'; used to turn a verbal phrase into a nominal phrase, commonly in the form of 'a person who does X' i.e. 耕者 (*gēngzhě*) 'a person who was ploughing', 'a ploughman', see p 83. ⑥ 中 **zhōng**: n. 'middle'; 田中 (*tián zhōng*) is an ellipsis for 於田之中 (*yú tián zhī zhōng*) 'in the middle of the field'; in practice 中 (*zhōng*) is used as a postposition (a preposition that follows the noun it refers to) meaning 'in' or 'among'; here 'in the field'. ⑦ 走 **zǒu**: vb 'run' or 'flee'; cf. the MC meaning of 'leave'. ⑧ 而 **ér**: conj. 'and', 'but', 'yet', 'when' etc.; used to link verbal units (*not* nouns) either in a co-ordinating function with two main verbs (broke its neck and died) or in a subordinating function, with a subsidiary verb followed by a main verb (having broken its neck, it died). ⑨ 因 **yīn**: adv. 'then'; the core meaning is as a verb 'follow'. From this comes the adverbs 'then' indicating a temporal relationship (following on in time) or 'because of' indicating a causal relationship (following on as a consequence). ⑩ 其 **qí**: poss. pron. 'his'; used for 'his', 'hers', 'its', 'theirs' and, less commonly, 'mine', 'yours', see p 59. ⑪ 得 **dé**: vb 'get'; this is the commonest sense of this character in CC where it is rarely used as a particle, and rarely as *děi* 'must'; when used with a following vb in CC it means 'manage to vb'. ⑫ 為 **wéi**: prep. 'by' introducing the agent in a passive construction using 笑 (*xiào*) as the verb 'to laugh', see p 65-66 i) e).

Story 3: 宋國富人 *(sòng guó fù rén)*①

sòng	yǒu	fù	rén	tiān	yù	qiáng	huài	qí
❶宋②	有	富	人，	天	雨	牆	壞③。	其
[In] Sòng	exist	rich	person,	sky	rain	wall	collapse.	His

zǐ	yuē	bù	zhú	bì	jiāng	yǒu	dào	qí	lín
子	曰：	「❷不	築④，	必⑤	將⑥	有	盜⑦。」	其	鄰
son	say:	"[If] not	[re-]build,	certainly	will	have	robbery."	His	neighbour

rén	zhī	fù	yì	yún	mù	ér	guǒ	dà	wáng
人	之	父	亦⑧	云。	❸暮	而⑨	果⑩	大⑪	亡
person	...'s	father	also	say so.	[In the] evening	and	[rich man] indeed	greatly	lose

qí	cái	qí	jiā	shèn	zhì	qí	zǐ	ér	yí
其	財。	❹其	家	甚⑫	智⑬	其	子，	而	疑
his	wealth.	His	family	very	consider wise	the	son,	but	suspect

lín	rén	zhī	fù
鄰	人	之	父。
neighbour	person	...'s	father.

94

Story 3: **A Wealthy Man from Sòng**

❶There was a rich man in Sòng. It rained and his wall collapsed. His son said: ❷"If you don't [re-]build it, you can be sure there will be a burglary." His neighbour's father said the same thing. ❸That evening, they indeed suffered a great loss of property. ❹The family thought the son very wise, but suspected the neighbour's father.

Original text (traditional)

宋國富人(韓非子)

❶宋有富人，天雨牆壞。其子曰：❷「不築，必將有盜。」其鄰人之父亦云。❸暮而果大亡其財。❹其家甚智其子，而疑鄰人之父。

Original text (simplified)

宋国富人(韩非子)

❶宋有富人，天雨墙坏。其子曰：❷「不筑，必将有盗。」其邻人之父亦云。❸暮而果大亡其财。❹其家甚智其子，而疑邻人之父。

Grammar and textual footnotes:

① Story taken from **韓非子 Hán Fēizǐ** written by the philosopher Hán Fēi (韓非), ca. 288-230 BCE.   ② **宋 Sòng**: prop. n. Sòng: a minor state in the Eastern Zhou Spring and Autumn period (東周春秋 *Dōngzhōu Chūnqiū*), 770-476 BCE. Its capital was Shāngqiū (商丘) in Hénán (河南) Province.   ③ **天雨牆壞 tiān yù qiáng huài**: n. vb n. vb 'sky rained, wall collapsed'; there is no need to make explicit the grammatical relationship by adding e.g. 而 (*ér*) between these two phrases; CC likes conciseness and balance. In a different context, it might also be read as a conditional phrase (see ④). It should be noted, too, that in CC, the character 雨, which in MC is always read third tone, takes on a fourth tone when it is used as a verb.   ④ **不築…將有 bù zhú … jiāng yǒu**: adv. vb … adv. vb '[if] not build, [then] will have…' the juxtaposition of the two clauses implies a conditional sentence; this is reinforced by the 必 (*bì*) 'inevitably' and 將 (*jiāng*) 'will'.   ⑤ **必 bì**: adv. 'inevitably', 'bound to'; although 必 (*bì*) sometimes has the MC sense of 'must', it is safer to think of it as an adverb indicating certainty in CC.   ⑥ **將 jiāng**: adv. 'will'; indicates future. A second common meaning in CC is as a noun 'general' (army) and a verb 'command', 'lead'. In such cases, it would be read *jiàng*.   ⑦ **盜 dào**: both vb 'rob' and n. 'thief'; here could be understood either as 'thief' or 'a case of robbery'.   ⑧ **亦 yì**: adv. 'likewise', 'similarly'.   ⑨ **暮而 mù ér**: n. conj. 'evening, and'; the 而 (*ér*) links verbal units, but is commonly used with nouns of time in a verbal sense e.g. as here 'become evening'.   ⑩ **果 guǒ**: adv. 'indeed'; signals something happens 'as expected'; cf. MC 果然 (*guǒrán*) adv. 'really', 'as expected', 'sure enough'.   ⑪ **大 dà**: adv. 'to a great extent' 'greatly'; cf. MC more common adjectival use meaning 'big'.   ⑫ **甚 shèn**: adv. 'extremely', 'very'.   ⑬ **智 zhì**: n. 'wisdom' or adj. 'wise'; here used in the putative sense 'consider wise', a common feature in CC.

Story 4: 鄭人買履 (*zhèng rén mǎi lǚ*)①

zhèng	rén	yǒu	qiě	mǎi	lǚ	zhě	xiān	zì
●鄭②	人	有③	且④	買	履	者⑤ ，	先	自⑥
[Amongst] Zhèng	people	exist	about to	buy	shoes	one who,	first	self
			(i.e. someone who was about to buy shoes)					

dù	qí	zú	ér	zhì	zhī	qí	zuò	zhì	zhī
度	其	足 ，	而	置	之⑦	其	坐 。	●至⑧	之
measure	his	foot,	and	put	it/them	[on] his	seat.	When	go to
					(i.e. measurements)				

shì	ér	wàng	cāo	zhī	yǐ	dé	lǚ	nǎi	wèi
市	而	忘	操	之⑦ 。	●已⑨	得	履 ，	乃⑩	謂
market	but	forget	to take	them.	[He] already	find	shoes,	then	declare

yuē	wú	wàng	chí	dù	fǎn	guī	ér	qǔ	zhī
曰：「吾	忘	持	度 ！」	●返	歸⑪	而	取	之 。
saying: "I	forget	bring	measure-ments!"	[He] turn around	[and] go home	and	fetch	them.

jí	fǎn	shì	bà	suì	bù	dé	lǚ	rén	yuē
及⑫	反⑬ ，	市	罷 ，	遂⑭	不	得	履 。	●人	曰：
When	return,	market	stop,	so	[he] not	get	shoes.	[A] person	said:

hé	bù	shì	zhī	yǐ	zú	yuē	nìng	xìn	qí
「何	不	試	之	以⑮	足 ？」	●曰：「	寧	信	其⑯
"Why	not	test	them	with	feet?"	[The man] said:	"[I] prefer	trust	the

dù	wú	zì	xìn	yě
度 ，	無⑰	自	信	也⑱ 。」
measure-ments,	should not	self	trust	{explan. fin. part.}."

Story 4: **A Man from Zhèng Buys Shoes**

❶A man from Zhèng was about to buy a pair of shoes. He first measured his own feet and put [the measurements] on his seat. ❷When he went to the market he forgot to take them with him. ❸When he had already found some shoes, he declared: "I forgot to bring the measurements." ❹He turned round and went home and fetched them. By the time he got back [to the market], the market was over, and so he did not get his shoes. ❺Someone said: "Why didn't you try them on your feet?" ❻He said: "I'd rather trust the measurements than myself!"

Original text (traditional)

鄭人買履(韓非子)

❶鄭人有且買履者，先自度其足，而置之其坐。❷至之市而忘操之。❸已得履，乃謂曰：「吾忘持度！」❹返歸而取之。及反，市罷，遂不得履。❺人曰：「何不試之以足？」❻曰：「寧信其度，無自信也。」

Original text (simplified)

郑人买履(韩非子)

❶郑人有且买履者，先自度其足，而置之其坐。❷至之市而忘操之。❸已得履，乃谓曰：「吾忘持度！」❹返归而取之。及反，市罢，遂不得履。❺人曰：「何不试之以足？」❻曰：「宁信其度，无自信也。」

Grammar and textual footnotes:

① Story taken from **韓非子 Hán Fēizǐ**: a famous legalist text.   ② **鄭 Zhèng**: prop. n. Zhèng: an ancient state in modern Hénán (河南) Province.   ③ **鄭人有...者 Zhèng rén yǒu ... zhě**: uses the general topic, 鄭人 (*zhèng rén*) 'people of Zhèng' followed by 有...者 (*yǒu ... zhě*) 'there was one who ...' to define the specific person.   ④ **且 qiě**: adv. 'about to', indicates future action.   ⑤ **買履者 mǎi lǚ zhě**: vb n. pron. 'one who buys shoes', see p 83.   ⑥ **自 zì**: pron. 'self', 'himself', etc; often used reflexively preceding a verb.   ⑦ **之 zhī**: pron. obj. 'it' etc.: the 之 in 置之 (*zhì zhī*) 'placed it/them' and 操之 (*cāo zhī*) 'took it/them' refers implicitly to the measurements.   ⑧ **至 zhì**: prep. 'when'; basic meaning vb 'arrive'.   ⑨ **已 yǐ**: adv. 'already'; cf. MC 已經 (*yǐjīng*) 'already'. In both CC and MC, 已 (*yǐ*) precedes the verb, see p 21.   ⑩ **乃 nǎi**: adv 'then', often used like a MC 才 (*cái*), i.e. 'only then'.   ⑪ **返歸 fǎn guī**: vb vb 'return'; both verbs separately mean 'return'; 歸 (*guī*) strongly suggests 'go home'.   ⑫ **及 jí**: prep. 'when'; like 至 (*zhì*) originally a verb meaning 'reach' or 'arrive'.   ⑬ **反 fǎn**: vb 'return'; here used like 返 (*fǎn*) (see ⑪).   ⑭ **遂 suì**: conj. 'thereupon', 'hence'.   ⑮ **以足 yǐ zú**: prep. n. 'with [your] foot'; the 以 (*yǐ*) introduces the instrument, see p 74, i) a).   ⑯ **其度 qí dù**: pron. n. 'the measurement'; the reference point for 其 (*qí*) 'his' etc is not clear: it could be 'my' or 'its' or 'the', see p 59.   ⑰ **無 wú**: vb 'there is not' 'has not'; the negative of 有 (*yǒu* 'have' 'exist'), i.e. it could be read 'there is not self belief'. However, 無 (*wú*) is also used like 勿 (*wù*) or 毋 (*wú*) as a negative imperative 'don't' or 'should not'.   ⑱ **也 yě**: fin. part. explanatory function, see p 71, iii).

Story 5: 攫金 (*jué jīn*) ①

xí	qí	rén	yǒu	yù	jīn	zhě	qīng	dàn
❶昔	齊②	人	有	欲	金	者③ ，	清	旦 ，
Formerly	[amongst] Qí	people	exist	want	gold	one who,	clear	morning,
				(i.e. someone who wants gold)				

yì	guàn	ér	zhī	shì	shì	yù	jīn	zhě	zhī
衣	冠④	而⑤	之⑥	市 ，	❷適⑦	鬻	金	者	之
put on clothes	put on hat	and	go to	market,	happen upon	sell	gold	one who	...'s
						(i.e. one who sells gold)			

suǒ	yīn	jué	qí	jīn	ér	qù	lì	bǔ	dé
所⑧ ，	因⑨	攫	其⑩	金	而	去⑪ 。	❸吏	捕	得⑫
place,	thereupon	grab	his	gold	and	depart.	Constable	catch	get

zhī	wèn	yuē	rén	jiē	zài	yán	zǐ	jué	rén
之 ，	問	曰 ：「	人	皆⑬	在⑭	焉⑮ ，	子	攫	人
him,	ask	saying:	"People	all	be present	there,	[yet] you	grab	[other] person

zhī	jīn	hé	duì	yuē	qǔ	jīn	zhī	shí	bù
之	金⑯	何⑰ ？」	❹對	曰⑱ ：「	取	金	之	時 ，	不
...'s	gold,	why?"	[He] reply	saying:	"[I] take	gold	...'s	time (i.e. when),	not

jiàn	rén	tú	jiàn	jīn
見	人 ，	徒⑲	見	金 。」
see	people,	only	see	gold."

Story 5: **A Man from Qí Snatches Gold**

❶Once upon a time in Qí, there was a man who wanted gold. Early one morning, he put on his coat and hat and went to the market, ❷where he went along to a goldsmith's shop and there snatched some gold and went off. ❸When the police caught him, they asked: "Why did you snatch someone else's gold with all those people around?" ❹He replied: "When I took the gold, I didn't see the people: I only saw the gold.

Original text (traditional)	*Original text (simplified)*
# 攫金(列子)	# 攫金(列子)
❶昔齊人有欲金者，清旦，衣冠而之市，❷適鬻金者之所，因攫其金而去。❸吏捕得之，問曰：「人皆在焉，子攫人之金何？」❹對曰：「取金之時，不見人，徒見金。」	❶昔齐人有欲金者，清旦，衣冠而之市，❷适鬻金者之所，因攫其金而去。❸吏捕得之，问曰：「人皆在焉，子攫人之金何？」❹对曰：「取金之时，不见人，徒见金。」

Grammar and textual footnotes:

① Story taken from **列子 Lièzǐ**: The *[Book of] Master Liè*, a Daoist text attributed, probably spuriously, to Liè Yǔkòu/Yùkòu (列圄寇/列禦寇), ca. 400 BCE. ② **齊 Qí**: prop. n. Qí; a powerful state centred around Línzī (臨淄) in Shāndōng (山東) Province. Its defeat in 221 BCE signified the unification of China. ③ **齊人有…者 Qí rén yǒu … zhě**: uses the general topic, 齊人 (*qí rén*) 'people of Qí' followed by 有…者 (*yǒu … zhě*) 'there was one who …' to define the specific person. ④ **衣冠 yì guàn**: vb vb these are normally first tone nouns, but here they are used as verbs and in CC the tone changes to fourth. ⑤ **而 ér**: conj. 'and'; links verbal phrases, either coordinately or subordinately, see p 54. ⑥ **之 zhī**: vb 'go'; see pp 84-87 for other uses. ⑦ **適 shì**: vb 'arrive'; here a full verb rather than adverb 'by chance', 'just'. ⑧ **所 suǒ**: n. 'place', for part. usage, see pp 62-64. ⑨ **因 yīn**: adv. 'then'. ⑩ **其 qí**: poss. pron. 'his' etc., see p 59. ⑪ **去 qù**: vb 'leave'; in CC 去 (*qù*) is not 'go' as in MC, but either transitively 'get rid of' or intransitively 'depart'. ⑫ **捕得 bǔ dé**: vb vb 'arrest', 'catch'; this is similar to MC, where 捕 (*bǔ*) refers to the action 'pursue' and 得 (*dé*) to the result 'get'. ⑬ **皆 jiē**: adv. 'all'; cf. MC 都 (*dōu*). ⑭ **在 zài**: vb 'be present'. Unlike MC, 在 (*zài*) is not typically a preposition in CC, but rather a verb meaning 'exist', 'be present'. ⑮ **焉 yán**: fusion particle of 於+之 (*yú+zhī*), see pp 67-68. ⑯ **人之金 rén zhī jīn**: n. part. n. 'someone else's gold'; 人 (*rén*) often has connotations of 'other person' or 'someone else'. 之 (*zhī*) is here used in an attributive function i.e. /…'s/, see pp 84. ⑰ **何 hé**: interrog. part. 'why'; 何 (*hé*) can carry a 'why on earth' sense, especially, as here, in the less common final position in the sentence. ⑱ **對曰 duì yuē**: vb vb 'reply, saying'; the 对 (*dui*) indicate the action 'reply' and the 曰 (*yuē*) introduces the citation. ⑲ **徒 tú**: adv. 'only', 'just'; adverbs normally precede the verb.

Dictionary

Dictionary for Grammar Section

The entries here contain all the characters used in the example sentences in this handbook. For completeness, characters used only in Modern Chinese (MC), but which are cited in this handbook, are also, for the most part, included. In the main, though, it is the Classical Chinese senses of the characters that are given. It should be remembered, too, that a character, in context, may have a causative or putative force, adjectives, even though they are quasi-verbs may also, in context, function as nouns or adverbs; nouns may act as verbs or adjectives, too, and vice-versa. A dictionary of Classical Chinese-English is usually only an initial step to reaching an understanding of a text and students will often need to turn to more comprehensive modern or classical Chinese-Chinese dictionaries for further information.

A

a	啊	MC fin. exclam. part.
āi	哀	sympathise with; pity; wail; alas!
ài	愛/爱	love; be fond of; like; covet; begrudge; be sparing of
ān	安	interr. part.: how, where (see pp 48, 49); quiet; still; peace; place; fix on; arrange; with intent
ān	鞍	saddle
àn	暗	dark
àn	案	table
àn	岸	shore; bank; beach; coast
áo	敖	ramble; proud; tall

ǎo	媼	old woman; ps-pron.: I, me etc.

B

ba	吧	MC fin. part.: sign of imp. or interr.: may also show emph. or prob.
bā	八	eight
bá	拔	pullout; draw; choose; lift; capture
bǎ	把	direct obj. marker in MC
bái	白	white; consider as white
bǎi	百	hundred; all; every
bàn	伴	accompany; companion

bàn	半	half; to halve
bàn	辦/办	manage; do business; provide
bāo	包	wrap; parcel; include
bǎo	寶	treasure; precious
bǎo zàng	寶藏/宝藏	precious (mineral) deposits
bǎo	堡	military camp; walled village
bào	報/报	report; reward; inform; remunerate
bào	抱	hold in arms; embrace; cherish
bào	鮑/鲍	abalone; surname

bēi	悲	grieved; sorry; sad; lament; sympathise
běi	北	postpos.: to the north of (see p 38); north; to be defeated
bèi	倍	double; ~fold; act contrary to
bèi	輩/辈	pl. sx (see p 11); generation; a series; a row of carriages
běn	本	root; source; origin; basics; pron.: I, my etc.
bǐ	彼	pron.: he, she, it, they etc. (see p 11); dem.: that, those, there (see p 14)
bǐ	筆/笔	write; pen
bì	玼	a gem
bì	必	adv.: for sure, certainly, necessarily, must
bì	璧	a round, flat piece of jade with a hole in the centre

bì	閉/闭	close; shut; stop up; obstruct
bì	辟	avoid; keep clear of; sovereign
bì	避	take leave; be excused; shun; avoid; hide
bì	壁	wall (indoors)
bì	躄	to limp; lame
bì	蔽	my; shabby; cover; hide
bì	陛	steps to the throne; the emperor
bì xià	陛下	ps-pron.: Your /His/ Her Majesty (lit. under the steps)
biān	邊/边	postpos.: to the side of (see p 42); border; edge; frontier
biàn	變/变	change; alter; transform; rebellion
biǎo	表	postpos.: outside, beyond (see p 38); display

bié	別	category; separate; part; other
bīng	兵	soldier; weapons; arms
bīng fǎ	兵符	military tactics
bīng fú	兵符	military tally
bǐng	炳	bright; illumine; (occ. alt. char. 秉, *bǐng* = hold, grasp)
bǐng	秉	hold; grasp; master; control; preside over
bìng	病	illness; be ill; fault; defect; vice
bìng	並	side by side; together
bìng	并	to annex (states); combine
bó	伯	older brother; uncle; count (feudal rank)
bó	博	wide; universal; substantial
bǔ	捕	catch; seize; apprehend; arrest

bù	布	cotton cloth
bù	不	neg. part.: not (see p 22)
bù rán	不然	no; not be so; (see p 61)
bù rú	不如	had best (see p 22)

C

cái	材	potential; material
cái	財/财	wealth; property; valuables
cān	參/参	counsel; consult; take part in; consider; compare; visit a superior; (read *chén* = uneven); (see also *shēn*)
cān	驂/骖	chariot horses
cán	殘/残	remaining; left
cāng	倉/仓	granary; storehouse; warehouse
cáng	藏	store; hide; conceal; (read *zàng* = storage place; short

		name for Tibet)
cáo	曹	pl. sx (see p 11); official; class; surname
cǎo	草	grass; straw; hasty; careless
cè	冊/册	volume; register; list; to appoint
cè	側/侧	postpos.: to the side of (see p 38); side; awry; prejudiced
cè	策	whip; plan
chā	叉	cross (arms); fold hands (bowing); fork; prong
chá	察	to examine (judicially); to find out
chái	儕/侪	pl. sx (see p 11); a class; a company
chái	柴	brushwood; faggots; fuel; firewood; 高柴, Gāo Chái, name of a Confucian disciple
cháng	常	often; normal;

		constant; invariable
cháng	長/长	long; height (trad. alt. pr. *zhàng*); (read *zhǎng* = grow; increase; excel)
cháng	嘗/尝	sign of past tense: once, before now (see pp 21, 78); taste; prove; experience
cháo	朝	court; dynasty; visit; towards; (see also *zhāo*)
cháo	巢	nest
chén	臣	minister; pspron.: I, me etc. (see p 11); make a minister of
chén	陳/陈	arrange; spread out; make a statement; a long time; seasoned; expose; a path; name of ancient state; surname; (read *zhèn* = alt. char.

		for 陣/阵, i.e. battle)
chén	沉	sink; perish; heavy; very
chéng	成	to complete; succeed; become finished; whole; perfect
chéng	城	city wall; city
chéng	懲/惩	to correct; punish; warn; punishment
chéng	盛	fill; contain; (see also *shèng*)
chéng	稱/称	call; talk about; mention; praise; weigh; raise; suitable
chī	笞	to beat/flog (with a bamboo)
chí	池	pond; moat
chí	持	hold; take hold of; support
chǐ	恥/耻	shame; humiliation
chǐ	尺	a foot (14.1" or 0.3581m)
chì	叱	shout at; abuse

chì	赤	red; naked; destroy
chì zǐ	赤子	baby
chóu	籌/筹	consider; prepare; plan
chū	出	payout; surpass; demote; leave; go out
chū	初	beginning; first
chú	雛/雏	chick; rear a brood
chǔ	楚	sharp; keen; clear; distinct; name of an ancient state
chù	處/处	postpos.: at (see p 38); place; office; condition (read *chǔ* = dwell; decide; punish; manage; have use for)
chuán	傳/传	hand on; bequeath; (read *zhuàn* = a commentary on the classics; a biography)
chuāng	窗	window

chuáng	床	(alt. char. 牀, *chuáng*); bed
chuò	輟/辍	pause; rest; stop
cí	祠	ancestral temple; worship ancestors
cí	辭/辞	(alt. char. 辤); words; speech; message; resign; decline; make excuses
cí	詞/词	sayings; musings; words; expression; stories; a form of poetry
cǐ	此	dem.: this, here (see p 14)
cì	次	second; next; occasion; (see p 17); inferior; lower
cì	賜/赐	bestow; give; confer upon; grant; gift (from superior); 端木賜/赐, Duānmù

		Cì, name of a Confucian disciple
cóng	叢/丛	clump of trees; thicket
cóng mǎng	叢莽/丛莽	under-growth
cóng	從/从	follow; obey; comply with; clan; (read *cōng* = lax; perpendic-ular; plough from north to south); (see also *zòng*)
cóng zhèng	從政/从政	have political office; engage in politics
cù	猝	sudden; abrupt; hurried
cù	簇	small bamboos; crowd; crowded; bunch; cluster; bouquet
cuàn	爨	cook (with a fire); a cooking stove; a mess

cūn	村	village; hamlet
cún	存	exist; keep; retain; preserve; inquire after

D

dá	答	respond to; reply; (read *dā* = reply; agree to)
dá	怛	grieved; distressed
dá huà	怛化	die; pass away
dà	大	great; big
dà fū	大夫	*dàfū* (trad. senior officials)
dà shèng	大聖/大圣	great sage
dà shì	大市	high street; town square
dà shuǐ	大水	flood
dài	待	treat; wait for; behave; (read *dāi* = MC stay)
dài	代	era; take place of; dynasty; generation
dài	殆	danger; func. part.: nearly, even, probably,

		almost (see pp 58, 73)
dàn	旦	morning; dawn
dàn rì	旦日	tomorrow
dàn	但	but; only; merely; yet; still
dàn	彈/弹	crossbow pellet; (see also *tán*)
dāng	當/当	ought; should; must; sign of imp. (see p 22); correct; suitable; fill a position; in; at; when; to match; (see also *dàng*)
dàng	當/当	treat as; regard as; serve as; stand in place of; fitting; just; (see also *dāng*)
dāo	刀	knife; sword
dào	道	the Way; road; say
dào	盜/盗	steal; rob; robber; bandit
dé	得	get; find; obtain; to

		effect; attain; can; may; able to be done
dé	德	morals; virtue; ethics; power; kindness
děng	等	pl. sx (see p 11); wait; rank; grade
dí	敵 / 敌	enemy; to oppose
dí	翟	(alt. pr. *zhái*); pheasant; surname
dì	地	earth; ground
dì	棣	the bush cherry; a wild plum; (see also 棠棣, *táng dì*)
dì	弟	younger brother; ps-pron.: I, me etc. (see p 11); (see also *tì*)
dì zǐ	弟子	disciple; a junior
dìng	定	fixed; settle; decide; forehead; name of a star

dōng	冬	winter
dōng	東 / 东	postpos.: to the east of (see p 38); east; master; owner; host
dòng	動 / 动	move; start; take action; rouse
dòng xīn	動心 / 动心	excite the mind; moved
dòng	洞	cave; hole; see through; comprehend
dòu	竇 / 窦	hole; surname
dú	獨 / 独	alone; only; independent
dù	渡	ford/cross (a river)
dù	杜	shut out; restrict; impede; stop
dù juān	杜鵑 / 杜鹃	cuckoo
duān	端	upright; proper; principle
duàn	斷 / 断	sever; decide
duì	對 / 对	opposite to; oppose; face; suit; compare
dùn	盾	(alt. trad. pr. *shǔn*); shield

duō	多	mostly; usually; many; much; only
duó	奪 / 夺	snatch; grasp; take away; settle; decide; surpass; determine; (read *duì* = name of a place)
duò	惰	lazy; careless;

E

ē	婀	graceful; elegant; unstable
é	俄	suddenly; lean
é ér	俄而	after a while; presently; (see p 56)
è	惡 / 恶	evil; foul; wicked; wrong; (see also *wū* and *wù*)
è	厄	in difficulty; in distress; a ring
ēn	恩	kindness; grace; favour; mercy
ēn chǒng	恩寵 / 恩宠	imperial favour

ér	兒/儿	boy; son; child
ér	洏	tears; tearful
ér	而	func. part.: and, but, whereas, then etc. (see pp 54-57); occ. alt. char. for 爾/尔, *ěr* = pron.: you, your etc. (see p 11)
ér hòu	而後/而后	func. part. set: then, and then, after that (see p 57)
ér kuàng	而況/而況	func. part. set: still more, with still stronger reason (see p 57)
ér qiě	而且	func. part. set: and, moreover, furthermore (see p 57)
ér yǐ	而已	fin. part. set: only, that's all (see p 57)
ér yǐ hū	而已乎	fin. part. set (see p 57)
ěr	爾/尔	(alt. char. 尒, *ěr*); pron.: you, your etc. (see pp 2, 11); so; like that; ~like; thus; only
ěr xǔ shí	爾許時/尔许时	so long
ěr	耳	ear; handle; a fungus; soft; as a fus. char. of 而已 (*ér yǐ*) = merely, only
èr	二	two; second; twice

F

fā	發/发	issue; send forth; issue stores; set off; manifest
fá	伐	to fell; cut down; attack; to act as a go-between; make a show of
fǎn	反	turn (over); oppose; but; contrary; instead of; return (alt. char. 返, *fǎn*)
fǎn	返	revert to; return (alt. char. 反, *fǎn*)
fāng	方	square; upright; direction; func. part.: then, just then, now, just at the/that moment (see p 21)
fāng jiāng	方將/方将	cont. tense part. set (see p 21)
fāng qiě	方且	cont. tense part. set (see p 21)
fāng yù	方欲	cont. tense part. set (see p 21)
fēi	非	neg. fus. cop. (不+惟/唯, *bù+wéi*): not be, is not the case of, without etc. (see pp 19, 20, 68, 69); wrong
fēi	飛/飞	fly; go quickly
fèi	廢/废	forgo; do away with
fèi	沸	boil; bubble up; gush
fēn	分	divide; share;

		separate; distinguish; (read *fèn* = alt. char. 份, i.e. a part; a share; function; duty)
fēng	風/风	wind; practice; customs
féng	逢	meet with; to happen; to hit upon
fèng	奉	accept; offer; receive orders; esteem; have the honour to
fèng	縫/缝	a crack; seam; joint; (read *féng* = sew; stitch; mend)
fǒu	否	neg. part.: no, not (see p 61); used in interr. (see p 48); (read *pǐ* = wicked; evil; clogged)
fū	夫	husband; sage; a man; artisan; a labourer; (see also *fú*)
fū rén	夫人	lady; ladies of high

		rank; wives of high officials
fūzǐ	夫子	a sage; master; ps-pron.: you, your etc. (see p 11)
fū	鈇/铁	axe
fú	扶	support; prop up; help
fú	弗	neg. fus. part. (不 + 之, *bù*+ *zhī*): not it etc. (see pp 12, 22, 87)
fú	伏	hide; lurk; prostrate; yield; suffer
fú	符	agree with; tally; spell; amulet
fú	夫	init. func. part.: the, now, then, therefore, however, moreover etc. (see pp 14, 51); (see also *fū*)
fú	服	clothes; wear; mourning garments; serve; submit; think of

fú sāng	服喪/ 服丧	to be in mourning
fǔ	甫	func. part.: just (now), recently (see p 21); to begin; (read *pǔ* = garden)
fǔ	斧	axe; hatchet
fǔ jīn	斧斤	axe; hatchet
fǔ	釜	cauldron; cooking pot
fù	富	rich; enrich;
fù	鮒/鲋	crucian carp; perch
fù	賦/赋	irreg. prose poem; give; bestow; levy
fù	附	adhere to; enclose
fù	赴	go against; attend; go to
fù dí	赴敵/ 赴敌	go to fight the enemy
fù	復/复	again; return; repeat
fù	父	father
G		
gāi	陔	step; grade; ledge
gǎi	改	alter; correct; change;

		repent; reform
gài	蓋／盖	cover; hide; seal; erect; (occ. alt. 概, *gai* = generally; for the most part; probably)
gǎn	敢	dare; presume
gāo	高	high; tall
gāo	皋	(alt. char. 皐, *gāo*); praise; bless; high; eminent; marsh; announce
gǎo	槁	withered; rotten; dry
gào	告	tell; inform
gào	誥／诰	to grant a title of honour (or nobility)
gē	割	carve (out); cut
gé	革	hides; human skin; remove; instead (see p 24)
gé	葛	kudzu vine; grass-cloth
gé	隔	on the other side; separated

		by; (see p 40)
gè	各	dem.: each, every, all (see pp 14, 16)
gēng	更	change; alter; night-watch; (see also *gèng*)
gēng	耕	to plough; to till
gēng	庚	age; seventh heavenly stem; compensate; change
gěng	耿	brilliant; dedicated; bright
gèng	更	still; again; more; much more; another; (see also *gēng*)
gōng	攻	attack; assault; apply oneself
gōng	公	public; gentleman; sir; duke
gōng zǐ	公子	prince
gōng	功	merit; achievement
gōng chén	功臣	meritorious minister

gòng	共	altogether; all; (read *gōng* = fulfil one's duties); (read *gǒng* = alt. char. 拱, i.e. to fold the hands)
gòng	貢／贡	tribute; contrib-ution; surname
gōu	勾	hook; arrest; entice; surname
gōu	溝／沟	ditch; drain; aqueduct; penetrating
gǒu	狗	dog
gǒu	苟	if; only; careless; of small importance
gū	姑	girl; maiden; lenient; just; for now; meanwhile
gù	故	reason; for this reason; therefore; (see p 71)
gǔ	鼓	drum; to drum; rouse; swell
gǔ	骨	bone
gǔ	谷	valley; ravine; surname

gǔ	古	ancient; antiquity
gǔ zhě	古者	in ancient times (see p 51)
gǔ	賈／贾	merchant; to trade; (read *jiǎ* surname)
guǎ	寡	few; little; friendless; alone
guǎ ren	寡人	ps-pr.: I, we etc. (used by kings)
guà	掛／挂	hang; suspend; suspense; anxious; think of
guà	絓	coarse silk; fasten; (alt. char. 罣) obstructed
guān	官	official; public; a term of respect; excellent; the senses
guān	觀／观	behold; travel; (read *guàn* = Daoist monastery)
guān	關／关	frontier pass; close; relation

guǎn	管	govern; control; care for; tube; surname
guàn	貫／贯	to thread; implicate; a string of 1,000 cash
guāng	光	light; favour; brightness; honour; illumine
guāng yīn	光陰／光阴	time
guǎng	廣	vast; wide; extensive
guī	龜／龟	tortoise; turtle; (read *jūn* = chapped)
guī	歸／归	return (home); belong to; restore; send back; marriage (of a woman)
guǐ	鬼	ghost; spirit
guì	桂	cassia; cinnamon
guì	貴／贵	expensive; costly; honourable; prized
guó	國／国	kingdom; nation; state; country;

		dynasty; capital
guǒ	果	certainly; surely; as predicted; fruit; obstinate
guò	過／过	visit; pass; through; cross over; blame; fault; mistaken; excessive

H

hái	孩	child; son; daughter
hǎi	海	sea; maritime; vast; large; marshes
hài	害	injure; harm; destroy; kill
hǎn	罕	rare; few; seldom; strange
hàn	漢	name of an ancient state; name of a dynasty
háo	豪	unrestrained; bold
hào	好	to like; love; be fond of (read *hǎo* = good; well)
hào shì zhě	好事者	idlers; onlookers

111

hào	號/号	style as; call; number; mark
hé	河	river; Yellow River
hé	河伯	Hé Bó (Yellow River God)
hé	曷	interr. part.: why, how, when, what, where (see pp 22, 48); to stop
hé	盍	interr. fus. part. (何 +不, *hé+bù*: or 胡+不, *hú+bù*) why not, wouldn't it be better to etc. (see p 49); sign of imp. (see p 22)
hé	和	peace; mild; harmony; on good terms with
hé	何	interr. part.: why, what, how, which, what sort of (see pp 14, 24, 48-49)
hé cóng	何從/ 何从	interr. part. set: from where, through

		where (see p 48)
hé gù	何故	interr. part. set: what reason, why (see p 48)
hé nǎi	何乃	interr. part. set: why
hé rén	何人	interr. part. set: who
hé rú	何如	interr. part. set: be like what, how about, wouldn't it be better to etc. (see pp 48, 69); (see also 如何, *rú hé*)
hé shí	何時/ 何时	interr. part. set: when (see pp 43, 48)
hé yǐ	何以	interr. part. set: by what means, how (see p 48)
hé yóu	何由	interr. part. set: from where, through where (see p 48)
hé zì	何自	interr. part. set: from where, through where (see pp 40, 48)

hóng	鴻/鸿	vast; profound; wild swan
hóng gōu	鴻沟/ 鸿沟	Hónggōu (name of an ancient city)
hóu	侯	marquis; archery target; beautiful
hòu	後/后	postpos.: behind (see p 38); later; descendant
hòu rén	後人/ 后人	successors; posterity
hòu shēng	後生/ 后生	young man; descendants; ps-pr. I, me etc.)
hòu shì	後世/ 后世	later generations
hòu	厚	thick; deep; rich; kind; substantial
hū	乎	interr. part. (see pp 20, 48-49, 57); pause part. (see p 58); fin. exclam. part. (see pp 24, 58); prep.: at, in, to, etc. (see p 58); use in imp. (see p 58); used in conjecture (see p 58);

112

		(alt. dial./ char. var. for 於/于, _yú_)
hū ěr	乎爾/ 乎尔	fin. func. part. set (see p 59)
hū zāi	乎哉	fin. part. set (see pp 49, 59)
hū	虖	rare alt. char. for 乎, _hū_
hū	呼	call out; try out; exhale; name
hū	膴	dried meat
hū	忽	suddenly; unexpect- edly; disregard; despise
hū ér	忽而	suddenly; unexpect- edly
hú	胡	interr. part.: why, what, where, how (see p 48)
hú	狐	fox
hǔ	虎	tiger
hù	戶	individual; door; family; population
huā	華/华	flower (orig. form for 花,

		huā); (read _huá_ = glory; splendour; China)
huà	化	change; transform
huà	畫/画	paint[ing]
huái	懷/怀	bosom; carry in the bosom; cherish
huài	壞/坏	demolish; spoil; ruin; bad
huán	還/还	go back; return; restore; repay; (read _hái_ = MC still, yet)
huán	環/环	ring; bracelet; encircle
huàn	患	be upset about; calamity; evil; worried; aggrieved
huáng	黃	yellow; the imperial colour
huáng	皇	supreme; imperial; ruler; sovereign
huí	回	to return to (or from); 顏/颜回,

		name of a Confucian disciple
huǐ	悔	repent; regret; reject; (occ. alt. char. 誨/诲, _huì_, i.e.: teach)
huǐ	毀/毁	destroy; ruin; (as alt. char. 譭, _huǐ_ = slander)
huì	賄/贿	bribe; bribery
huǒ	火	fire; flame
huò	或	in one case; in some cases; someone; somebody; (see pp 14, 27, 31-33); perhaps; sometimes
huò	獲/获	catch; seize; obtain
huò	貨/货	sell; goods; produce; cargo
huò	禍/祸	misfortune; calamity; judgement from heaven

J

jī	幾/几	almost; nearly;

		about; (see also *jǐ*)	jí	吉	disease; urgency			supervise; prison
jī	几	bench; small table; quiet; (see also *jī* above and *jǐ*)			auspicious; lucky	jiàn	見/见	see; have an audience; interview; mark of pass. agent (see p 42)
			jǐ	幾/几	interr. part.: how many; (see also *jī*)			
jī	擊/击	strike; rout	jì	既	since; when; already; to finish	jiàn	劍/剑	sword (double-edged)
jī gǔ	擊鼓/击鼓	strike a drum	jì	跡/迹	track; footprints	jiàn	踐/践	tread upon; trample; walk; follow
jī	機/机	changes; motions; machine; secret; (occ. alt. char. 几, *jī*, i.e. a small table)	jì	冀	hope; desire	jiāng	將/将	sign of fut.: will, about to (see pp 22, 24); interr. part.: or (see p 20); take; hold; nourish; care for; escort; lead; side of; strong; (read *qiāng* = beg; impose); (see also *jiàng*)
			jì	繫/系	(alt. pr. *xi*); tie; bind; be attached to			
jī	雞/鸡	chicken; fowl	jì	濟/济	aid; cross; relieve; stream; up to standard; success; complete (read *jǐ* = numerous)			
jī	其	fin. part.: (see p 61); (see also *qí*)						
jí	及	catch up with; extend; come up to; when; as to	jiā	家	house; home; relative; family	jiāng	江	large river; the River; the Yangtse
			jià	價/价	price; value	jiāng pàn	江畔	the bank of a river
jí	即	in fact; at once; then; even if; go to	jiān	間/间	postpos.: among, in, on, space between (see p 38); divide; separate; blame			
jí	急	swift; anxious; hasty; hurried; urgent				jiàng	將/将	a general; leader; (read *qiāng* = beg; ask);
jí	疾	sickness; illness;	jiān	監/监	inspect; oversee;			

		(see also *jiāng*)
jiāo	教	teach; instruct; cause; allow; command; (see also *jiào*)
jiāo	交	go around with; hand to; deliver; join; intertwine
jiǎo	矯/矫	dissemble; usurp; strong; martial; reform
jiǎo jiǎo	矯矯/矯矯	bold; strong; courageous
jiào	教	education; teaching; sect; religions; doctrines; (see also *jiāo*)
jiē	皆	all; every; entirely
jiē kě	皆可	either of them will suit; any will do
jié	桀	Jié - last ruler of Xià (夏) dynasty; cruel

jié	潔/洁	clean; pure; clear
jié	節/节	beat (music); rhythm; verse; regulate; save; joint
jiě	解	loosen; release; explain; understand
jiè	戒	warn; caution; guard against; avoid
jiè zāi	戒哉	beware!; take care!
jiè zhī	戒之	beware!; take care!
jīn	金	gold; piece of gold; precious; metals; weapons
jīn	斤	catty (1⅓lb); pierce; penetrating
jīn	今	at present; now
jīn rì	今日	today
jīn zhě	今者	present; today; now; nowadays
jǐn	謹/谨	carefully; with care

jìn	晉/晋	promote; name of a dynasty
jìn	盡/尽	utmost; wholly; exhaust
jìn xīn	盡心/尽心	whole-heartedly
jìn	燼/烬	cinders; ashes
jīng	京	capital (of a country)
jīng shī	京師/师	capital (of a country)
jīng	經/经	classic books; pass through; manage; plan; rule; invariable constant
jǐng	井	well; pit; mine
jìng	鏡/镜	mirror
jìng	敬	reverant; respectful; respect
jiū	鳩/鸠	pigeon; turtledove; collect; assemble
jiǔ	久	for a long time; long-enduring
jiǔ ér jiǔ zhī	久而 久之	in the course of time

115

jiù	舅	uncle, i.e. mother's brother
jiù	就	just; simply; to come; go to; to approach; near
jiù	救	save; deliver; rescue; relieve; aid
jū	居	inhabit; live; reside; dwell; bent on; (read *jī* = fin. part.)
jū	且	fin. func. part. (see 也且, *yě jū*); dignified; many; great; (see also *qiě*)
jǔ	舉	raise (with hands); all; the whole; begin; recommend
jù	拒	refuse; resist
jù	巨	huge; great; very; a carpenter's square
jù	聚	gather; assemble; meet together; collect
juān	鵑 / 鹃	cuckoo

jué	厥	pron.: he, she, it, its etc. (see p 11)
jué	掘	dig; excavate
jué	絕 / 绝	cut short; break off; interrupt; very
jué	決 / 决	decide; sentence; cut off; bid farewell to; slay; execute; thumb ring
jué	钁 / 镢	a pick; a hoe
jūn	君	lord; ruler; sovereign; gentleman; ps-pron.: you, your etc. (see p 11)
jūn zǐ	君子	gentleman (Confucian ideal)

K

kě	可	may; can; all right; able; acceptable; sign of imp. (see p 22); 可+pass. vb = ~able (see pp 24, 72)

kè	客	visitor; guest; stranger; traveller
kōng	空	empty; hollow; reduced to extremities
kǒng	恐	afraid; to fear; apprehensive
kǒng	孔	opening; hole; to penetrate; great; very; surname
kǒng zǐ	孔子	Confucius (551-478 BCE) a philosopher
kǒu	口	mouth; hole; speech; talk
kòu	寇	bandit; robber; pirate; invade
kòu	叩	kowtow; knock; ask
kòu	扣	knock; fasten; deduct
kuāng	筐	basket; chest
kuī	窥 / 窥	peep; spy
kuì	喟	(alt. pr. *wèi*); sigh deeply; breathe heavily

kǔn	閫/阃	door to women's quarters; city wall
kùn	困	tired; distress; poverty
kuò	闊/阔	broad; rich; separated

L

lái	來/来	come; cause to come
láng	狼	wolf
láng	稂	grass; weeds
láo	勞/劳	labour; work
lǎo	老	old; aged; venerable; term of honour and respect
lè	樂/乐	pleasure; to take pleasure in; happy; joy; (see *yuè*)
léi	雷	thunder
léi	累	(alt. char. 縲, *léi*) join, bind, trammels, burdens; read *lèi* = tired, implicate; read *lěi* = accumulate

lí	梨	pear
lí	犁	a plough; to plough
lǐ	李	plum; surname
lǐ	禮/礼	rules of propriety; etiquette; ceremony; rites
lǐ	里	⅓ mile; lane; neighbourhood
lǐ	裡/里 or 裏/里	postpos.: inside, in, within
lì	立	stand; stand up; set up; establish; straight away
lì	力	strength; force; power
lì	勵/励	urge; incite; encourage
lián	廉	pure; honest
lián	簾	curtain; loose hanging screen
liàn	練/练	practise; drill; select; (alt. char. 楝, *liàn*, = a chinaberry [tree])

liáng	梁	bridge; roof beam; name of ancient dynasty; surname
liáng	良	good; virtuous; respectable; innate
liǎng	兩/两	two; pair; MW = ounce/tael
liè	列	dem.: all the, the various (see p 14)
liè	獵/猎	hunt
lín	林	forest; woods
lín	臨/临	stand over; be adjacent to; next to
lín	麟	a mythical beast usu. translated as a (Chinese) unicorn
lín	鄰/邻	neighbour; near to; connected
líng	靈/灵	spirit; divine (powers); efficacious; smart; coffin
liú	流	flow; drift; circulate; descend;

		unstable; banish
liú	劉 / 刘	battle-axe; kill; destroy; surname
liǔ	柳	willow; pleasure; dissipation; gaiety
liǔ shù	柳樹 / 柳树	willow tree
lóng	龍 / 龙	dragon
lú	蘆 / 芦	rushes; reeds
lǔ	魯 / 鲁	dull; rude; stupid; common; vulgar; name of an ancient state
lù	路	road; path; way; journey
lù	露	dew; disclose; expose
lù	祿 / 禄	blessing; happiness; prosperity
lù	戮	execute; kill; slaughter
lú	驢 / 驴	ass; donkey; mule
lǔ	旅	guest; stranger; travel; lodge; order; troops

lǚ	履	shoes; footwear; tread; walk on
lǜ	慮 / 虑	consider; think
luǎn	卵	egg
luàn	亂 / 乱	disorder; rebellion; confuse
lüè	略	roughly; outline; abduct
lún	淪 / 沦	ruined; lost; eddying water

M

mǎ	馬 / 马	horse
mǎi	買 / 买	buy; purchase; win over
mài	賣 / 卖	sell; betray; show off
mǎn	滿 / 满	fill; all over
mǎng	莽 / 莽	disorderly; under-growth; jungle; rude
māo	貓 / 猫	cat
máo	矛	lance; spear
máo	毛	hair of an animal; feathers; fur; grass
mào	貌	outward appearance

méi	枚	stalk; item; MW for coins, fruits etc.
měi	美	beautiful; delicious
měi	浼	contaminate; request; buy
mèi	妹	younger sister
mén	門 / 门	door; gate; profession; sect
méng	蒙	cover; stupid; untaught child; I, my etc.; place name; (read *mēng* = cheat)
měng	猛	fierce; cruel
mèng	夢 / 梦	dream
mèng	孟	great; eminent; elder; Mencius; rude; press forward
mèng zǐ	孟子	Mencius (a Confucian philosopher, 372-289 BCE)
miǎn	勉	urge; consrain; exert oneself

miáo	苗	a sprout; seedling; grow corn; progeny
miè	滅/灭	annihilate; eliminate; perish
mín	民	people; mankind
míng	名	name; reputation; fame
míng	明	bright; clear; intelligent; understand; illustrate
míng rì	明日	tomorrow; next day
mìng	命	advise; advice; order; fate; destiny; command; mandate
mò	莫	dem.: in no case, nobody (see pp 14, 27, 31-33); decide; fix; plan for; shave; pare; (read *mù* = evening; late)
mò ruò	莫若	...had best; sign of imp. (see p 22)

mò	默	silent; quiet
mò mò	默默	silently; quietly
mò	末	end; finally; powder; mean; insignificant
mò	墨	ink; black; 墨翟, Mò Dí (aka 墨子, Mòzǐ), a 5th Cent. BCE pacifist philosopher
móu	謀/谋	discuss; plan
móu	侔	equal; similar; like
mǔ	母	mother; female
mǔ	畝/亩	a Chinese land measure = ⅙ of an acre
mù	木	tree; wood; numb
mù	暮	evening; sunset
mù	穆	solemn; quiet; respectful

N

nǎi	乃	in fact; but; and then; only then; namely; pron.: you, your, their etc. (see

		p 11); dem.: that, those etc.; sim. to cop. it is (see p 19)
nài	奈	but; how; bear; endure; a remedy; resource
nài hé	奈何	do what [about it]?
nán	南	postpos.: to the south of (see p 38); south
náng	囊	bag; sack
něi	餒/馁	hungry; feeble
nèi	內	postpos.: inside, in (see p 38); (read *nà* = alt. char. 納, i.e. to enter)
néng	能	can; able to; power; talent; ability
nǐ	擬/拟	plan; intend; determine; compare; resemble
nì	逆	disobey; rebel; oppose; contrary; accord with

nián	年	year; age; harvest
niǎo	鳥/鸟	bird
nìng	寧/宁	func. part.: how could ...! (see p 57); prefer; rather; (read *níng* = peaceful; tranquil)
niú	牛	cow; ox; buffalo; bull
nú	奴	slave; servant; term of deprecation
nù	怒	anger; passion; rage
nǚ	女	girl; daughter; (read *nù* = give a daughter in marriage); (read *rǔ* = you, your etc., see alt. char. 汝, *rǔ*)
nuò	諾/诺	respond; answer; promise
P		
pān	攀	climb up; drag down; implicate
pán	磐	a huge rock

pán	盤	check; game; set; tray; gift
pàn	叛	rebel; revolt
pàn	畔	postpos.: by the side of (see p 38); bank; leave; rebel; a path between fields
páng	旁	postpos.: by the side of, next to (see p 38)
páo	庖	cook; kitchen
pèi	沛	copious; abundant; tall; high; to fall prostrate
pèi rán	沛然	in torrents (e.g. of rain)
pén	盆	bowl; basin
pǐ	匹	one of a pair (e.g. in marriage); a common man; MW for horses; as MW = occ. alt. char. 疋, *pǐ*)
pǐ	疋	bolt; roll (cloth); the foot
piān	偏	slant; lean; stubborn;

		(alt. char. 翩, *piān*, lightly, elegantly)
pín	貧/贫	poor
pǐn	品	grade; actions; conduct; classify; estimate; think
píng	平	level; even; just; equal; average; common
pò	破	broken; ruined; break; take by storm; destroy
pū	撲/扑	hit; beat; strike; rush on
Q		
qī	妻	a (legal) wife; (read *qì* = give in marriage)
qī	欺	deceive; cheat; bully
qí	岐	forked
qí	其	poss. pron.: his, her, its, their etc. (see p 11); dem.: the, that, this,

120

		etc. (p 14); sign of imp. (see p 61); interr. part.: or (see pp 20, 60); probably (see p 60); nom. part. (see pp 59-60); attrib. part. (see p 61); func. part. (see pp 13, 59-61); (see also *jī*)
qí dài	其殆	func. part. set (see p 61)
qí yōng	其庸	func. part. set (see p 61)
qí zhū	其諸	func. part. set (see p 61)
qí	齊/齐	even; all alike; arrange; name of an ancient state; (read *zhāi* = alt. char. 齋/斋, to fast; penance; pure; a study; library)
qǐ	豈/岂	interr. part.: surely not (see pp 24, 49, 57)

qǐ	啟/启	open; explain; inform; begin
qǐ	起	get up; rise; start; begin
qì	泣	cry; weep
qì	棄/弃	abandon; cast aside
qì	氣/气	vital energy; air; vapour
qiān	千	thousand; many
qiān	遷/迁	move; change (house, capital)
qián	前	postpos.: in front of, before (see p 38); formerly
qián	錢/钱	money; copper coin; cash; wealth
qiāng	槍/枪	spear; lance
qiáng	牆/墙	wall
qiáo	喬/乔	tall; lofty; proud; stately
qiǎo	愀	to blush
qiǎo rán	愀然	miserable; sad-looking
qiē	切	cut; slice; feel; urge; pressing

qiě	且	sign of fut.: will (see pp 22, 24); sign of imp. (see p 22); only; almost; just; (see also *jū*)
qiè	妾	concubine; ps-pron.: I, my etc. (see p 11)
qiè	竊/窃	steal; stealthy; I, my (term of deprecation)
qīn	親/亲	marriage; marriage ties; parents; relatives; intimate; self
qín	秦	Qín dynasty (221-207 BCE); name of an ancient state
qín	琴	5-stringed (now 7-stringed) Chinese lute
qín sè	琴瑟	Chinese lutes; matrimony
qín	擒	capture; catch; arrest
qín	禽	birds; animals; (as alt. char. 擒, *qín* = arrest; capture etc.)

121

qín shòu	禽獸/禽兽	animals (i.e. birds and beasts)
qīng	卿	minister; ps-pron.: you, your etc. (see p 11)
qīng	輕/轻	light (opp. heavy); frivolous; reckless
qīng	傾/倾	upset; collapse; fall flat; pour out; incline; to lean to
qīng	青	green; blue; azure; black
qíng	情	emotion; affections; feelings; desires; facts (of a case)
qǐng	請/请	invite; request; ask a favour; please; may show imp. (see p 22)
qǐng	頃/顷	instant; short time; 100 mǔ (畝) = 15.1 acres
qǐng zhī	頃之/顷之	after a while (see p 87)
qiū	秋	autumn; period; time

qiú	求	seek; implore; beseech; beg; pray; may show imp. (see p 22)
qiú	球	(alt. char. 毬, *qiú*); ball; sphere
qiú	毬	(alt. char. 球, *qiú*); ball; sphere
qiú	裘	fur coat; surname
qū	趨/趋	hasten; goal; (read *cū* = to urge)
qū	屈	bend; submit; injustice
qú	渠	drain; gutter; pron.: he, she, it etc. (see p 11)
qǔ	取	take; choose; (occ. alt. char. 娶, *qǔ*, i.e. to take a wife)
qǔ yǒu	取友	choose friends (according to certain standards)
qǔ	娶	marry; take a wife

qù	去	go (away); be distant; (read *qǔ* = remove e.g. from office; kill; get rid of)
quán	泉	fountain; spring; wealth
quán	全	completely; perfect; entire; to keep
quàn	勸/劝	exhort; advise; persuade; encourage
què	確/确	solid (like a rock); actual; really
qún	群	dem.: all the, the various (see p 14); in groups
R			
rán	然	yes; be so; thus; func. part. (see pp 61-62)
rán ér	然而	func. part. set: it is so, but... (see p 62)
rán hòu	然後/然后	func. part. set: then

		and only then (see p 62)
rán zé	然則 / 然则	func. part. set: if it is so, then... (see p 62)
rǎn	冉	tender; weak; gradual
rǎn rǎn	冉冉	slowly; gradually
rǎng	壤	rich (soil)
rǎng rǎng	壤壤	(alt. char. set 攘攘, *rǎng rǎng*); disorderly; chaotic; in turmoil
rǎng	攘	seize; steal; drive out; lay bare; throw into confusion
rǎng rǎng	攘攘	throw into confusion
ràng	讓 / 让	yield; cede; resign
rǎo	擾 / 扰	disturb; cause trouble
rén	人	dem.: one, people, others, a, someone's, (see p 14);

		man; person; mankind
rén	仁	altruism; benevolent; humanity
rěn	忍	bear; suffer; endure; tolerate
rèn	任	allow; tolerate; office; official position; put in office; apointment
rèn	刃	sword; kill
rēng	扔	throw away; reject
rì	日	sun; day
rì shí	日食	solar eclipse
róng	戎	pron.: you, your etc. (see p 11); weapons, war, chariot
ròu	肉	flesh; meat
ròu shí zhě	肉食者	meat eaters (i.e. high-ranking officials)
rú	如	like; as if; equal to; if; supposing; should; ought;

		(read *rù* = proceed; go to; follow)
rú hé	如何	interr. part. set: be like what, how about, wouldn't it be better to etc. (see p 48); (see also 何如, *hé rú*)
rú zhī	如之	(be) like this; thus
rǔ	乳	milk; give birth
rǔ	汝	pron.: you, your etc. (see p 11);
rǔ	女	pron.: you, your etc. (see p 11); (see also *nǔ*)
rù	褥	cotton-padded mattress
rù	入	enter; make; put in
ruò	若	pron.: you, your etc. (p 11); like; seem; as; if
ruò áo	若敖	surname
S		
sān	三	three
sāng	桑	mulberry tree

sāng	喪／丧	mourn for parents; (see also *sàng*)
sàng	喪／丧	lose; die; destroy; (see also *sāng*)
sè	瑟	25-stringed Chinese lute
sēng	僧	Budd. priest; monk
shā	殺／杀	kill; destroy
shān	山	hill; mountain
shān shuǐ	山水	landscape; water from a mountain
shàn	善	good; well; good at; friends with
shāng	商	merchant; to trade; discuss; to deliberate; name of a dynasty
shāng	傷／伤	wound; hurt
shàng	上	postpos.: on, above (see p 38); upper; ascend; go up; supreme
shàng	尚	still; yet; and besides; honour;

		esteem; proceed to; go to
shǎo	少	few; short of; scarce; seldom; briefly; (see also *shào*)
shào	少	young (see also *shǎo*)
shē	奢	extravagant; wasteful
shé	蛇	snake
shě	捨／舍	leave; part; give alms; bestow
shè	涉	cross; ford; pass through; involve; concern
shè	社	land god; sacrifice to local gods; a village or hamlet (with an altar for sacrifice to land god)
shè	射	archery; project; aim at
shēn	身	pron.: self (see p 12); body
shēn	深	deep; profound;

		intimate; long; old
shēn	參／参	ginseng; 曾參／参, Zēng Shēn, name of a Confucian disciple; (see also *cān*); (read *chén* = uneven)
shén	神	magical; make magical; spirit; god; divine; the mind; nerves; energy; used as an exclam.
shěn	瀋／沈	pour out (water); leak; liquid
shěn	審／审	to judge; hold an official enquiry; investigate; examine
shèn	甚	very; intense
shèn	慎	careful; cautious
shèn	脤	raw meat for sacrifice
shēng	牲	livestock; cattle; animals

shēng	聲／声	sound; note; voice; reputation; make known
shēng	生	(young) gentleman; student; lay (eggs); be born; birth
shéng	繩／绳	cord; string; measure; estimate
shěng	省	province; frugal; diminish; save; reduce; (read *xǐng* = watch; examine)
shèng	勝／胜	overcome; excel; (read *shēng* = to be equal to; worthy of)
shèng	盛	flourishing; luxuriant (see also *chéng*)
shèng	聖／圣	holy; sacred; divine; imperial
shèng rén	聖人／圣人	wise man; sage
shī	施	bestow; give; carry out

shī	師／师	teacher; troops; army division; capital city; 顓孫師／颛孙师, Zhuānsūn Shī (one of disciples of Confucius)
shī	屍	corpse; arrange; superintend
shí	十	ten; complete
shí quán	十全	perfect; entire
shí	石	stone; rock; mineral; barren; (read *dàn* = 120 catties or 133⅓lb; as a liquid measure = one gallon)
shí	時／时	season; time; period; when (see p 86)
shí	實／实	solid; full; to fill; real; true; sincere; genuine; fruit
shí	食	eat; food; (read *sì* = to feed)

shǐ	使	make; cause to; send (as envoy); use; employ; if; (read *shì* = messenger; an envoy)
shǐ	矢	arrow; aim at
shǐ	始	only now; begin; in the beginning
shì	氏	a family; a clan; a female; a surname
shì	世	generation; world
shì	逝	pass away; depart; die
shì	市	market; fair; to trade; execution ground
shì	事	matter; affair; to serve
shì	視／视	look at; regard; inspect; equal to
shì	仕	serve as an official
shì	適／适	go to; reach; marry (of women); happen to; suddenly;

		just now; (see p 21); (read *dí* = rightful heir; preside over; read *zhé* = alt. char. see 謫/谪, *zhé*)
shì	試/试	try (out); test; examine
shì	識/识	(alt. pr. in China = *shí*) know; recognise; distinguish; judge; (see also *zhì*)
shì	柿	persimmon
shì	恃	rely on; depend on
shì	士	knight; scholar; gentleman; soldier
shì	室	room; home; house; chamber
shì	是	yes; right; dem.: this, that (see p 14); which; vb to be (rare in CC)
shì gù	是故	for this reason (see p 71)

shì yǐ	是以	for this reason (see p 71)
shǒu	手	hand
shǒu zú	手足	hands and feet; brothers
shǒu	首	first; head; chief; leader
shǒu	守	guard; defend
shòu	獸/兽	animals; wild beasts
shū	書/书	book; letter; writings
shū	叔	uncle, i.e. father's younger brother
shú	孰	interr. part.: which, what, who (see pp 14, 49); ripe (orig. form for 熟, *shú*)
shǔ	鼠	mouse; rat; a mole
shǔ	屬/属	belong to; subject to; class; kind (read *zhǔ* = enjoin; assemble; entrust to)
shǔ	數/数	count; scold; discriminate;

		(see also *shù* and *shuò*)
shù	束	arrest; tie up; keep in order
shù	樹/树	tree; to plant; appoint
shù	數/数	number; several; fate; an art; (see also *shǔ* and *shuò*)
shuāi	衰	decrease; decline; weak
shuài	率	lead; follow and obey; all; for the most part; (read *lǜ* = ~rate)
shuí	誰/谁	(alt. pr. *shéi*); interr. part.: who, which, whose (see pp 14, 49)
shuǐ	水	water; river; fluid; liquid
shuì	說/说	to influence; persuade; (alt. char. 稅, *shuì* = to halt, put up at); (see also *yuè*, *shuō*, *tuō*)

shùn	舜	Shùn (a legendary monarch)
shuō	說／说	speak; say; tell; talk; discuss; (see also *shuì*, *tuō*, *yuè*)
shuò	數／数	frequently; annoy; bothered; (see also *shǔ* and *shù*)
sī	斯	dem.: this; these; (see p 14); thus; such
sī	司	an officer; control; manage; sub-division of a district
sī	私	favour; personal
sī	思	think; consider
sǐ	死	die; put to death
sì	四	four; on all four sides; (see p 17)
sì	祀	ancestral sacrifices; to sacrifice to the gods or spirits of the dead; year
sǒng	竦	respectful

sòng	宋	name of an ancient state; name of a dynasty
sòng	訟／讼	litigation; dispute; demand justice
sòng	送	see off; accompany; escort
sǒu	叟	old person; old man; ps-pron.: you, your etc. (see p 11)
sū	蘇／苏	rest; revive; plentiful; gather grass; species of thyme
suī	雖／虽	supposing; even; if; still; though; dismiss
suī rán	雖然／虽然	albeit; notwith-standing; although; (see p 62)
suí	隨／随	follow; accord with; accompany; forthwith; subsequent
suì	遂	comply with; follow; proceed to;

		then; thereupon; next
sǔn	損／损	to harm; injure; destroy
suǒ	索	rope; rule; to demand; to exact; think
suǒ	所	rel. func. part.: that which, who, what, whatsoever (see pp 28, 33-37, 62-64); place; cause
suǒ cóng	所從／所从	rel. part. set: from which, from where, through which etc. (see p 35)
suǒ wéi	所為／所为	that which one does (see p 64); the reason why (see p 64); behaviour
suǒ wèi	所謂／所谓	as it is said; that which is called (see p 64)
suǒ yǐ	所以	rel. part. set: how, the means by

		which, why etc. (see p 35); MC = hence; therefore
suǒ yóu	所由	rel. part. set: from which, from where, through which etc. (see p 35)
suǒ zì	所自	rel. part. set: from which, from where, through which etc. (see p 35)
T		
tā	他	elsewhere; other; (see p 14, alt. trad. pr. *tuō* in the above meanings); MC = pron.: he
tā rì	他日	another day
tài	太	too; very; excessive; term of respect used in titles
tài zǐ	太子	crown prince
tān	貪/贪	greedy; avaricious; corrupt; covet; desire

tán	彈/弹	pluck; play on stringed instrument; rebound; accuse; (see also *dàn*)
tàn	探	grope; search out; spy; inquire after; (read *tān* = try; attempt)
tàn	歎/叹	sigh; lament (alt. trad. char. 嘆)
tāng	湯/汤	hot water; soup; scald; heat; dissipated
táng	唐	name of a dynasty; bold; hasty
táng dì	唐棣	the Chinese bush cherry; a kind of white poplar; sparrow/ aspen-plum, *amelanchier asiatica* or *prunus japonica*
tǎng	倘	supposing; if; in the event of; unforseen; accidental
tè	特	only; alone; on purpose;

		special; eminent; a male animal; a bull; stallion
tì	弟	(alt. char. for 悌); fraternal piety; respect one's elder brother; (see also *dì*)
tiān	天	sky; heaven; nature; god; divine
tiān hū	天乎	my God!
tiān xià	天下	the world
tián	田	fields; land;
tián liè	田獵/ 田猎	hunt; hunting games
tiǎn	忝	disgrace; be ashamed
tiāo	挑	pick; choose (see also *tiǎo*)
tiǎo	挑	push; poke; incite; (see also *tiāo*)
tīng	聽/听	allow; listen; hear
tǐng	梃	club; cudgel
tōng	通	through; understand;

tóng	同	together; same
tóng	桐	name of a tree; (b.f. see 梧桐, *wú tóng*)
tóu	投	throw at; jump into
tóu	頭／头	head; top; chief; ends
tú	徒	only; disciple; follower
tú	塗／涂	mud; mire; spread on; apply
tú	徒	follower; disciple; go on foot; only; merely; empty
tǔ	土	soil; earth; items made of earth
tù	兔	rabbit; hare
tuī	推	push; decline; yield; expel; extend; infer; promote; give up
tuì	退	retire; withdraw; recede; decline; keep back

tūn	吞	swallow; to bolt; to appropriate
tuō	托	carry on the palm; (as alt. char. 託／讬, *tuō* = entrust to; request; ask; depute)
tuō	說／说	(alt. char. 脫, *tuō*); take off; (see also *shuì*, *shuō* and *yuè*)
tuō	脫	take off; undress; cast off; abandon; renounce; escape from
tuō	他	see *tā*
tuó	橐	bag; knapsack

W

wài	外	postpos.: outside, beyond (see p 38)
wài rén	外人	outsider; people of a different clan
wàn	萬／万	10,000; lots; many
wàn wù	萬物／万物	animals; all living things

wáng	亡	lose; die; flee; abandon; forsake; (read *wú* = not have, i.e. sim. to 無／无, *wú*)
wáng	王	king; prince; ruler; royal ps-pron.: I, we etc. (see p 11); (see also *wàng*)
wǎng	往	go to; depart; formerly
wàng	王	rule; be king over; govern; (see also *wáng*)
wàng	望	expect; hope; look towards; gaze at; may show imp. (see p 22)
wàng	忘	forget; neglect
wàng	妄	wanton; dissolute; presumptuous; rash
wēi	危	peril; danger; lofty
wēi	微	tiny; subtle; obscure; mean; pron.: I, my etc.;

		not have (used like 無/无, *wú*)
wēi	巍	lofty; eminent
wēi wēi	巍巍	majestically; lofty
wéi	為/为	be (see pp 18-19); do; make; become; act; think; as pass. agent (see pp 65, 65-66); as conj.: if, when, and (see p 66); as adv. modifier: then (see p 66); as exclam. part. (see pp 66-67); as interr. part. (see p 67); used with 之, *zhī* (see p 66); (see also *wèi*)
wéi	惟	(alt. char. 唯, *wéi*); only; and; with; think
wěi	尾	extremity; tail; end
wèi	位	position; situation; seat; rank or degree

wèi	未	neg. part: not, not yet (see p 21)
wèi bì	未必	uncertain; improbable; not necessarily
wèi cháng	未嘗/未尝	neg. part. set: never, never yet (see p 21)
wèi	魏	high; lofty; name of an ancient state
wèi	為/为	because of; on account of; for; by; to; (see pp 65-66); (see also *wéi*)
wèi	謂/谓	say; tell; call; name; be called
wèi	畏	fear; afraid of; respect
wèi	遺/遗	bestow; (see also *yí*)
wén	文	elegant; cultured; literature
wén	聞/闻	hear; smell; (read *wèn* = make known to; to state)
wèn	問/问	ask; consult; inquire; investigate

wǒ	我	pron.: I, me, we, us etc. (see p 11)
wò	臥/卧	lie down; rest
wū	惡/恶	interr. part.: how, where, wherein (see pp 24, 48); (see also *è* and *wù*)
wū hū	於乎	sign of praise; an interj. (see p 80)
wū xì	於戲/於戏	sign of praise; an interj. (see p 80)
wú	吾	pron.: I, we, my, our etc. (see p 11)
wú	蕪/芜	a vigorous growth of weeds; jungle
wú	梧	name of a tree (see b.f. 梧桐, *wú tóng*)
wú tóng	梧桐	wútóng (the Chinese parasol tree)
wú	無/无	not have (opp. of 有, *yǒu*); neg. imp.: do not (see p 22)

130

wú yǒu	無有/无有	non-existence
wú zuì	無罪/无罪	innocent
wǔ	舞	dance; posture; to fence
wǔ	五	five
wǔ	武	military; fierce; violent
wù	勿	neg. imp.: not, don't (see p 22)
wù	物	thing; creature
wù	惡/恶	dislike; hate(ful); (see also *è* and *wū*)

X

xī	西	postpos.: to the west of (see p 38); west
xī	奚	interr. part.: how, why, where, what (see p 48)
xī	兮	a poetic pause part.
xī	熙	bright; splendid; intelligent
xī xī	熙熙	peaceful and happy; crowds

xī	昔	formerly; of old; in the past; a long time; a night
xī zhě	昔者	in the past; once upon a time; once; formerly
xǐ	喜	delighted; pleasure; joy; pleased with
xǐ	洗	wash; bathe; purify
xiá	狹/狭	narrow; limited; narrow-minded; stingy; to pinch
xià	下	postpos.: under, below (see p 38); lower; get down from; go down
xià	夏	summer; great; spacious; ancient name for China; name of a dynasty
xiān	先	foremost; first; in front

xiān shēng	先生	sir; master; ps-pron.: you, your etc.
xián	賢/贤	worthy; virtuous
xiǎn	顯/显	manifest; display; seem; appear; evident
xiàn	獻/献	offer; present; show; display
xiāng	香	fragrant; incense
xiāng	相	mutual; reciprocal; it, him etc. (see p 12); (see also *xiàng*)
xiāng	鄉/乡	district; country (opp. town); village; neighbour-hood
xiāng rén	鄉人/乡人	locals; villagers
xiāng yì	鄉邑/乡邑	countryside and towns
xiáng	詳/详	detailed (alt. char. 祥, *xiáng*); lucky (alt. char. 祥, *xiáng*); to examine;

		carefully; report to a superior
xiáng	祥	auspicious; lucky; good omen; (as alt. char. 詳, *xiáng* = detailed)
xiàng	相	minister of state; look at; see; looks; (see also *xiāng*)
xiàng	項/项	nape of the neck; item; surname
xiàng	象	elephant; stars; chess; (as alt. char. 像, *xiàng* = resemble; image)
xiàng	嚮/向	formerly; in the past; a little while
xiàng zhě	嚮者/向者	hitherto; formerly; in the past; once upon a time
xiāo	嚻/嚣	shout; make noise; clamour
xiǎo	小	small; slightly
xiào	笑	laugh; smile; laugh at; ridicule

xiào	孝	filial; honour one's parents; mourning
xié	偕	accompany; together; sign of imp. (see p 22)
xié	攜/携	lead by the hand; take with; become disaffected; leave
xiě	血	(alt. pr. *xuè*); blood
xiě qì	血氣/血气	(alt. pr. *xuè qì*); animal desires; vigour
xiè	謝/谢	to thank; be grateful for; to decline; to confess (faults); die; fade; hand over
xīn	心	heart; mind; affections; intention; moral nature; centre
xīn	欣	joy; delight; happy
xīn rán	欣然	with pleasure; joyfully

xīn	馨	pervasive fragrance
xìn	信	believe; trust; confidence; pledge; free; aimless
xìn	釁/衅	consecrate (with a blood sacrifice); annoint with blood
xíng	形	form; shape; appearance; demeanour; to take shape
xíng	刑	law; punish; punishment; example; imitate
xíng	行	walk; move; travel; about to; soon; will; behaviour
xíng dāng	行當/行当	about to; soon
xíng jiāng	行將/行将	about to; on the verge of; soon
xìng	性	nature; disposition; spirit; temper
xìng	興/兴	flourish; prosper; increase; raise; rise

xiōng	兄	(elder) brother; ps-pron.: you, your etc. (see p 11)
xiōng	匈	name of a tribe
xiōng nú	匈奴	the ancient Xiōngnú (Hun) nationality
xiōng xiōng	匈匈	(alt. char. 訩 訩／讻讻, *xiōng xiōng*) in an uproar
xiū	休	rest; cease; resign; divorce; good fortune
xū	虛	false; unreal; untrue; vacant; abstract; humble; pure
xū	胥	lowly; petty official
xú	徐	grave; slow; dignified; surname
xú xú	徐徐	carefully; slowly; steadily
xǔ	許	promise; thus; allow; betroth; agree; a fin. part.

xuǎn	選／选	select; choose; a little while; an ancient weight
xué	穴	hole; cave
xué	學／学	study; learn; imitate
xuè	血	(alt. pr. *xiě*); blood
xuè qì	血氣／血气	(alt. pr. *xiě qì*); animal desires; vigour
xùn	訊／讯	news; information; inquire into; announce to; to make a judicial investigation

Y

yǎ	雅	refined; elegant; your
yān	煙／烟	smoke; mist; vapour
yān	燕	ancient state; surname; (read yàn = a swallow; comfort; enjoy)
yān	焉	interr. part.: how, why, where (see pp 24, 68); to replace

	然, *rán* (see p 68); as fin. part. (see p 69); (see also *yán*)
yān ěr	焉耳	fin. part. set (see p 69)
yān ěr	焉爾／焉尔	fin. part. set (see p 69)
yān ěr yǐ	焉耳矣	fin. part. set (see p 69)
yān yǐ	焉矣	fin. part. set (see p 69)
yān zāi	焉哉	fin. part. set (see p 69)
yán	言	discuss; talk about; speak; remarks; language
yán	嚴／严	severe; serious; stern
yán	岩	rock; cliff; high and dangerous
yán	炎	flame; blaze; brilliant
yán	焉	func. fus. part. (於／于 +之, *yú+zhī*): of it etc., there (see pp 67-68); as obj. pron. (see p 68); used in pass. (see pp

		67-68); (see also *yān*)
yǎn	掩	cover; shield; conceal
yàn	雁	wild goose
yàn zú	雁足	foot of wild goose; letter
yàn	嗲	coarse; rude; condole with
yàn	晏	clear sky; bright; quiet; peaceful
yáng	陽/阳	clear; bright; sun; of this world; male element in nature (opp. of 陰/阴, *yīn*)
yáng	羊	sheep; goat; (alt. char. 祥, *xiáng*, = lucky; auspicious)
yǎng	養/养	raise; rear; bring up; support
yáo	堯/尧	Yáo (a legendary emperor, ca. 2200 BCE)
yáo	遙/遥	in the distance; distant; remote

yé	邪	fin. interr. part. (see p 48)
yé	耶	fin. interr. part. (see p 48)
yě	也	func. part.: pause/exp. (see pp 70-71); fin. part.: tense, mood or sign of cop. (see pp 19, 71-72); used in neg. (see p 72); used in interr. (see p 73); used in exclam. (see p 73); MC = also
yě fú	也夫	fin. part. set (see p 73)
yě hū	也乎	fin. interr. part. set (see p 74)
yě hū zāi	也乎哉	fin. interr. part. set (see p 74)
yě jū	也且	fin. part. set (see p 73)
yě yé	也邪	fin. interr. part. set (see p 74)
yě yé	也耶	fin. interr. part. set (see p 74)

yě yǐ yǐ	也已矣	fin. part. set (see p 73)
yě yú	也與/也与	fin. interr. part. set (see p 74); (alt. char. set: 也歟/欤, *yě yú*)
yě zāi	也哉	fin. interr. part. set (see p 74)
yè	夜	night; dark; darkness
yè chā	夜叉	a *yaksha* (an evil Budd. spirit)
yè	葉/叶	leaf; petal; generation; age; (read *shè* = name of a place in Hénán Province, 河南省, *hénán shěng*)
yè	業/业	job; trade; occupation; already
yè	曳	trail; tow; drag; pull
yī	一	one; once; unite; all; a
yī	伊	pron.: he, she, it etc. (see p 11)
yí	宜	ought; should; suitable; right; fitting

yī	郪	name of an ancient state
yí	遺／遗	inherit; bequeath; lose; omit; forget; involuntary discharge of urine; (see also *wèi*)
yí	夷	ancient barbarian tribe
yí	疑	doubt; suspect; hesitate
yǐ	已	sign of past: already (see pp 21, 78); come to an end; finished; stop; too
yǐ	以	to use; func. part. - as prep.: with, using, by means of, in, according to, on, because of (see pp 74-75); marking a dir. obj. (see p 75); 以…為／为, *yǐ...wéi*, (see pp 75-76); as a conj.: in

		order to, and thereby, as a result, and (see p 76); used in dir./time (see p 76); this, like this (see pp 76-77); as adv. modifier: too, only, already (see p 77); as noun: reason, means (see p 77)
yǐ shì gù	以是故	for this reason (see p 74)
yǐ	矣	fin. part.: change of state (see pp 77-78); used in an assertion (see p 78); used in imp. (see p 78); used in interr. (see pp 78-79); as a pause marker (see p 79)
yǐ fú	矣夫	fin. part. set (see p 79)
yǐ hū	矣乎	fin. interr. part. set (see p 79)

yǐ zāi	矣哉	fin. interr. part. set (see p 79)
yì	亦	also; and; moreover; further; then
yì	邑	town; district city; depressed
yì	義／义	just; kind; justice
yì	易	change to; the *Book of Changes*; clear (fields); treat lightly; easy
yì	抑	interr. part.: or; or if; else; either; press down; restrain
yì	益	increase; benefit; profit
yì	異／异	different; strange; unusual
yì	繹／绎	explain; continuous
yì	弈	chess (the boardgame called 圍／围棋, *wéiqí*, in MC and *Go* in Japanese)
yīn	殷	abundant; many;

		highest degree of; to determine exactly; name of a dynasty; (read *yān* = a dark red)
yīn	陰／阴	shady; secret; dark; female element in nature (opp. 陽／阳, *yáng*)
yǐn	飲／饮	drink; swallow; (see also *yìn*)
yǐn	尹	ancient official title; surname
yǐn	隱／隐	hidden; secret; mysterious; grieved; conceal; pity; small; painful; (see also *yìn*)
yǐn chù	隱處 隐处	a hiding place; live in seclusion
yìn	隱／隐	(trad. alt pr.) lean on; (see also *yǐn*)
yìn	飲／饮	to cause to drink; to water (of

		animals); (see also *yǐn*)
yīng	應／应	ought; should; must; right; proper; (see also *yìng*)
yīng	嬰／婴	baby (usu. girl); infant; run against; entangle; attend to
yīng ér	嬰兒／ 婴儿	child; baby; infant
yíng	迎	greet; meet; welcome; receive
yíng	營／营	build; camp; barracks; regulate; manage; found; plan
yíng	盈	full; surplus; to fill
yìng	應／应	reply; respond; echo; fulfill; (see also *yīng*)
yōng	庸	interr. part.: how could ...! (see p 57); employ; use; simple; ordinary; merit; harmony
yǒng	俑	burial image

yǒng	勇	brave; daring; courage
yǒng qì	勇氣／ 勇气	bravery; courage
yòng	用	use; employ; consume; thus
yōu	憂／忧	be anxious about; worry; grieve
yōu	悠	far-reaching; drawn-out; leisurely
yóu	游	(alt. char. 遊, *yóu*); swim; float; roam; travel; wander; friends with; play
yóu	逌	please; smiling; complacent
yóu	遊	(alt. char. 游, *yóu*); swim; float; roam; travel; wander; friends with; play
yóu	猶／犹	still; yet; like; as if; even; (as alt. char. 猷, *yóu* = to plan; to scheme)

yóu	由	cause; means; from; by way of; through; because of; 仲由, Zhòng Yóu, name of a Confucian disciple
yóu	油	oil; fat
yóu rán	油然	plentifully; amply
yǒu	友	friend; companion
yǒu	卣	ancient wine vessel
yǒu	有	have; there is; existence; (opp. of 無/无, _wú_); (read _yòu_ = alt. char. 又, _yòu_, i.e.: and, also, in addition)
yǒu shí	有時/有时	sometimes; occasionally
yǒu sī	有司	Magistrate's Office; officials; civil authorities
yǒu yǐ	有以	to have as one's reason or purpose
yǒu zhū	有諸/有诸	fin. interr. part. set:

		have this?, is it true that ...? etc. (see p 88)
yǒu	牖	window
yòu	又	and; also; in addition
yòu	右	postpos.: to the right of (see p 38)
yū	淤	silt; mud; filth
yú	愚	simple; stupid
yú	魚/鱼	fish
yú fū	漁夫/渔夫	fisherman
yú	于	alt. char. see 於 (_yú_)
yú	踰	exceed; transgress; cross over
yú	餘/余	-odd; the rest
yú	余	pron.: I, me, we, us etc. (see p 11)
yú	予	(alt. char. 余, _yú_); I, me, we, us etc.; (see also _yǔ_)
yú	於/于	prep.: at, in, on, to, from, by, than (see pp 37-46, 79); towards (see p 34);

		and, moreover (see pp 79-80); alt. dial./char. var. for 乎, _hū_); (see also b.f. _wū xì_ and _wū hū_)
yú cǐ	於此/于此	hereof; in this place; here; thereupon
yú shì	於是/于是	thereupon; henceforth
yú sī	於斯/于斯	here; in this place
yú zī	於茲/于茲	this; here; thereupon
yú	與/与	(alt. char. 歟/欤, _yú_); interr. fus. part. of 也+乎, _yě+hū_, (see pp 20, 48, 81); (see also _yǔ_)
yú	輿/輿	bottom of a carriage; a carriage; chariot; sedan chair
yǔ	禹	Yǔ, the founder of the Xià (夏) Dynasty (2205-1766 BCE)

yǔ	予	(alt. char. 與/与, *yǔ*); give; grant; confer; (see also *yú*)
yǔ	語/语	talk; words;
yǔ	羽	feather; wing; plume
yǔ shì	羽士	a Daoist priest
yǔ	雨	rain; (see also *yù*)
yǔ	與/与	give; help; approve; be friendly with; follow; conform with; wait; permit; pay; conj.: and (see p 80); prep.: with, be at, along with, to, for, by (see pp 80-81); adv.: all (see p 81); exclam. or rhet. part. (see p 81); func. part: if (see p 81); pause part. (see p 82); (read *yù* = participate in; interfere in); (see also *yú*)

yǔ qí	與其/与其	func. part. set: rather than (see p 81)
yǔ	庾	grain store
yù	欲	will; want; desire; about to; (alt. char. 慾, *yù* = lust; passion)
yù	雨	trad. alt. pr. = vb to rain; (see also *yǔ*)
yù	玉	jade; gem; your
yù	遇	meet; bump into; happen; occur; receive; entertain
yù	馭/驭	drive a carriage
yù	鬻	sell; nourish; (occ. alt. pr. *zhōu*, i.e. alt. char. 粥 = rice gruel)
yù	豫	beforehand; prepare; pleased; excursion
yù	愈	more; excel; surpass; (alt. char. 癒,

		yù or *yú* = recover)
yuān chú	鵷雛/鹓雏	b.f. a *yuānchú*: a myth. bird sim. to the phoenix
yuán	原	source; origin; cause; reason; plateau; plain
yuán	圓/圆	round; full (moon)
yuǎn	遠/远	far; distant
yuàn	願/愿	wish that; desire; may show imp. (see p 22)
yuàn	怨	complain; enmity; resentment; grudge; blame
yuē	曰	to speak; it is said; is (in lists); (see pp 18-19)
yuē	約/约	agree; make a date
yuè	躍/跃	jump; skip
yuè	說/说	(alt. char. 悅, *yuè*); take pleasure in; pleased; (see also *shuì*,

		shuō and *tuō*)
yuè	越	Yuè (an ancient state); overpass; exceed; transgress; thereupon
yuè	月	moon; month
yuè	樂/乐	music; (see also *lè*)
yún	云	to speak; say
yún	雲/云	cloud

Z

zāi	哉	fin. interr. part.; a part. expressing surprise or admiration; (see pp 24, 49)
zǎi	宰	slaughter; butcher; govern
zài	再	twice; again
zài	在	be at; rest with; consist in; be present; be alive
zāng	臧	skillful; happy; good; right; surname
zé	責/责	upbraid; punish;

		duty; responsibility; alt. char. 債/债, *zhài* = debts)
zé	擇/择	select; choose; pick out
zé	則/则	rule; standard; norm; example; imitate; follow; linking statements: then, already, turned out that, but (see p 82); if (see pp 82-83); expos. part. (see p 83); interr. mood part. (see p 83)
zé ān	則安/則安	func. part. set (see p 83)
zé àn	則案/則案	func. part. set (see p 83)
zé yǐ yǐ	則已矣/則已矣	fin. part. set (see p 83)
zéi	賊/贼	robber; thief; injure; plunder
zèng	贈/赠	to give a present;

		confer; bestow
zèng	甑	rice steamer
zhāi	摘	pluck; pick (e.g. fruit)
zhái	宅	residence; home
zhān	粘	(alt pr. *nián*); to stick up; attach
zhān	旃	silken banner; func. fus. part. of 之 +焉, *zhī* +*yán*
zhàn	戰/战	war; battle
zhāng	張/张	draw a bow; stretch; set forth; extend; boast; surname
zhāo	朝	dawn; morning; early; (see also *cháo*)
zhāo	昭	bright; luminous; show; display
zhào	趙/赵	hasten to; to visit; surname; name of an ancient state
zhé	謫/谪	blame; find fault; to

		disgrace (an official)
zhě	者	this (one); rel. pron.: the one who, he who, that which etc. (see pp 19, 51, 83-84); exp. part. (see pp 19, 51, 68, 84); after time express. (see pp 51, 67, 84)
zhè	這／这	this (MC)
zhěn	枕	pillow; neck-rest; a stake (to tether cattle)
zhèn	朕	pron.: I, we etc. (used only by the emperor)
zhēng	爭／争	fight (for)
zhèng	政	rule; laws; admin-istration; government
zhī	知	conscious-ness; know
zhī	織／织	weave; knit
zhī	之	to go; this; attrib. part.: /...'s/ (see pp 9, 11, 84); obj. pron.:

		him, it, her, them, etc. (see pp 11-12); used in rel. clauses (see pp 28-35, 85-86); used in nom. (see pp 13, 84-85); used in causal clause (see p 86); used in temp. clause (see p 86); fus. of 於之, *yú zhī* (see p 87); used as dummy obj. (see p 87); used in names (see p 87); used with 為／为, *wéi* (see p 66)
zhí	執／执	hold (in hands); carry out
zhǐ	止	only; stop; stay; detain
zhǐ	指	finger: toe; point; direct; indicate
zhì	至	arrive (at); reach
zhì	擲／掷	throw; fling away

zhì	智	clever; wise
zhì	志	ambition; will; aspirations; records; aims; ideals; frame of mind
zhì	制	restrain; regulations; control; system; institutions
zhì	識／识	(trad. alt. pr.) remember; record; see also *shi* (Taiwan pr.) = know; recognise; distinguish
zhì	質／质	hostage; pledge
zhì	置	put; place
zhì jiǔ	置酒	give a party; hold a banquet
zhì	致	cause; bring about; result in; retire; resign; extend to; to apply to; send; convey to; transmit
zhì zhì	致志	driven; concentrate one's energies on

zhōng	中	postpos.: inside, in, middle of (see p 38)
zhōng yōng	中庸	the Constant Mean
zhōng	終/终	the end; finally; death; the whole of; after all
zhōng	鐘/钟	bell; clock
zhōng	忠	loyal; honest; faithful; patriotic
zhǒng	踵	ankle; follow in the footsteps of; reach
zhòng	仲	the second (in order of birth)
zhòng	重	heavy; weighty (i.e. important); to secure respect for
zhòng	眾/众	dem.: all; the whole of (see p 14); a crowd
zhōu	周	encircle; all round; everywhere; complete; whole; near; place and

		dynasty name; surname
zhōu	舟	boat; ship
zhòu	胄	helmet; descendants; posterity
zhū	誅/诛	punish; put to death
zhū	諸/诸	dem.: all the, the various (see p 14); pl. sx (see p 87); func. fus. part. of 之+於/于, *zhī+yú*; (see pp 87-88); interr. fus. part. of 之+乎, *zhī+hū* (see pp 48, 88)
zhū	銖/铢	ancient unit of weight
zhū hóu	諸侯/诸侯	the feudal lords; the feudal princes
zhú	竹	bamboo
zhú	燭/烛	candle; light up
zhú	竺	a kind of bamboo; India
zhú	逐	expel; follow;

		pursue; in order to; in succession
zhǔ	主	master; owner; lord; to act as lord; ruler
zhù	箸	chopsticks
zhù	助	aid; help; assist; system of mutual aid
zhù	築/筑	build; erect; building
zhuān	專/专	only; alone; specially; solely
zhuān xīn	專心/专心	focussed; absorbed in
zhuāng	莊/庄	village; farm; correct in conduct; serious
zhuāng zhōu	莊周/庄周	Zhuāngzǐ/ Chuang-tzu, a Daoist philosopher 369-286 BCE
zhuàng	狀/状	shape; form; appearance; state; accuse
zhuī	追	pursue; follow; escort; go back
zhuì	墜/坠	fall (down); sink

zǐ	紫	purple; violet
zǐ	子	son; child; ps-pron.: you, your etc. (see p 11); officer; viscount; gentleman; occ. lady
zì	自	self (see p 12); from (see p 40); since
zòng	從/从	a follower; (read *cōng* = lax; perpendicular); (see also *cóng*)
zǒu	走	run; walk; travel; go
zú	族	family; clan; tribe; collect together

zú	足	foot; worth ~ing; ~able; enough; satisfied; complete; pure (metal)
zú yǐ	足以	sufficient to; competent to; fit to; qualified to (see p 24)
zǔ	祖	grandfather; ancestor; founder
zuì	醉	drunk
zuì	罪	crime; wrong; suffering; retribution; to blame
zūn	尊	dignified; respectful
zuó	昨	yesterday; lately

zuó rì	昨日	yesterday
zuǒ	左	postpos.: to the left of (see p 38); left; inferior; second to
zuǒ yòu	左右	left and right; servants; attendants
zuǒ zhuàn	左傳/左传	*Zuǒ Zhuàn*, commentary on the *Spring and Autumn Annals*
zuò	作	make; do; act; write; compose
zuò	坐	sit; seat; travel by; be situated; to assign
zuò	座	a seat; a throne

Index

Index for Grammar Section

CPSIA information can be obtained at www.ICGtesting.com
Printed in the USA
LVOW112008161211

259728LV00004B/48/P